U0164665

教育的目的

［英］懷特海 著

莊蓮平　王立中　譯注

The Aims of Education
by Alfred North Whitehead

香港大華文化出版社

作者小傳

艾爾弗雷德·諾思·懷特海（Alfred North Whitehead，1861年2月15日-1947年12月30日），英國數學家、邏輯學家、哲學家和教育理論家；過程哲學創始人，他創立了20世紀最為龐大的形而上學體系。

懷特海在數學、哲學和教育等領域留下了大量著作，主要有《泛代數論》、《相對論原理》、《自然知識原理》、《科學與近代世界》、《宗教的形成》、《過程與實在》、《觀念的歷險》、《思維的方式》、《科學與哲學論文集》和《教育的目的》等。

懷特海與羅素合著的《數學原理》，標誌着人類邏輯思維的巨大進步，被稱為永久的偉大學術著作之一；羅素起初是他的學生，後來他們成為同事和朋友。

懷特海10歲開始學習拉丁文，12歲開始學希臘文。一直到19歲半，除了節假日外，他每天都要翻譯幾頁拉丁文和希臘文作家的作品，還要考拉丁文和希臘文的文法。去學校之前，他用拉丁語複述幾頁拉丁文文法規則，並用引文來舉例說明。他的古典著作的學習還伴隨着數學學習。

1880年秋天，19歲的懷特海開始了在劍橋大學三一學院的大學生活；一直持續到1910年的夏天，先是作為學生，然後作為研究生，並應聘得到一個教職。

1910年夏天，懷特海離開劍橋遷往倫敦。1910-1911年間，寫作《數學導論》。從1911年到1914年夏季，他在附屬於倫敦大學的大學學院擔任數個不同職位；從1914年到1924年夏，任肯辛頓帝國科技學院的教授。在長達14年時間裡，處理

倫敦大學的這些問題的體驗，改變了他對現代工業文明中高等教育的看法。

1924年，在他63歲時，應聘接受了哈佛大學哲學系的教職。

1936年至1937年學年結束時，成為榮譽退休教授。1947年12月30日，懷特海在美國麻塞諸塞州劍橋逝世。

1890年12月，懷特海和伊芙琳·威洛比·韋德結婚，妻子有軍事和外交的背景經歷，對他的世界觀影響很大：道德的和美學意義上的美，是生存的目的；善良、愛和藝術上的滿足是實現它們的形式；邏輯和科學揭示相關的模式，也可以避免不相關的事物。他們的三個孩子出生於1891-1898年之間，都參加了第一次世界大戰：大兒子在整個戰爭期間隨軍轉戰法國、東非和英國；女兒隨外交部在英國和法國工作；小兒子在空軍服役，1918年3月，他駕駛的戰機在法國被擊落，不幸以身殉職。

1861年2月15日，懷特海出生於英國東南部的肯特郡，他的祖父是當地一位有名望的教育家，曾任當地一所私立學校的校長。他的父親先後從事教育、宗教工作，十分關心教育事業。受家庭的影響，他對教育很感興趣。他早年就讀並留校於英國劍橋大學，中年任教職於英國倫敦大學，晚年受聘於美國哈佛大學。

《教育的目的》（1929）是他的教育代表作，其深刻的教育思想得到了廣泛認同，並影響深遠，閃耀着不朽的智慧光芒。

中文版推薦序

茅于軾

　　思考教育的目的，事關我們下一代的成功或失敗，他們將如何塑造我們這個世界。這絕不是小事。

　　這本由一個英國人懷特海寫的書，討論教育的目的。讀了之後，感到它簡直就是專門為當前的中國人寫的。書中討論的問題對中國非常有針對性。我國從初等教育到高等教育普遍的問題是把人當成工具來培養，要把人塑造成建設社會主義的人才。人是為建設服務的，只不過是一種工具而已。懷特海在書中寫道「我們的目標是，要塑造既有廣泛的文化修養又有專業知識的人——專業知識是奠基起步的基礎；而廣泛的文化修養，使他們既有藝術般的優雅，又有哲學般從容，通達高遠深邃之境。」

　　我國的教育曾經非常成功。在抗戰期間西南聯大（由北大，清華，南開三校組成）培養出幾位後來獲得諾貝爾科學獎的大師，引領世界微觀物理學的發展幾十年。可是正如這本書中所說，「時過不久，他們已經被那些呆滯的思想完全束縛。就教育而言，填鴨式灌輸式的知識，呆滯的思想不僅沒有什麼意義，往往極其有害——最大的悲哀莫過於最美好的東西遭到了侵蝕。

　　在人類歷史的長河中，除了某些時候思想活躍，具有創新之外，其他時候都背上了沉重的知識包袱。」我們不能不佩服，懷特海在英國這塊土地上思考的結果，還能適用於千萬公里之外的中國。可見世界的歷史有其共同性。

　　懷特海在這本書中不但詳盡地討論了教育的目的，也討論了學習的方法。我覺得他最精闢的一段話是說：學校裡教授的知識

都是二手貨，甚至是三手貨。一切學問都是從生活中來的，是從對自然和社會的觀察中歸納出來的。如何歸納，這在書本上是不講的。學生學了別人歸納出來的二手貨，未必真正懂得這些知識和原始的觀察有着什麼聯繫。而這才是學生最最需要的東西。

我認為，學習的第一目標還不是知識本身，而是學獲取知識的方法。有了這個方法再學什麼都不難。所以重要的是告訴學生如何觀察世界，如何整理觀察得到的素材，如何通過分析比較抽象出規律性的知識。或者說如何創造發明知識。我經常告訴學生，學習經濟學重要的是對經濟學裡的規律重新發現一遍，順着前人走過的道路再走一遍。其實，不僅僅學經濟學如此，學一切學科都如此，都要重新發現一遍。這樣，知識才會變成你自己的東西，才會應用，而不是食古不化。

阿基米德洗澡時發現了水的浮力定律，興奮得光着身子從浴缸裡跳出來，叫喊着「我發現了！」現在老師教大家浮力定律時絕沒有那種興奮感。學生對這條定律的理解也絕不像阿基米德那樣深。我們現在所知道的各種知識都是前人冥思苦想發現的，經過多少次從迷惑，到開朗；走了多少彎路，做了多少次嘗試，才變成一條學問。當你廢寢忘食，絞盡腦汁尋求問題的答案時，你正在創建一個新學問。人和動物的一個重要區別就在於人有好奇心，因而人具有知識。每當你通過觀察獲得新知識時，你會感到比得頭獎還興奮的滿足。所有獲得諾貝爾科學獎的人無一不經過這樣的，從黑暗來到桃花源，豁然開朗的經驗。老師所需要的就是保護孩子們天性中就有的好奇心，進而表揚他們提出問題，啟發創造性思維。不是填鴨式和灌輸式的教育，更不是打擊學生獨立思考，限制他們的追求真理、海闊天空的思想自由。這也是中國13億人口至今沒有一個人能獲得諾貝爾科學獎的問題所在。

其實，我們的日常生活中有許多現象值得我們關注，進而尋求答案，增加我們對周圍世界的認識和理解。比如你坐在馬路旁，觀察計程車裡有沒有載客，有多少車有客人，多少車是空駛的。你能發現計程車的成本和什麼有關，計程車應該如何定價，你在打的時平均要等多長時間才能招呼到一輛車，一個城市應該有多少計程車等等。你還可以統計所有經過的車輛的載客情況，從而對城市交通問題做更深入的思考。你在十字路口，觀察紅綠燈開啟的時間和東南西北四個方向來車數有什麼關係。你會對此提出改進意見嗎。如果你騎腳踏車上下班，你能知道你騎車的平均速度嗎？進而問，你能不能從觀察中統計出當地人騎車的平均速度。你學了熱傳導定理，就應該能回答，冬天要不要給樹木保溫。如果你把這個問題提給周圍的人，你會發現答案是很不相同的。這說明了什麼？你學過物理學，就應該知道一立方米空氣在常溫常壓下有多重，壓在我們身上的幾萬米厚的空氣一共有多大的壓力。

　　上面就是我讀了這本書後的，對教育的目的的一些想法。思考教育的目的，事關我們下一代的成功或失敗，他們將如何塑造我們這個世界。這絕不是小事。

　　*茅于軾，中國著名經濟學家，天則經濟研究所榮譽理事長（創始人之一兼首任所長）、人文經濟學會理事長。2012年CATO研究所頒發的「密爾頓·弗里德曼自由獎」得主。2014年入選世界思想家名單，排名第4。出版中、英文著作10餘部，代表作《擇優分配原理——經濟學和它的數理基礎》。所著《中國人的道德前景》一書獲1999 Sir Antony Fisher 國際紀念提名獎。曾擔任亞洲開發銀行註冊顧問、中國環境與發展國際合作委員會能源工作組中方專家、太平洋經濟合作委員會能源組國際顧問組成員和中國能源研究會副理事長等職。1929年出生於南京。

譯者前言：這是一本奇書！

這是一本奇書！

奇在它是影響歐美命運的一本書。

英國與美國甚至整個西方國家，為什麼如此之發達？與這本書有很大的關係。

本書從一定意義上來說，是對英美教育的觀察與總結、指導與推動；時至今日，那些智慧的光芒依然璀璨閃耀——毫不過時，更顯生命力——這就是經典。

這是一本奇書！

奇在它一針見血地洞悉教育的目的。

人是有意識的動物，做任何事情，先要明白：目的是什麼？

作為孩童，作為學子，您明白教育的目的嗎？

作為老師，作為家長，您明白教育的目的嗎？

活到老，學到老，終生教育，您明白教育的目的嗎？

可是——「教育的目的」究竟是什麼？

中華人民共和國教育法的解釋是「教育必須為社會主義現代化建設服務，必須與生產勞動相結合，培養德、智、體等方面全面發展的社會主義事業的建設者和接班人。」

台灣地區教育法的解釋是「教育之目的以培養人民健全人格、民主素養、法治觀念、人文涵養、強健體魄及思考、判斷與創造能力，並促進其對基本人權之尊重、生態環境之保護及對不同國家、族群、性別、宗教、文化之瞭解與關懷，使其成為具有國家意識與國際視野之現代化國民。」

近百年前，本書就一針見血地指出——就是——學生是有血有肉的人，教育的目的是為了激發和引導他們的自我發展之路。

您知道嗎？您明白嗎？

您想知道嗎？您想明白嗎？

這是一本奇書！

奇在它關乎所有人的命運！

我們每一個人，都是受教育者，我們也都是教人者；家庭教育、學校教育，社會教育，自我教育，等等，可以說，教育——它與每一個人都息息相關。

不光僅僅關乎歐美人，日本人，更是關乎您個人、家人、親戚、朋友，以及所有你所愛人的命運。

這是一本奇書！

奇在它翻譯與注釋齊舉，中文共英文一書。

我們深知，通過中文瞭解西方教育思想，需瞭解西方文化背景。為了便於您的閱讀與理解，我們進行了較為詳細的注解。譯者水準有限，不達意或錯漏之處，在所難免，懇請方家批評指正。

我們深知，翻譯不可能完全呈現原著，所以，我們將英文原版一併呈上，當讀者諸君對字裡行間有疑問時，可對照英文再看一下。

也許我們錯了，但是您更明白了——

這是我們希望竭盡全力為您做到的。

此外，我們特別建議有一定英文基礎的人，讀一讀我們為您特別呈上的原著英文版。

這是一本奇書！

錯過——遺憾一輩子！

遲讀——遺憾一陣子！

知而不讀——後悔一輩子！

知而細讀——幸運一輩子！

所以，這是一本值得所有人認真研讀的奇書！

給你一縷前所未有的有神清新①！
給你一個千載難逢的拍案叫絕！
給你一個今生難得的相見恨晚！

幸運的你，從現在開始，
儘快擁有、盡情地享受吧！

王立中
2020年6月，戰略家書苑

---

① 清·宋匡業《梅花》詩：不染紛華別有神，亂山深處吐清新。

前 言

本書的主要側重點在於智力的教育，因此在所有的章節中，都將始終貫穿着這樣一個主題，並從多個視角進行說明——簡單地說，就是——學生是有血有肉的人，教育的目的是為了激發和引導他們的自我發展之路。

從這個意義上來說，我們也可以得出一個結論，那就是老師也必須有活躍的思想。

本書斷然反對灌輸生硬的知識，反對沒有火花的使人呆滯的思想。

本書除了第四章外，都是我在一些教育和科學團體的演講，它們都是有實踐證明的經驗之談，或是教育實踐後的反思，還有一些對該主題的批判。

文中談及的教育體系來自於英國，這個體系在英國的失敗和成功可能與美國有所不同，但是這些例子具有說明性，主要的原理對兩國同樣適用。

A·N·懷特海
1929年1月，美國哈佛大學

目　錄

第一部分　教育的目的（中文譯註）

第一章　教育的目的

　　文化是思想的活動，是對美和人類情感的感受。零零碎碎的信息或知識對文化毫無幫助。如果一個人僅僅是見多識廣，那麼他在上帝的世界裡是最無用且無趣的。我們的目標是，要塑造既有廣泛的文化修養又有專業知識的人——專業知識是他們奠基起步的基礎；而廣泛的文化修養，使他們既有藝術般的優雅，又有哲學般從容，通達高遠深邃之境。

　　我們必須要記住：自我發展才是最有價值的智力發展，這種發展通常在16—30歲之間發生。訓練這種自我發展，最重要的應該是12歲之前從母親那裡所受到的教育。大主教坦普爾①說過的一句名言可以佐證我的觀點。一個年少時在拉格比公學②表現平平的男孩子，在其長大成人後卻非常成功，人們對此感到非常驚訝。大主教在解釋人們的困惑時說道：「問題不在於他們18歲時怎麼樣，重要的是他們之後將成為怎樣的人。」

　　在訓練兒童的思維活動時，我們需要特別注意的是那種我所說的——「呆滯的思想」（inert ideas）——那些僅僅被大腦所接收、卻沒有經過實踐或驗證而不具有普世性的知識。就是說，正確的知識必須實用過，驗證過，並在不同的條件下都能成立，「放之四海而皆準」，套用現在時髦詞彙就是「普世」。

　　在教育史上，有個非常有意思的現象，某些學校在某個時期，充滿天才創造的活力，人才輩出，群星璀璨，然而不久，開始淪為賣弄炫耀，墨守成規。原因就在於，他們的大腦已經被呆滯的思想塞滿了。就教育而言，充斥呆滯思想的教育不僅無用，反而有害，因為其極具腐蝕性；這種腐蝕性會生成人的劣根性（pessima）。在人類歷史的長河中，除了某些時候思想活躍、具有創新之外，其他時候都背上

了沉重的知識的包袱。那些沒有受過正規教育卻聰明智慧的女性，她們見多識廣，把世界看得通透，當她們步入中年，成了社會中最具智慧和文化修養的群體，就是因為她們曾經免遭那些呆滯思想的侵蝕。每次對人類社會進步舉足輕重的知識革命，都是一次對陳腐呆滯思想的反抗和反叛。但是，可悲的是，由於對人類心理的忽視，某些所謂的教育制度又重新用呆滯的思想來蒙蔽人們的眼睛。

現在，讓我們來談談在我們的教育體制中，如果要避免思想上的僵化，就要特別注意兩條戒律：（一）不要同時教授太多科目；（二）如果要教，就一定要教得透徹。

教授大量的科目，如果只是蜻蜓點水地教授一點皮毛，那麼就會造成一些毫不相干的知識碎片的被動接受，不能激起任何思想活力的火花。如果只給兒童教授一些少而精的科目，讓他們對所學的東西進行自由的想象和組合，他們就會利用這些所學的知識去認識世界，並在現實生活中加以運用。孩子自己的發現（discovery），就會是一些普遍的、基礎的概念，這些概念能夠幫助他們理解生活中不斷湧現的各種事情。孩子就是要這樣來生活。

我所說的「理解」，不僅僅是一種邏輯上的認識，而是那句法語格言「理解一切，即寬恕一切」③層面上的「理解」。那些學究或許會嘲笑具有實用性的教育，但是，如果教育是沒有用的，那麼它又是什麼呢？！它是一種藏而不用的才能嗎？教育當然應該是有用的。不管你生活的目的是什麼，它對聖·奧古斯丁④有用，對拿破崙⑤也有用，對你、對我都有用。教育是有用的，因為去理解這個世界是有用的──好的教育，能讓人更好地理解這個世界。

我不想多談文學教育意義上的那種理解，我並不想對古典的或是現代的課程的優點下斷言，我只想說，我們想要的「理解」，是堅定不移地對現在的理解。知識的唯一用途，就是武裝我們的現在，沒有比輕視現在對年輕人的危害更大的了。現在包涵了一切。現在是一個

神聖的所在，因為它既聯繫着過去，又包含着未來⑥。同時，我們需要瞭解，一個兩千年前的年代並不比一個二百年前的年代更為久遠，不要被所謂的「時代」所蒙蔽，莎士比亞⑦、莫里哀⑧的時代和索福克勒斯⑨、維吉爾⑩的時代同樣古老。與先賢聖哲的交流是一種偉大且令人激情迸發的集會，這種集會只能在一個地方進行，那就是現在，至於先賢們誰先到達誰後到達並沒有多大的意義。

　　當我們轉而考察科學和邏輯方面的教育時，我們必須記住：不能加以利用的知識是相當有害的。所謂知識的利用，是指要把它和人類的感知、情感、慾望、希望，以及能調節思想的精神活動聯繫在一起，因為那是我們的生活。如果只是一味地通過被動記憶一些支離破碎的知識來塑造自己的精神生活的話，簡直不可想象。人性不是這樣，生活更不應該這樣，或許某些報紙雜誌的編輯才需要這樣。

　　在科學領域，學習一個概念的首要途徑就是去證明它。請允許我先來說明一下什麼是「證明」，我的意思是證明它的價值。一個概念，除非包含它的命題是正確的，否則就沒有多大價值。所以，證明一個概念的一個必要條件就是證明包含它的命題的正確性，無論是通過實驗還是邏輯推理。但是證明一個命題的正確與否，並不構成最初採用這一概念的必要條件。畢竟，那些受人尊敬的老師的權威斷言，是我們開始討論一個命題的重要依據。

　　在我們最初接觸一系列命題的時候，總是會先分辨其重要性，這也是我們在日後生活中經常會做的。從嚴格意義上來說，我們並不會主動地證明或反駁任何事物，除非其重要性值得我們那樣去做。（狹義上的）證明和（正確的）評價，這兩個過程在順序上並不需要進行嚴格地區分，幾乎可以同時進行。如果一定要有個優先順序的話，那就是（正確的）評價。

　　此外，我們不應該孤立地使用各種命題。我的意思是絕不用一系列簡單的實驗來說明命題一，然後證明命題一；再用一系列簡單的實

驗來說明命題二，然後證明第二個命題；依次類推，直至本書的最後一頁。如此這番，您肯定會感到乏味至極！

相互關聯的知識要從整體上加以利用，各種各樣的命題按不同順序可反復使用。在一個理論科目中，選擇一些可以應用的知識，同時用系統的理論說明來研究它，這個理論說明必須簡單、精煉，盡可能地嚴謹準確，那樣就容易真正地為人所正確地理解。擁有太多一知半解的知識是悲哀的，理論和實踐不應該混為一談，兒童在證明和利用某個知識的時候，應該毫不懷疑地知道什麼時候是在證明，什麼時候是在利用。

我的觀點是：凡是被證明的東西都應該加以利用，凡是被利用的東西都應該（只要可行）加以證明。我不認為證明和利用是同一回事情。

講到這裡，我可以用一個看似離題的方式來進一步闡述我的觀點。我們剛剛才意識到教育的藝術和科學需要天賦，需要對這種藝術和科學進行研究。這種天賦和研究絕不僅僅是某門科學或文學知識，這個道理上一代人已經部分地覺察到了；而那些多少有點不成熟的中小學校長，傾向於要求他們的老師會玩保齡球，或對足球有所涉獵，而不是讓老師對教育的藝術和科學進行研究。文化畢竟不僅僅是保齡球，不僅僅是足球，也不僅僅是淵博的知識。

教育是教人們如何運用知識的藝術，這是一種很難掌握的藝術。

每當一本真正有教育價值的教科書出現時，肯定會有一些評論家說，這本教科書很難用於教學。誠然，一本真正有教育價值的教科書理應是難教的。

如果它很容易，那麼這本教科書就應該被付之一炬，因為它是不可能有教育價值的。

和其他任何領域一樣，在教育領域，平坦的享樂之路，往往通向糟糕的結局。

　　如果一本書和一些講座的目的，是為了使學生能夠記住所有考試中可能會出現的問題，那麼，這本書或這些演講就代表了一條邪惡之路。我可以附帶說一句，學生在任何一次考試中，可能被問到的每一個問題，都應該由這門課程的老師事先設計或修改，否則，任何教育制度都不會成功。外部的評審人員可以就課程或學生的成績寫出報告，但是絕不應該被允許去問學生一個連該課程的老師都沒有嚴苛審察過的問題，或是至少和學生談話後碰撞出來的問題。會有一些例外，但只能是例外，是在總的規則下的例外，總的規則不容破壞。

　　現在，讓我們回到我先前的觀點，就是理論知識必須在學生的課程裡具有可應用性，這不容易付諸實踐，也很難實行。因為理論知識本身就需要解決這樣的問題：不能讓知識僵化，而要讓它生動活潑起來——這是所有教育的核心問題。

　　最理想的教育取決於幾個不可或缺的因素：（一）教師的天賦；（二）學生的智力類型；（三）他們對生活的期望；（四）學校外部（鄰近環境）所賦予的機會，以及（五）其他相關的因素。這就是為什麼統一的校外考試⑪非常有害的原因。我們不會公開指責它，因為我們都害怕自己被認為是怪人，好像喜歡公開指責一些既成事實的東西。這樣的考試檢驗學生是否懈怠有一定的作用，但是，我們不喜歡這樣的考試，因為歷史與現實都已經證明，它抹殺了文化的精髓。

　　當你根據自己的經驗來分析教育的首要任務時，你會發現：教育的成就取決於對諸多可變因素的精妙調整，因為我們是在與人的思想打交道，而不是與沒有生命的物質打交道。激發學生的求知慾，提升其判斷力，鍛造其對複雜環境的掌控能力，使學生能夠運用理論知識對特殊事例做出預見——所有這些能力的塑造，不是單靠幾張考試科目表中羅列的幾條既定規則就能傳授的。

　　那些有實際經驗的老師，我在這裡提個醒：良好的課堂紀律，總是可能讓教師把大量無活力的知識灌輸到一班學生的腦子裡去，比如

你們拿起一本教科書，讓學生學習，一切看似順利。然後，學生學會了如何解二次方程。

那麼，教會學生解二次方程的目的是什麼呢？

對於這個問題，有一個傳統的答案，就是人的大腦像是一件工具，你必須先把它磨鋒利了，才能去使用它，獲得解二次方程能力就是一個磨礪的過程。這種觀點在幾個世紀的時間裡，都被廣泛地接受。

儘管這種觀點有一定的道理，但是它包含了一個根本的錯誤，從而可能扼殺這個世界上天才的產生。把人的大腦比喻成工具的人，我不知道誰是第一個，我所瞭解的可能是希臘七賢⑫之一，或者是他們集體討論的結果。不管提出這種觀點的人是誰，歷代傑出人物大多贊同此說，使其有了不容置疑的權威性。但是，不管這種說法有多麼權威，不管什麼樣的傑出人物對此深表贊同，我都毫不含糊地抨擊這種說法——這是引入教育領域最致命、最離譜、最危險的一種觀點。人的大腦不是被動地接受知識，它是永恆活動着的，它能對外部的刺激做出最精密的反應。你不能像對待工具一樣，把它磨鋒利了才去使用它。

不管學生對你的課程有什麼樣的興趣，必須在此時此刻激發這種興趣；不管你想要加強學生何種能力，必須在此時此刻練習這種能力；不管你想怎樣建構學生未來的精神世界，必須現在就去展示它——這是教育的金科玉律，這是很難遵循的一條規律。

困難在於，對一般概念的理解，思考的習慣，思考的樂趣，不是任何形式的文字所能激發出來的。具有實踐經驗的教師都知道，教育是需要精雕細琢的，一分鐘又一分鐘，一小時又一小時，一天又一天，一年又一年，反反復復。學習無捷徑。「見樹不見林」，這句俗語形容得好，那種因為「只看見『樹木』而看不見『樹林』的問題」所帶來的困難，就是我想要強調的。教育的問題是——如何讓學生借

助「樹木」來認識「樹林」。

我極力主張這樣的解決方案：必需根除科目之間毫無關聯的狀態，這種各自為營的局面扼殺了現代課程中的生動性。教育只有一個主題——那就是多姿多彩的生活。

我們提供給學生的必須是獨一無二的整體，而不是教給學生代數——後面沒有了；幾何——後面沒有了；歷史——後面又沒有了。不是教他們幾門語言，但他們又從未真正地掌握。最沉悶的就是文學，所謂的文學就是幾部莎士比亞的戲劇，一些需要學生記憶的語言學特點、情節的分析或對人物的認識。我們從來沒有教學生如何把各種知識綜合起來運用。這樣一系列的課程能代表生活嗎？充其量不過是上帝在思考如何創造這個世界時在大腦中閃過的一個要目表而已，根本沒有想好怎樣才能把它們融為一體。

現在，讓我們回到二次方程，我們還沒有解決這個問題呢。

孩子為什麼要學習二次方程的解法呢？除非二次方程完美地契合在相關的課程中，否則，就沒有理由教任何關於二次方程的東西。此外，數學在整個文化領域中具有廣泛的意義。我有點兒懷疑，對不同類型的孩子而言，二次方程可以有不同類型的解法？而不是只依賴於那種數學專業性的解法。我在這裡提醒大家，我沒有對心理學或學科專業性的內容作任何評論，雖然這兩者是理想教育不可或缺的部分。如果那樣做，就是對我們提出的實際問題的一種逃避，我在這裡提及，只是為了避免諸位誤解我的觀點。

二次方程是代數的一部分，代數是用來量化世界的一種智力工具。你無法迴避它，數量每時每刻地存在於這個世界，要想說話有道理，就得用數字來描述。說這個國家很大毫無意義——到底有多大？說鐳很稀有也毫無用處——到底有多稀有？你無法逃避數量的概念。哪怕轉向詩歌或是音樂，數量和數字還是會在節奏和音階裡與你碰面。有些故作優雅的學者輕視數量的理論，這是不正確的，與其譴責

他們，不如憐憫他們，他們在學校裡所學的那些所謂的代數知識值得反思。

　　無論表面上還是在事實上，代數都已經退化成了一堆無用的知識碎片，這樣可悲的例子不勝枚舉。比如，我們希冀在孩子生動活潑的大腦中喚起一些美好的品性，但是如果連我們自己對這些品性都沒有一個清晰概念的話，就盲目地推行關於教育改革的計劃，結果肯定是白費力氣；如果你沒有明確的教育目的，那麼你的一切教育方案都是徒勞！

　　幾年前，有人大聲疾呼，學校的代數需要改革。最終所有人都認為圖表可以解決所有問題。於是其他東西都被逐出了學校，圖表取而代之。但就目前我所看到的而言，在那之後，除了圖表（只剩下圖表了），根本沒有一點代數的思想和概念了。現在，每一次代數考試總會有一兩道關於圖表的題目。

　　我個人是圖表法分析的熱烈擁護者，但我始終懷疑，我們是否達到了預期目標。

　　生活與所有智力或情感的認知有關，如果不能成功地展示出兩者之間的關係，那麼，就不可能把生活嵌入到任何通識教育的計劃之中。

　　這句話很難表達，但卻是大實話，我不知道怎樣才能把它表達得更為通俗易懂些。學校所進行的那些小小的形式上的改變，最終還是被事物的本質所羈絆。正如你們在與一個非常老練的對手作戰，自以為得計，以為用計可戰而勝之，卻不幸被其將計就計，反為其縛，反受其害。

　　改革應該從另一頭開始。首先，必須確定這個世界上有哪些簡單得完全可以應用到通識教育中的數量關係；其次，應該擬定一份代數課程計劃，這份計劃大致能在這些數量的應用中找到例證。

　　我們不用擔心我們所熱愛的圖表會消失，當我們開始把代數作為

一個嚴肅的可以用來認識世界的工具時，圖表就無所不在了。對社會進行簡明精確的研究時，可以用某些簡單的圖表來進行描述。描述歷史的曲線圖顯然要比一連串乾巴巴的名字和年代表要生動得多，而後者常常佔據了學校裡沉悶教學的大部分。那麼多不為人知的國王、王后的名字一覽表能說明什麼呢？

湯姆、迪克或哈里，他們都已經逝去了。一般的革新最後都被證明完全失敗了，最好被暫時擱置起來。現代社會中各種力量的變動，都可以用數量來進行簡明的表達。同時，關於變量、函數、變化速率、方程式及其解法，消元（elimination）的概念⑬，都可以作為一種純粹的抽象科學來進行研究。當然，我們不應誇大其辭，而是用適合教學的既簡單又具代表性的例子來反復說明。

如果沿着這個思路，那麼從喬叟⑭到黑死病，從黑死病⑮再到現代勞工問題，這條線索將把中世紀朝聖者的傳說和代數這門抽象的科學聯繫起來，兩者都從諸多不同的側面反映了一個獨一無二的主題——生活。

我知道你們大部分人對這個觀點的看法，我所勾勒出來的這條線索未必是你們想選擇的，甚至其效果你們也懶得去想。對此我頗為贊同。我也不能說我自己就能做到這一點。但是，你們的反對恰恰說明——為什麼統一的校外考試制度對教育極其有害。知識應用的過程若要成功，只能取決於學生的品性和教師的天賦。當然，關於量的科學，如力學和物理學，我沒有提到我們日常生活中都熟悉的某些最簡單的應用。

用同樣的方法，我們可以繪製出對應時間的社會現象統計圖表。然後，挑出類似的兩種現象來進行對比，除去時間上的差異，我們可以看到其中的內在聯繫，或只是一種暫時的巧合。我們注意到，對不同的國家，我們可以用不同的社會現象統計圖表，然後通過對科目的適當挑選，可以得出或許只是巧合的一些統計圖表，而其他的圖表可

能表現出明顯的因果聯繫。我們想知道如何分析這些統計圖表……我們樂此不疲。

　　但是，在考慮這種描述的時候，我請求你們記住我上面一直堅持的東西。首先，一種思維訓練方式不可能適合所有的兒童。比如，偏愛手工的兒童可能考慮得更具體，動作更敏捷，超乎想象。也許我錯了，但我必須做這樣的猜想。其次，我不敢奢望一次出色的演講就可以一勞永逸地激勵出一個令人贊賞的班級。這不是教育應該採取的方式。一直以來，學生非常努力地解題目，畫圖表，做實驗，直到他們對一門課程有了透徹的掌握。我在描述各種解釋和方向，就是希望說明：應該引導孩子的思維。學生應該覺得他們是在真正地用腦子學習，而不是在進行智力表演。

　　最後，如果你所教的學生需要通過某些統一的普通考試，那麼如何實施完美的教學就變得複雜起來了。你們有沒有注意到諾曼底式拱形門上那彎曲的鋸齒形花紋？古代的藝術品是那麼地雋永美麗，而現代的卻顯得有些醜陋粗鄙。原因在於：現代的工藝品多按精確尺寸設計製作，而古代的藝術品則隨工匠的風格有所變化；現代的緊湊局促，古代的舒展開闊。

　　現在，為了讓學生順利地通過考試，對所有的科目都要給予同樣的關注。但是，人的天性各不相同，有很大的差異。有的人可以鳥瞰甚至融會貫通整個課程，而另外的一些人可能發現一些不相干的例證。對於一個為了培養廣泛文化修養而設計的課程來說，允許差異化的存在是有點矛盾的。但是，這個世界如果沒有矛盾，就會變得空乏無味。我相信，在教育中如果排除差異化，那就是在毀滅生活。

　　現在，我們再來看看一般數學教育中的另一分支——幾何學，同樣的原則亦適用於此。理論部分必須明確、嚴謹、簡潔且有重要意義。表達概念之間的主要關係但又不是絕對必要的命題，都應當捨棄；不過，重要的基本概念應當保留。有些概念不能省略，如相似形

和比例。我們必須記住，由於圖形具有形象化的特徵，幾何學是訓練大腦在推理演繹能力方面必不可少的一門學科。還有，幾何作圖可以很好地訓練手與眼的協調。

　　但是，像代數一樣，幾何和幾何作圖必須超越幾何學自身的範疇。在工業領域，機械和車間操作實踐是幾何學的適當延伸。比如，在倫敦工藝專科學校，這方面已經取得了令人矚目的成功。我想，就許多中等學校而言，測量和繪製地圖是對幾何學極好的運用。特別是，繪製平面圖，有助於學生對幾何原理的運用有更為生動的理解。簡單的繪圖工具，比如測量員常用的測鏈⑯和羅盤，都能夠使學生從對一塊地的勘定和測量，提高到對一小塊地的地圖繪製。**最好的教育是用最簡單的工具獲得最大限度的知識。**我們堅決反對提供給學生精密的儀器。通過繪製一小塊地區的地圖，研究它的道路、輪廓、地質、氣候，與其他地區的聯繫，以及居民的狀況，這些都將教會孩子更多的歷史和地理，超越任何關於柏金·奧貝克（Perkin Warbeck）⑰和白令海峽⑱知識。我不想就某一學科做一個含糊其辭的演講，而是說要進行認真的調查研究，用準確的理論知識探明真正的事實。一個典型的數學習題應該是，測量某一塊地，按比例繪製地圖，然後計算面積，等等。這是很好的一種方式，即提出很好的幾何命題，但不立馬進行證明；而是在進行測量的同時，自然而然地學會了命題的證明。

　　幸運的是，專業教育的問題要比通識教育的問題相對簡單一些，原因是多方面的。其一，許多必須遵守的程序原則在兩種情況下是相同的，因此不必重新改過。其二，專業訓練發生在學生學習的較高階段——也應當發生在這個時候，因為對學生來說，有比較容易的材料可供研究使用。但是，不容置疑的是，專業學習對學生來說通常是一種特殊的興趣，他去學習它，因為他想瞭解它。這就有了本質的區別，通識教育旨在鼓勵心智活動，而專業課程則是利用這種活動。不

必過多地強調兩者的對立，就像我們已經看到的那樣，在通識教育的課程中，學生會對某些內容產生特殊的興趣；而在專業化學習中，課程之間的外在聯繫也會拓展學生的視野。

還有，在學習中，不存在一種課程僅僅傳授通識知識，而另一種課程僅僅傳授專業知識。為通識教育而設置的科目，都是需要專門學習的特殊課程；或者說，鼓勵一般心智活動的方式之一，就是培養一種專門的愛好。不可能把這種渾然一體的學習過程進行分割。教育所要傳達的是對思想的力量、思想的美妙和思想的邏輯的深刻的認識，以及特殊的知識——這種知識與學習者的生活有着特殊的關係。

對思想邏輯的欣賞，是有教養的一種表現，這是在專門學習後才可能具備的一種能力。這種能力是一種洞察力，既有全局觀，有通盤認識，又能看到一組思想與另一組思想之間的聯繫。只有通過專門學習，人們才能欣賞一般思想的確切表達，領會這些思想在表達時彼此之間的相互聯繫，以及它們在理解生活方面的幫助。在抽象思維的理解和對具體事實的分析過程中，人們的思維能力得到了訓練，經過如此訓練的大腦，其思維能力，既能極為抽象，又能極為具體。

最後，我們必須培養所有精神品質中最難得的一點——對風格的鑒賞。這是一種對風格的感知——審美感——是對可預見結果的不由自主、發自內心的讚美。藝術的風格，文學的風格，科學的風格，邏輯的風格，實踐的風格，都有同樣的美學特質，即實現和約束。對學科本身的熱愛，不是反復思考所產生的那種讓人昏昏欲睡的快感，而是對在學習過程中所展現出來的那種清晰風格的熱愛。

這樣，我們就又回到了我們開始的地方，即教育的功用。風格，按其最美好的意義，就是最終獲得有教養的心智；風格是最有用的東西。它無所不在。有風格的管理人員討厭浪費，有風格的工程師盡可能地節約原料，有風格的工匠更喜歡創造精美的作品。**風格是人類精神世界最後的道德歸宿。**

在風格之上，在知識之上，還有一樣模糊的東西，就像希臘眾神之上有種命運般捉摸不定的東西一樣，那就是力量。風格是力量形成的形式，是對力量的約束。但無論如何，達致預期目標的力量才是最為根本的。首先要達致目標。不要為你的風格所困擾，而要去解決你的問題，證明上帝給予人類的方式是正確的，去履行你的職責，去完成擺在你面前的任何其他任務。

那麼，風格能夠幫到你什麼呢？有了風格，你可以避開細枝末節的東西，直達目標，而不會生出一些令人不快的插曲；有了風格，你可以達到你本來的目標，而不會是其他東西；有了風格，你可以預見你的行為的效果，而遠見是神賜予人類最後的禮物；有了風格，你的力量將得以提升，因為你的思想不會被一些不相干的事務所打擾，你就能更為專心致志於你的目標。但，風格是專家獨享的特權。誰聽說過業餘畫家的風格？誰聽說過業餘詩人的風格？風格是專業化學習的產物，是專業化對文化的特殊貢獻。

英國現階段的教育缺乏一種明確的目的，深受外部機構的損害，這種外部力量正在扼殺教育的生命力。在這次演講中，我始終在思考那些對教育起決定性作用的目的。在這方面，英國一直在兩種意見中猶豫不決：到底是培養業餘愛好者，還是造就專家型人才。十九世紀，世界發生的深刻變化之一——就是知識的增長給予了我們預見未來的能力。業餘愛好者本質上是這樣一群人，他們有鑒賞力，在完成常規性工作時表現出非常出色的靈活多面。但是，他們缺乏專業知識所賦予的預見能力。這次演講的目的，就是建議如何在保留業餘愛好者優點的同時，造就專業性人才。我們中學教育的誤區，就是在應該富有彈性的地方僵化刻板，而在應該嚴謹嚴厲的地方卻放任自流。所有的學校都要承受這樣的痛楚：為了學校的生存而不得不訓練學生去應付一些考試。沒有校長可以無所顧慮地根據學校的境遇，去發展適合自己的通識教育或專業教育；這種境遇是由學校的教職員工、學

校所處環境、學生和學校所得到的捐贈所決定的。我認為，所有以考察單個學生情況為基本目的的外部考試制度，都不可能有效，徒然造成教育的浪費。

首先，被考察的應該是學校而不是學生。每所學校都應該有權利根據自己的課程頒發畢業證書，這些學校的標準應該經過查驗和修正。教育改革的第一要務是，學校必須作為一個獨立的單位，必須有經過自己審核後批准的課程，這些課程應該根據學校自身的需要由其在校教師開發出來。如果我們不能確保這一點，那麼我們就很容易從一種形式主義走向另一種形式主義，從一堆無用呆滯的思想走向另一堆無用呆滯的思想。

在說到學校作為國家機構中唯一真正的教育單位時，我把學生的校外考試看作是一種可供選擇的制度，但是，在斯庫拉和卡律布狄斯之間⑲，或者，用通俗的話來說，就是每條道路的兩邊都有壕溝。如果我們落到某個主管部門的手中，而這個主管部門以為它能夠把全部學校分成兩三種嚴格的類型，各種類型又必須採用一種僵硬的課程，那麼，這對教育來說，是災難性的，是致命性的。當我說學校是教育單位時，我的意思是指，那種獨立完整的單位。每所學校都有權考慮自身的特殊情況。為了某種目的把學校進行分類是可以的，但是絕對不要有僵硬的、未經學校老師修正過的課程；同樣的原則，經過適當修改，也完全適用於大學和技術學院。

當全面考慮教育對一個國家民族尤其是年輕一代是如何重要時，當看到因為輕浮且遲鈍地處理教育問題所造成的破碎的生活、受挫的希望、民族的失敗，我們難抑心頭的百般憤慨。在現代生活條件下，規律是絕對的，凡是不注重智力訓練的民族是注定要滅亡的。無論你們有怎樣的英雄氣概，怎樣的社交魅力，怎樣的聰明智慧，你們在陸地上或海洋中取得的勝利，都不能夠挽回這一命運。今天，我們尚能維持現在的地位；明天，科學將會更進一步，那時，當命運之神對未受良好教育的人進行裁決時，將不會有人為他們提出上訴。

我們可以對人們普遍信仰的教育理想感到滿意，因為人類自有文明史以來，教育的本質便在於它那虔誠的宗教性。

　　那麼，什麼是宗教性的教育呢？

　　宗教性的教育是諄諄教導我們要有責任感和敬畏感，責任來自於我們對事件發生過程中潛在的掌控能力。當習得的知識可以改變結果的時候，無知就成了罪過。敬畏的基礎在於這樣的一種感覺：現在包含着全部的存在，向前──一切的過去，抑或，向後──一切的未來，直到永遠──直到永恆。

---

①坦普爾（Archbishop Temple，1821-1902），英國坎特伯雷大主教，自由主義思想家，社會改革家，教育改革家，曾任牛津大學講師和拉格比公學校長。1896年任坎特伯雷大主教，成為英國聖公會的精神領袖。他長期從事教育與教會工作，認為宗教與教育是改善勞苦人民生活的重要手段。他在任拉格比公學校長期間（1858-1869），根據當時科技發展和工業革命的現實需求，將自然科學納入課程體系，使諸如化學、地質學、植物學和物理學等成為必修課，並且建立被戲稱為「罐狀教堂（Tin Tabernacle）」的簡易教學實驗室。拉格比公學為諸多公學進行自然科學的教學帶了個好頭。──譯者注

②拉格比公學（Rugby School），位於英格蘭西北部Warwickshire郡的Rugby市，是英國歷史最悠久及最有名望的貴族學府之一，全英排名前20位。學院於1567年創立，是一所男女兼收寄宿學校，以卓越之學術成就享譽全球，每年約有超過20之畢業生能成功入讀牛津及劍橋大學。世界名著《愛麗絲漫遊奇境記》的作者劉易斯·卡羅爾（Lewis Carroll，1832-1898）、香港第25任總督麥理浩勳爵（Crawford Murray MacLehose，1917-2000）等曾在此就讀。這裡是英式橄欖球運動發源地。

1865年初版的童話、玄幻小說《愛麗絲漫遊奇境記》是英國文學、世界文學名著。

它講的是小女孩愛麗絲有一天在室外午睡進入夢中奇境，看到一隻穿背心的白毛紅眼的兔子從身邊跑過，而且邊跑邊從背心口袋里掏出一隻懷錶，口中還念念有詞，叨念自己要遲到了。愛麗絲看到這些奇異的景象，不禁高叫「真是越來越奇怪」（Curiouser and curiouser）。於是，Curiouser and curiouser也成為是全世界千百萬人耳熟能詳的世界文學名句。──譯者注

③懷特海引用法語格言強調他所言的「理解」，是一種基督徒的精神的「理解」。就是運用上帝賦予人類的智性之光，理解了人類的苦難深層次的原因後，那麼，對於現實世界，就不會有什麼抱怨，而會產生一種憐憫。就會盡自己的力量，去減輕周圍人群的苦難做些事情。有了懷特海所言的「理解」，人的內心是平和的，才會在生活中，真正去「盡人事，順天意」。

顯然，這種「理解」，不是邏輯分析能夠獲得的，而是通過靈魂的蘇醒才能獲得。邏輯分析對於靈魂的蘇醒沒有幫助，靈魂的蘇醒，只有不斷追求造物主才能實現。當然，學習懷特海這樣偉大人物的著作，其實，就是在感觸造物主，肯定有助於靈魂的蘇醒。一個人的靈魂是否願意蘇醒，最終是取決於個人願景；因為，上帝也無法叫醒一個刻意裝睡的人。──譯者注

④聖·奧古斯丁（St. Augustine，354-430），古羅馬帝國時期基督教思想家，歐洲中世紀基督教神學、教父哲學的重要代表人物。在羅馬天主教系統，他被封為聖人和聖師，並且是奧斯定會的發起人。對於新教教會，特別是加爾文主義，他的理論是宗教改革的救贖和恩典思想的源頭。他 是聖孟尼迦的幼子，出生於北非，在羅馬受教育，在米蘭接受洗禮。

至今尚存的他的佈道約有500篇，書信200多封，他的最著名、最有影響的兩部著作是《論上帝之城》和《懺悔錄》。後一部是迄今為止最著名的自傳之一，是他在四十多歲時寫成的，被稱為西方歷史上「第一部」自傳，至今仍被傳誦。──譯者注

⑤拿破侖·波拿巴（Napoleon Bonaparte，1769-1821年），軍事家、政治家和數學家；法蘭西第一共和國執政、法蘭西第一帝國皇帝，出生於科西嘉島，是一位卓越的軍事天才。他多次擊敗保王黨的反撲和反法同盟的入侵，捍衛了法國大革命的成果。

他執政期間多次對外擴張，形成了龐大的帝國體系，創造了一系列軍事奇跡。1812年兵敗俄國，元氣大傷；1814年被反法聯軍趕下台。1815年復辟，隨後在滑鐵盧之戰中失敗，被流放到聖赫勒拿島。1821年病逝，1840年屍骨被迎回巴黎並隆重安葬於塞納河畔的榮譽軍人院。

拿破侖曾創立科學院制度、現代大學制度和整個大陸體系的成文法制度。當拿破侖戰敗被流放到聖赫勒拿島時曾說：「我真正的光榮並非打了四十多次勝仗，滑鐵盧一戰抹去了關於這一切的記憶。但是，有一樣東西是不會被人們忘卻的，它將永垂不朽──那就是我的民法典。」

《拿破侖法典》包括物權、債權、婚姻、繼承以及許許多多沿用至今的民法概念，是第一部把羅馬法的基本精神完整傳承到近現代社會的民法。確立了私人財產所有權的神聖不可侵犯，明確了市場經濟條件下的商品交換和價值秩序，進一步保護了資產階級革命的歷史成果，捍衛了法國普通民眾的基本人權，將《人權宣言》中關於財產權、名譽權等基本人權概念細化、具體化。

私有財產制度在拿破侖法典中「像數學邏輯一樣嚴格建立起來」。被黑格爾這種知識分子真心崇拜，稱為哲學理性在地上的代表，這種君主實在不多。

他的經典名言有：

1. 想得好是聰明，計劃得好更聰明，做得好是最聰明又是最好。
2. 總司令最重要的品質就是冷靜的頭腦。
3. 偉大的統帥應該每日自問數次，如果面前或左右出現敵人該怎麼辦？他若不知所措，就是不稱職的。
4. 我只有一個忠告給你──做你自己的主人。
5. 人不管處在什麼樣的情況下都可以幸福。
6. 無所謂幸福，也就無所謂不幸。幸福者的生活是在一幅銀色底片上顯示黑色的星星；不幸者的生活則猶如黑底版上的銀色星星。
7. 我不願意為取金蛋而殺掉我的老母雞！
8. 不想當將軍的士兵不是好士兵。（他24歲時榮升為準將）──譯者注

⑥中國朦朧詩人舒婷在《一切都是命運》一詩中有「一切的現在都孕育着未來，／未來的一切都生長於它的昨天。／希望，而且為它鬥爭，／請把這一切放在你的肩上。」兩者有異曲同工之妙。──譯者注

⑦威廉·莎士比亞（William Shakespeare，1564-1616），英國文藝復興時期偉大的劇作家、詩人，歐洲文藝復興時期人文主義文學的集大成者。他的代表作有《哈姆雷特》、《奧賽羅》、《仲夏夜之夢》、《威尼斯商人》、《羅密歐與朱麗葉》和《亨利四世》

等。他還寫過154首十四行詩，兩首長詩。他的名言雋語有：

1. 生存還是毀滅，這是一個值得考慮的問題。

2. 當我們還買不起幸福的時候，我們絕不應該走得離櫥窗太近，盯着幸福出神。

3. 最好的好人，都是犯過錯誤的過來人；一個人往往因為有一點小小的缺點，更顯出他的可愛。

4. 千萬人的失敗，都失敗在做事不徹底；往往做到離成功尚差一步就終止不前了。

5. 多聽，少說，接受每一個人的責難，但是保留你的最後裁決。

6. 在命運的顛沛中，最可以看出人們的氣節。

7. 不良的習慣會隨時阻礙你走向成名、獲利和享樂的路上去。

8. 對眾人一視同仁，對少數人推心置腹，對任何人不要虧負。

9. 真正的愛情是不能用言語表達的，行為才是忠心的最好說明。

10. 忠誠的愛情充溢在我的心裡，我無法估計自己享有的財富。

11. 書籍是全世界的營養品。生活裡沒有書籍，就好像沒有陽光；智慧裡沒有書籍，就好像鳥兒沒有翅膀。

12. 沒有什麼事是好的或壞的，但思想卻使其中有所不同。——譯者注

⑧莫里哀（法語：Molière，1622年1月15日-1673年2月17日），法國喜劇作家、演員、戲劇活動家，法國芭蕾舞劇的創始人，莫里哀為其藝名。他以整個生命推動了戲劇的前進，以滑稽的形式揭露了社會的黑暗，是法國古典主義文學以及歐洲文藝復興運動的傑出代表，是世界戲劇史上與莎士比亞共同彪炳史冊的偉大戲劇家。他給後人留下了三十多部喜劇，主要代表作品有《無病呻吟》、《偽君子》、《吝嗇鬼》和《唐璜》等。

莫里哀是位喜劇大師，但是他的死卻是一場悲劇。為了維持劇團開支，他不得不帶病參加演出。1673年2月17日，在演完《無病呻吟》最後一幕以後，莫里哀咳血倒下，當晚就逝世了，終年51歲。莫里哀去世後，法蘭西學院在其大廳裡為他立了一尊石像，底座上刻着這樣的題詞：他的榮譽什麼也不缺少，我們的光榮卻缺少了他。

莫里哀說：「喜劇的責任，就是通過娛樂來糾正人們的弊病，通過令人發笑的描繪，抨擊本世紀的惡習。」這也是其基本創作綱領。——譯者注

⑨索福克勒斯（Sophocles，約前496—前406），雅典人，古希臘三大悲劇作家之一。他既相信神和命運的無上威力，又要求人們具有獨立自主的精神，並對自己的行為負責，這是雅典民主政治繁榮時期思想意識的特徵。他根據他的理想來塑造人物形象，即使處在命運的掌握之中，也不喪失其獨立自主的堅強性格。代表作品有《安提戈涅》、《俄狄浦斯王》等，其悲劇以莊嚴、崇高和雄壯的詩句震撼人心。他的名言有：

莫做見不得人之事，時間知道一切，也會揭露一切。

思想比武力更有力量。

倘若我還是我，我就沒有發瘋；倘若我已瘋了，我就不再是我。——譯者注

⑩維吉爾（拉丁語：Vergilius，英語化為Vergil或Virgil，前70年10月15日-前19年9月21日），古羅馬最偉大的詩人，在西方思想和藝術領域的影響堪與荷馬比肩。他出生於阿爾卑斯山南高盧曼圖亞附近的安得斯村；在家鄉受過基礎教育後，去羅馬和南意大利，攻讀哲學與數學、醫學；約公元前44年回到故鄉，一面務農，一面從事詩歌創作。他是古羅馬奧古斯都時期最重要的詩人，著有長詩《牧歌》、《愛奈特》和史詩《埃涅阿斯紀》等。

由於羅馬基督教會從公元4世紀起，就認為他是未來世界的預言家和聖人，他在中古時代一直享有特殊的尊榮地位。他是詩人但丁最崇拜的作家，但丁認為他最有智慧，

最瞭解人類，在《神曲》中，後者稱他為「老師」，虛構他解救了迷路的自己，並邀請自己去遊覽地獄和天國。

維吉爾的史詩沒有人民口頭文學的特點，是歐洲「文人史詩」的開端，使古代史詩在人物、結構和詩歌格律等方面進一步獲得了定型。文藝復興以後，許多用史詩詩體裁寫作的歐洲著名詩人，如彌爾頓等，都以維吉爾的史詩作為他們自己的範本。在古代希臘羅馬文學作家中，公認維吉爾是荷馬以後最重要的史詩詩人。——譯者注

⑪指由政府教育主管機構等來出題或評卷的考試。——譯者注

⑫古代希臘七位名人的統稱，現代人瞭解較多的只有立法者梭倫和哲學家泰勒斯兩人，剩餘五人一般認為是契羅、畢阿斯、庇塔庫斯、佩利安德、克萊俄布盧，但無法確定。

雅典的梭倫（Solon of Athens），他的格言相傳是「避免極端」（Nothing in excess）。

斯巴達的契羅（Chilon of Sparta），他的格言相傳是「莫妄想不可能之事」（Do not desire the impossible）或「認識你自己」（first Know yourself）。

米利都的泰勒斯（Thales of Miletus），他的格言相傳是「維穩帶來毀滅」（To bring surety brings ruin）或「認識你自己」（Know thyself）。

普林納的畢阿斯（Bias of Priene），他的格言相傳有「人多反而壞事」（Too many workers spoil the work）、「多數人皆惡人」（Most men are bad）。

林度斯的克萊俄布盧（Cleobulus of Lindos），他的格言相傳是「適度即至善」（Moderation is the chief good）。

米蒂利尼的庇塔庫斯（Pittacus of Mitylene），他的格言相傳是「認清你的時機」（Know thine opportunity）。

科林斯的佩利安德（Periander of Corinth），他的格言相傳是「事事都應做長遠考慮」（Forethought in all things）。——譯者注

⑬消元法，利用方程組的一些乘除加減，使得某個未知變量前面的系數變為零，方程組總的變量變少的方法。——譯者注

⑭傑弗雷·喬叟（Geoffrey Chaucer，約1340-1400），英國最偉大的詩人和作家，被譽為「英國詩歌之父」，他在英國文學史上的地位相當於但丁在意大利文學史上的地位。自從1066年諾曼人征服英國以後，英國存着用三種語言創作的文學：僧院文學使用拉丁文；騎士詩歌多用法語；民間歌謠則用英語。喬叟率先採用倫敦方言寫作，並創作「英雄雙行體」，對英國民族語言和文學的發展影響極大。他是後來十五世紀末葉 直到十七世紀四十年代以莎士比亞為代表的英國文藝復興的奠基人，也是英國詩歌從 民間歌謠進一步發展的創始人。在生活的最後十五年，他進行了《坎特伯雷故事集》（The Canterbury Tales，1387-1400）的創作，這是他最傑出的作品。喬叟於1400年10月25日在倫敦逝世，葬於威斯敏斯特教堂「詩人角」（Poets' Corner）。——譯者注

⑮黑死病（The Black Death），也叫鼠疫（plague），人類歷史上極嚴重的瘟疫之一，14世紀蔓延到歐洲和亞洲的鼠疫傳染病。一般認為起源於亞洲，一說起源於中亞，一說起源於喜馬拉雅山區，一說起源於黑海城市卡法，約在1440年代（1346-1353年）散佈到整個歐洲。這場瘟疫在全世界造成了大約7500萬人死亡，根據估計，瘟疫爆發期間的中世紀歐洲約有佔人口總數30%-60%（約2500萬）人死於黑死病。

同樣的疾病多次侵襲歐洲，直到1700年代為止，期間造成的死亡情形與嚴重程度各不相同。較晚的幾次大流行包括1629年到1631年的意大利瘟疫、1665年到1666年的倫敦大瘟疫、1679年的維也納大瘟疫、1720年到1722年的馬賽大瘟疫，以及1771年的莫斯科瘟疫。關於這些疾病的異同仍有爭議，但是其致命型態似乎於18世紀消失於歐洲。

　　黑死病對歐洲人口造成嚴重影響，改變歐洲的社會結構，動搖當時支配歐洲的羅馬天主教會的地位，並因此使得一些少數族群受到迫害，例如猶太人、穆斯林、外國人、乞丐以及癩瘋病患者。生存與否的不確定性，使得人們產生「活在當下」的一種情緒，如同薄伽丘在《十日談》（The Decameron）之中所描繪的一般。

　　14世紀發生於歐洲的事件，剛開始被當時的作家稱作「Great Mortality」，瘟疫爆發之後，又有了「黑死病」之名。一般認為這個名稱是取自其中一個顯著的症狀，稱作「acral necrosis」，患者的皮膚會因為皮下出血而變黑。而黑色實際上也象徵憂鬱、哀傷與恐懼。

　　歷史紀錄對於黑死病的特徵紀錄中，有一些關於淋巴腺腫的描述，與19世紀發生於亞洲的淋巴腺鼠疫相似，這使得科學家與歷史學家推測自14世紀開始的黑死病，與鼠疫相同，皆是由一種稱為鼠疫桿菌（Yersinia pestis）的細菌所造成。這些細菌是寄生於跳蚤身上，並藉由黑鼠（Rattus rattus）等動物來傳播。也有研究認為病源可能來自亞洲的小沙鼠（Gerbils）。不過由於其他疾病也有可能產生淋巴腺腫，因此也有人提出其他不同的觀點。黑死病第二次大流行時，9座城市中有7座透過人類身上衣物的跳蚤與頭蝨傳播。

　　目前普遍認為黑死病的病原體可能已經滅絕。——譯者注

　　⑯測鏈，測量用的一種工具，包含有100個相連的鋼鐵環，長66英尺（20.1米），為埃德蒙·岡特（Edmund Gunter，1581-1626，英國天文學家和數學家）所發明；他還發明了象限儀和標尺，並引進了兩個三角學術語，餘弦和餘切。——譯者注

　　⑰柏金·奧貝克（Perkin Warbeck，1474-1499），亨利七世處決了所有對他的王位構成威脅的約克家族成員，但是總有人假借死去的約克家族成員給他添亂，其中一人名叫柏金·奧貝克。他是一個船夫的兒子，但他卻聲稱自己是倫敦塔里被理查三世殺害的愛德華四世的次子。此前，沃貝克從可惡的騙子逐漸演變成了極具威脅的人物，因為他的表演十分成功，歐洲各國君主以及包括真正王子的姑姑在內的約克家族剩餘成員紛紛支持他的活動。沃貝克自稱「理查德四世」登陸英格蘭，後被抓住並判處絞刑。——譯者注

　　⑱白令海峽（Bering Strait），太平洋的一個海峽，位於亞洲最東點的迭日涅夫角（169°43'W）和美洲最西點的韋爾斯王子角（168°05'W）之間的海峽，位於大約北緯65°40'，寬約35-86公里。這個海峽連接了楚科奇海（北冰洋的一部分）和白令海（太平洋的一部分），位於俄羅斯和阿拉斯加中間，最窄處約82公里，水深30-50米。

　　它的名字來自丹麥探險家維他斯·白令。白令海峽正中間有代奧米德群島。

　　國際日期變更線位於大代奧米德島和小代奧米德島之間，因此這兩座島雖然只相隔約3公里，但時區並不相同，所以可在小代奧米德島這邊看到「明天」的俄羅斯。

　　白令海峽地區人口稀少。東部沿海的美屬阿拉斯加州的Nome城鎮（3,788人）和Teller聚居點（228人）。西部沿海則是位於俄羅斯聯邦遠東地區的楚科奇自治區，沿海峽城鎮Lorino（1,267人）和Lavrentiya（1,459人）。

　　冷戰時期，白令海峽作為蘇聯和美國的邊界，蘇聯的大代奧米德島僅距美國的小代奧米德島3.9公里。傳統上，當地人常常往返此邊界「例行訪問、慶祝節日及生活貿易」。但是在冷戰時期，這種做法被禁止，該邊界成為了「冰幕」（Ice Curtain），被完全封閉。直至1987年，美國游泳者琳·考克斯象徵性地游泳橫穿該邊界，才緩解了兩國間的緊張氣氛，她同時受到羅納德·里根及米哈伊爾·戈爾巴喬夫的嘉獎。——譯者注

　　⑲斯庫拉和卡律布狄斯，是古希臘神話中的女妖和魔怪。女妖斯庫拉（Scylla）住在意大利和西里島之間海峽中的一個洞穴裡，對面住著另一個妖怪卡律布狄斯（Charybdis），它們各自守護著墨西拿海峽（Strait of Messina）的一側，危害所有過往航海的人。

　　相傳，斯庫拉本來是一位美麗的仙女，因為女巫喀耳刻（Circe）妒忌她的美貌把她變成了怪物，性情大變的她抓住過往船隻的水手並且吃掉他們。卡律布狄斯是一個怪物，能夠在一天之內三次吸入又吐出海峽中的水。

　　據荷馬史詩說，女妖斯庫拉長着12只不規則的腳，有6個蛇一樣的脖子，每個脖子上各有一顆可怕的頭，張着血盆大口，每張嘴有3排毒牙，隨時準備把獵物咬碎。

　　在海峽中間，卡律布狄斯化身為一個大漩渦，波濤洶湧、水花飛濺，每天三次從懸崖下奔湧而出，在退落時將通過此處的船隻全部淹沒。它們每天在意大利和西西里島之間海峽中興風作浪，航海者在妖怪和漩渦之間通過是異常危險的，它們時刻在等待着穿過西西裡海峽的船舶。

　　短語「處於斯庫拉和卡律布狄斯之間」（Scylla and Charybdis），算是一個英語典故（相當於中國的成語、諺語），其意是「左右都是危險、左右為難」。現實世界中，墨西拿海峽靠近陸地的一側有一塊危險的岩石稱作「斯庫拉巨岩」；西西里島一側的一處漩渦被稱作「卡律布狄斯漩渦」。——譯者注

第二章　教育的節奏

所謂教育的節奏（rhythm of education），我指的是每一個有教育
經驗的人都熟悉並在實踐中運用的原則。因此，當我意識到我是在對
一群英國著名教育家發言的時候，我並不指望我能講出一些對你們來
說有新意的東西。但是，我確實認為，考慮到影響該原則應用的所有
因素，人們還沒有對這個原則進行充分的討論。

首先，我努力用最簡明的方法來闡述什麼是教育的節奏，希望這
種闡述足夠清晰地表達這次演講的重點——這個原則其實就是——

在學生心智發展的不同階段，應該採用不同的課程，採用不同的
學習方式。

你們或許與我一樣，認為這不過是眾所周知的老生常談，沒有人
懷疑過。我之所以選擇這個主題，一方面，我確實想強調我所演講的
基本思想其主要特徵就是這個，大家肯定也都發現這一特點；另一方
面，我認為這個顯而易見的真理在教育實踐中並沒有被真正地掌握，
沒有根據其中的規律對學生的心理給予應有的關注和重視。

幼年期的任務

首先，我要對一些原則提出異議，而學科的劃分就是按照這些原
則來進行的。對於這一點，只有清楚地說明這些原則，它們的正確性
才能為人們所理解和接受。我們先來討論一下難易的標準是什麼。人
們常常認為，較容易的科目應該先於比較難的科目學習，這種觀點並
不對。相反，有些最難的科目應該先學習，因為人的先天秉性如此，
亦是生存所需，學會這些東西對生活非常重要。幼兒面對的第一個智
力任務就是對口語的掌握，這是一件多麼艱難的任務！他們需要把聲
音和意思對應起來，需要對聲音和意思進行分析。但我們都知道，幼

兒自然而然地學會了。他的這種奇跡般的成功是可解釋的。所有的奇跡都是如此，可是對於智者來說，這些依然是奇跡。我希望，擺在我們面前的這個活生生的例子，是不是可以讓那些主張把最難的科目往後放的蠢話就此打住？！

幼兒需要學習的下一個科目是什麼？應該是書面語的掌握，也就是說，把聲音和形狀聯繫起來。天啊！這些教育家們瘋了嗎？他們給一個六歲的正在牙牙學語的小東西指定了一些任務，這些任務或許令聖賢都感到沮喪——他們窮其一生努力都未必能完成。同樣，數學學習中最難的部分是代數的原理，但這部分卻要放在相對比較簡單的微積分之前來學習。

我不想再多說什麼了，我只強調一點：在複雜的教育實踐中，把較難的內容往後放並不是解決問題的有效方法。

至於學科誰先誰後，我們可以按照必要優先原則。顯然，在這方面，我們更有依據。比如，你在學會閱讀之前是不可能欣賞《哈姆雷特》①這樣的文學作品的；同樣，你必須掌握了整數的概念，才能接着去學習分數。但是，如果細究的話，這個原則無疑也會失去效力。原則本身沒問題，但是這個原則只有在你對所學學科進行人為限制的時候它才是對的。這個原則也存在着一定的危險性，因為從某種角度來看，它是正確的；但是，從另一個角度去看，它卻是錯誤的。正常來說，你要先學會閱讀，才能去讀荷馬②；然而，很多兒童，甚至過去幾個世紀裡的很多成年人，卻是通過聆聽媽媽的講述或行吟詩人的歌唱，來「閱讀」《奧德賽》③的，在充滿傳奇色彩的大海上遨遊，大家的想像力通過一代代的口耳相傳。對這個原則不加區別地使用，人為地把一些科目放在另一個科目之前，只會製造出教育實踐中的撒哈拉沙漠，枯燥乾癟，了無生氣。

智力發展的階段

我之所以選擇這個題目作為我演講的主題，是源於對當前一些流

行觀念的批判。人們常常認為，學生的進步是一個勻速發展、持續穩定的進程，形式不變，速度一致。比如說，人們設想一個小男孩在十歲的時候開始學習拉丁語，按說在十八或是二十歲的時候，就會成長為一名古典文學的學者。對此，我不敢苟同，我始終認為，這種觀念是建立在對智力發展的錯誤認識基礎之上，極大地妨礙我們教育方法的有效性。

生命是有周期性的。它既有日常的周期，比如一天中，工作和娛樂的交替，活動和睡眠的交替；還有季節的周期，如學校學期和假期的交替；還有，一年春夏秋冬四季的交替，等等。這些周期就在那裡，任何人都無法視而不見，也無從迴避。

同樣，生命中存在着微妙的涉及智力發展的周期，它們循環往復地出現，每一個循環都各不相同，而且每次循環中又會再生出附屬的階段。我選擇「節奏」作為我的主題，主要是用它來表示在重複結構中的差異性。我們的教育呆板無效的主要原因是缺乏對智力發展節奏和特徵的認識。

我認為，黑格爾④把一般發展過程分為三個階段是正確的，這三個階段分別為正(thesis)、反(antithesis)、合(synthesis)⑤。不過，在把黑格爾的這個概念運用於教育理論的時候，我認為這三個名稱不是特別具有啟發性。因為涉及智力發展的過程，所以我更樂意把它們命名為：浪漫階段（the Stage of Romance）、精確階段（the Stage of Precision）和綜合運用階段（the Stage of Generalization）。

浪漫階段

浪漫階段是對萬事萬物開始有所領悟的階段。在這一階段，各種事物對於孩子來說，既新奇又生動，其本身包含着種種未經探索的可能聯繫，孩子懵懂地面對着若隱若現的大量內容，不知所措卻又異常興奮。在這一階段，知識不受系統化程式的支配，這裡所說的系統是

指為了特定目的而建立起來的系統。這時,孩子處於對事實的直接認知中,只是偶爾會對認識的事實進行系統化分析。浪漫的情感,主要表現為興奮,這種興奮是從我們所接觸的單純事實之間可能存在某種重要意義而產生的。比如,魯濱孫⑥僅僅是一個男人,沙灘僅僅是沙灘,腳印僅僅是腳印而已,荒島只是一個荒島,歐洲也不過是一個人潮湧動的世界。但是,當我們突然意識到在魯濱遜、腳印、沙地及與歐洲隔離的荒涼的小島之間存在着某種若隱若現的聯繫時,浪漫的遐想就開始了。

我之所以採用這個極端的例子來進行闡述,是希望使我的觀點變得簡單易懂些。這個故事可以很貼切地說明智力發展過程中的第一個階段——從本質上說,教育必須是對大腦中已經存在的紛繁複雜的騷動進行有序整理的過程,你不能對一個空白的大腦進行教育。在我們的教育概念中,我們趨向於把它框在智力發展的第二個階段,即精確階段。但是當我們對教育做這種限制時,必然會對整個教育產生誤解。我們必須對大腦最初混沌的騷動、掌握的知識,以及學習的成果給予一視同仁的關注。

精確階段

精確階段也代表了一種知識的積累。在這個發展階段,知識之間的廣泛關係居於次要地位,從屬於系統闡述的準確性。這是文法和規則的階段,包括語言的文法和科學的原理。在這個階段,要使學生一點一點地接受一些分析事實的特定方法。新的事實增加了,但是增加的是適合於分析的事實。

顯然,如果沒有前期的浪漫階段,精確階段是不會有結果的:如果沒有對這些事實廣泛且普遍的模糊認識,那麼之後的分析會變得毫無意義。這不過是對一系列蒼白事實展開的無意義的闡述,這些事實完全人為提出,並且沒有更進一步的關聯性。我想強調的是,在這個

階段，我們不能僅僅停留在浪漫階段所獲取的簡單事實。

　　浪漫階段的事實揭示了可能具有廣泛意義的種種概念，而在精確階段，我們按照條理化、系統化的方式，獲得其他一些事實，從而對浪漫階段的一般事實作出揭示和分析。

綜合運用階段

　　最後的綜合運用階段就是黑格爾所說的理論綜合。這是在增加了分類概念和有關的技能之後，重新回歸浪漫，不過，這是下一階段的新的浪漫。這是精確訓練的目的。這也是最後的成功。我恐怕對一些明顯的概念做了枯燥的分析，這也是不得已而為之，因為在我後面的評論中，我是假定大家對教育這三個階段的基本特點有清晰瞭解。

循環的過程

　　教育應該是這三個階段循環往復的疊加。從小的方面來說，每一堂課都應當自成一局。越是長周期越要確保有明確的收穫，以便形成新一輪循環的起點。我們應該堅決擯棄這樣的觀念：在教育中設定不切實際的長遠目標。在學生階段性的求知欲望中，如果教師能夠適時地對他們取得的成功進行鼓勵，學生就會為其階段性的某種成功感到欣喜，躊躇滿志地開始下一階段新的學習。

　　幼兒在浪漫階段的體驗，是他開始瞭解物體以及物體之間內在聯繫的起點。兒童智力發展的外在表現是把自己的身體行為和心理感知完美地協調起來。他在精確階段的第一步是掌握口語，使其成為一種工具，從而對他感興趣的物體進行分類並加強他與其他人的情感聯繫。他在綜合運用階段的第一步，就不僅是把語言作為一種媒介用來對物體分類，而是擴大他在認知事物過程中產生的快樂。

　　智力發展的第一個循環周期，即從感知事物到語言能力的獲得，再到分類思維的形成和對事物更敏銳的感知，每一階段都需要給予更

細緻的研究。這是唯一一個我們在它最自然的狀態下觀察到的循環發展周期（以後的諸多發展周期總是受到現行教育模式的影響）。這個發展周期有一個顯著特徵——那就是它獲得了完全的成功，可惜，這個特徵在以後的教育中消失了。這個發展周期結束時，孩子能夠說話了，他的觀念可以歸類了，他的感知能力變得更為敏銳了。這個發展周期達到了它的目的，遠遠超過了大多數學生在大多數教育體制下獲得的成就。為什麼會是這樣的呢？我猜想，是嬰兒周圍的環境，為他佈置了一項適合大腦正常發育的任務。無疑，一個新生嬰兒，當我們意識到擺在他面前的任務是多麼地困難的時候，我們都會誤以為他在智力發展方面毫無希望。孩子學會說話並開始更好地思考，我不認為這有什麼特別的神秘，但它確實啟發我們，對此該有相應的省察。

在接下來的教育中，我們還沒有找到另一個發展周期可以與之相媲美，既可以在有限的時間裡管理它們的全過程，又可以在自身領域獲得完全的成功。在幼兒自然成長的過程中，這種成功有着顯著的特徵。我們讓孩子在十歲時開始學習一門課程，比如說拉丁語，如果期許他通過統一的正規訓練讓他在二十歲的時候獲得成功，那麼無論是興趣還是最終的成就，結果自然是失敗。我這裡用「失敗」這個詞，是把學習拉丁語的結果與學習母語所取得的巨大成功比較而言。但我並不認為失敗是因為這些任務本身太艱巨了，我始終認為：幼兒的第一個發展周期是最艱巨的。之所以失敗，是因為我們設定的這個任務是以一種非自然的狀態出現的，沒有節奏，沒有中間階段成功帶來的即時鼓勵，沒有專注集中。

我還沒有談及專注集中所具有的顯著特徵，它與幼兒的進步息息相關。嬰兒全身心地專注於他的智力訓練，沒有其他東西可以打擾他的發展進程。在這一點上，這個自然發展周期和之後我們所看到的學生發展過程中的歷史記錄，存在着顯著的差別。顯然，生活是多姿多彩的，因而，人們的精神和智力自然也會多方面地發展，以適應這個

他們註定要生活於其中的繽紛世界。但是，在做出這種考慮之後，我們應該明智地多關注一下以後的幾個發展周期。我們特別要避免在同一個發展周期內進行不同科目的競爭。舊教育的弊端在於，對一個沒有明顯特徵的科目給予了毫無節奏的關注。我們今天的教育體制強調一種初級的普通教育，允許把知識分解到不同學科中去，這樣的做法不過是在雜亂無章地拼湊一些知識的碎片。我在這裡呼籲，我們要努力在學生的心靈中繪製一幅和諧的圖案，依據對學生的直觀理解，把各種具有內在價值的教學內容，分配到各個從屬的循環周期中去。我們必須在合適的季節收穫合適的作物。

青春期的浪漫

現在我們開始討論一下我前面所說觀點的具體應用。

最初的嬰兒階段其智力發展是非常成功的，緊接着就是青春期的智力發展，這個時期的發展依舊從浪漫階段開始。正是在這個階段，孩子的性格開始形成。孩子在青春期浪漫階段所表現出來的東西，決定了他將來的生活如何被理想和想像所塑造，決定了他將來生活的豐富多彩程度。緊接着就是伴隨口語和閱讀能力的掌握而獲得的綜合運用階段。綜合運用階段相對整個嬰兒期來說，是很短暫的，因為嬰兒期的浪漫元素很少。就「知識」這個詞而言，不管作何種解釋，孩子對於這個世界的最初認識都是從第一個循環周期結束之後，才開始進入到精妙絕倫的浪漫階段。各種概念、事實、關係、故事、歷史、可能性和藝術性，等等，它們以語言、聲音、形狀和顏色等等，一齊湧入孩子的生活，激發他的感情，刺激他的鑒賞力，激勵他去做相似的活動。但令人悲哀的是，孩子的黃金時期不幸籠罩在填鴨式教育的陰影之中。我所說的這個時期大概有四年的時間，從常規意義上來說，通常在八歲到十二或十三歲之間。這個時期兒童已經學會使用母語，並且已經學會觀察和處理問題。嬰兒不能應付身邊的環境，但是兒童

能；嬰兒不會觀察事情的來龍去脈，但是兒童能；嬰兒不能通過記憶來學會思考，但兒童能。於是，兒童相比嬰兒，進入了一個全新的世界。

當然，有些小周期在浪漫階段形成的渦流，精確階段通過這個周期的反復出現而使自身得以延長。提高書寫、拼寫和計算能力，掌握一系列簡單的事實（比如說英國的歷任國王），這些都是精確階段的基本內容。這些基本的能力和掌握的內容，對於訓練兒童的專注集中以及作為一種生活的基本常識十分必要。不過，這些東西在性質上是支離破碎的。更為重要的是，浪漫階段如滔滔江流，把孩子推向波瀾壯闊的精神世界。

蒙特梭利教育法⑦之所以成功，在於它承認了浪漫在孩子的智力發展過程中所起到的主導作用。如果這種解釋成立的話，那麼也意味着這種方法在實用方面有其局限性。蒙特梭利教育法在一定程度上對所有浪漫階段的教育都是必不可少的。它的精髓是在知識王國裡自由自在地遨遊以及激發大膽主動的創新，但是它缺乏精確階段所必要的克制和約束。

語言的掌握

當兒童的智力發展開始接近浪漫階段尾聲的時候，這種循環成長的過程使他開始傾向於精確知識的學習。語言就自然地成為他專注學習的主要內容。這是一種他非常熟悉的表達方式。他初步瞭解了一些他人的生活和其他文明社會的故事、歷史和詩歌等。因此，從11歲開始，他需要在精確知識的獲得方面增加注意力。最後，在12歲到15歲這三年的時間裡必須用大量豐富的語言詞彙充實自己；如果按此計劃進行的話，其結果必然值得期待。試想一下，在一定時間內，把注意力集中在一個地方，可以說在這個階段結束時，孩子既能掌握英語，順利地閱讀一些基本的法語，也可以完成拉丁語的初步學習；我的意

思是，能夠掌握比較簡單的拉丁語語法知識、拉丁語句子的結構，在優美譯文的幫助下能夠閱讀一些拉丁語作家的簡化版，通過閱讀原文並對照譯文的方法，掌握這本拉丁語文學原著的全部內容。我認為，用這種方法學習三種語言，對一般的兒童來說，完全是在他們的能力範圍之內，只要他們沒有被其他需要精確學習的科目分散精力。當然，一些有天賦的孩子可以學得更好，走得更遠。學習拉丁語對這些孩子來說並不困難，所以，在這個階段結束的時候，如果他們在文學方面有興趣，而且還想以後這方面多學習幾年的話，可以開始學習希臘語。其他科目在這個時期處於一個次要的地位，意味着我們在態度方面要有所區別。首先，我們要明白，這些半文學性質的科目，比如說歷史，將來會被融合在語言學習中。如果不學一點歐洲歷史的話，那麼很難閱讀英語、法語和拉丁語的文學作品。我並不是說要擯棄所有專門的歷史教學。不過，我確實建議：這門學科應該以我所謂的「浪漫精神」來表現，而不應當讓學生為了考試而去記憶大量的系統性的細節。

在這一時期，科學應該處於它的浪漫階段。學生應該自己觀察，自己實驗，只要求有局部的精確思維就可以了。不論是出於對科學理論的興趣，還是因為技術應用的目的，科學重要性的本質都是將科學應用於具體的實物，每一個這樣的應用都會喚起一個新的研究主題。因此，所有關於科學的訓練都應該以研究開始，以研究結束，自始至終都應該把握自然中所發生的事實材料。能否做出適合這個年齡的正確指導方針，取決於經驗豐富與否。但我依然呼籲，這個時期是以浪漫的方式來學習科學的最佳年齡。

科學的專注

到15歲的時候，語言的精確階段和科學的浪漫階段接近尾聲了，隨之而來的是語言的綜合運用階段和科學的精確階段。這是一個短

暫的階段，但是至關重要。我想這個時期大概會持續一年左右，毫無疑問，這個時期會打破之前課程之間的那種平衡。這個時期需要集中注意力學習科學，而相對減少語言課程學習。緊接着用一年的時間集中學習科學，可以讓學生深入瞭解諸如機械、物理、化學、代數和幾何學等學科中重要的原理。理解這些原理，並不意味着學習了這些課程，而是通過系統地闡述這些學科的概念從而把他們之前所學的東西融合在一起。以代數和幾何為例，我把它們作為例子是因為我多少對它們還有些瞭解。之前三年，學生們已經學習了如何用簡單的代數公式和幾何原理來解決測量方面的問題，或是其他關於計算的科學工作。通過這種方式，強調只有數字才能表達正確的結果，學生的算術能力得到了加強，他們熟悉了字母表達的公式和幾何命題的概念，懂得了一些簡單處理問題的其他方法。這樣，在熟悉科學概念的過程當中沒有浪費很多時間。學生們已經做好準備去學習那些他們應該徹底瞭解的少量代數和幾何原理。此外，在前面的階段中，一些男孩子在數學方面顯示出了一定的天賦，他們將在這方面繼續有所發展，在最後一年中，他們在數學方面的加強是以犧牲其他科目為代價的。我只是以數學來舉例說明而已。

　　與此同時，語言的周期正處於它的綜合運用階段。在這一階段，語法和作文的精確學習暫時告一段落，語言的學習僅限於文學作品的閱讀，着重於作品的思想及其所處的一般歷史背景；歷史學習將具體到某個時代的研究上。選擇時代作為歷史學習的重點，是為了確切地說明在這個重要時間段內所發生的事情，以便對有關的人和政策做出評判。

　　至此，我大概已經對從幼兒階段到十六歲半的教育做了一個大概的描述，這個大概輪廓是根據生命的節奏來安排的。普通教育以這樣的方式來進行是可行的，對學生專注學習的訓練以及保持飽滿的活力都有好處。因此，精確階段經常出現的是已經被理解但是需要迫切處

理的主題。每個學生都會依次把注意力集中在不同的學科上，並找出他的興趣所在。最後——這是所有目標中我最珍視的——理科生既得到了難能可貴的文學教育，又在最敏感的年齡養成了在科學領域獨立思考的習慣。

十六歲之後，新的問題又會出現。文科生的科學知識到了綜合運用階段，大部分是以講座的形式來學習科學的主要結果和大概思想。語言、文學和歷史的學習周而復始。

至於這些學科更多的細節則不再必需了。對學生而言，科學知識的學習，在精確階段會一直延續到中學結束，在這期間，學生會對廣泛的科學概念不斷地加深理解。

但是，在這個教育階段，問題的產生非常個性化，或者至少可以分解成很多的個案，以至於不可能有普遍適用的方法，但是我仍然強烈建議：所有的學習者都應該繼續學習法語，如果他們還沒有掌握德語，那麼也可以開始學習德語。

大學教育

如果你們還能忍受我繼續演講的話，那麼我還想和你們談談大學教育中思想的重要性。從嬰兒到成人的整個成長階段是一個巨大的循環周期。浪漫階段覆蓋了兒童前十二年的學習生活，精確階段包含了整個學校的中等教育，綜合運用階段是從少年邁向成人的階段。對於那些在中學教育後繼續接受正規教育的人來說，大學課程或相當於大學水準的課程是很重要的綜合運用階段，綜合運用的精神和理念佔據主導地位。大學的講座是面向那些已經熟悉細節和過程的人，也就是說，至少是和先前所受的訓練比較符合，因此容易掌握。在中學階段，學生伏案專注於自己的課業，而在大學階段，他應該站起來，環顧四周。正因為如此，如果學生在進入大學的第一年，把時間浪費在用過去的學習方式去溫習以前學過的東西，那將是致命的錯誤。在中

學階段，學生經過艱苦的努力，學會了從具體特殊的事例到一般抽象概念的瞭解；在大學，他必須學會從一般抽象概念向具體事例運用的轉變。一門設計出色的大學課程是對一般規律的廣泛研究。我並不是指與具體事實割裂的一般規律，而是我們應該研究具體事例，從具體事例來說明一般概念。

智力的培養

　　智力培養是大學教育的一個方面，着重於理論興趣和實際效用的結合——不管你向學生灌輸什麼細節，在他以後的生活中正好遇到這個細節的機會微乎其微；就算他真的遇到了，他可能早就忘記了你教給他什麼了。真正有用的教育是使學生透徹地理解一般原理，這些原理能夠運用到各種不同的具體細節中去。在以後的實踐中，人們可能已經忘記具體的細節是什麼，但是，在他們潛意識裡，曾經習得的判斷力會幫助他們把這些原理用於當時的實際情況。**當你丟掉你的課本、燒掉你的聽課筆記，忘掉你為了應付考試而背誦的細節，你的學習對你來說才是真正有用的。**你所需要的那些細節的知識就像頭頂上的太陽和月亮一樣，都是顯而易見的事實；而你偶爾需要的，也都能在任何參考文獻裡找到答案。**大學的功能在於使你能夠擺脫細節而保留原理。**當我說到原理的時候，我甚至不能用簡單的語言來進行描述。一個真正深入骨髓的原理，與其說是一種正式的語言闡述，倒不如說是一種思維習慣。這種思維習慣是大腦對一些刺激的反應方式，這些刺激具體表現為一些具體事例。沒有人在面對某種情況的時候，他所學的知識會清晰地、有意識地出現在他的面前。智力的培養無非就是人在執行某個活動的時候，大腦以一種令人滿意的方式運轉而已。學習常常被比喻成這樣一件事情：我們注視着我們讀過的所有書本，當一個時機來臨時，我們選取適當的那頁，對着世界大聲朗讀出來。

幸運的是，實際情況與上述不成熟的想法並不矛盾；因此，獲得純粹知識和取得專業成就之間的對立，應該沒有我們用一個錯誤的教育觀念來看待這個問題那樣嚴重。我用另外一種方式來闡述我的觀點，一所大學的理想，不是為了獲得知識，而是為了獲得力量。大學的職責就是把一個孩子的知識轉變為一個成人的力量。

智力發展的節奏特點

我將用以下兩點來結束我本次的演講，我希望用告誡的方式來闡明我的意思。這次演講的重點是智力發展有其內在的節奏性。人的精神生活是由很多條線串成的網。這些線不會按照統一的標準編織在一起。我曾經試圖用事實來說明這個真理，我觀察了不少天賦中等資質的孩子，他們在順利環境中發展的各種能力都是正常的。也可能我是錯的，是我曲解了這種正常的現象。因為用來證明這一點非常困難而且複雜。但是，不能因為某方面可能性的錯誤，而導致你們對我所強調的觀點產生偏見。智力發展的整個過程顯示出一種節奏性，這種節奏性包含着一種互相交織的循環，而某個階段作為整個發展中的小片段，又受到同類型循環周期的控制。而且，這種節奏是對大部分學生都有效的一般規律，我們的教育品質必須要適應學生的智力發展節奏。課程設置不僅僅是規劃出一系列科目就可以了，最關鍵的是要在智力發展的萌芽階段開始學習。因此說，真正重要的順序是教育過程中定性順序。

我的第二個告誡是：不要過分誇大循環周期中任何一個階段的特點。我猜大家在聽到我說這三個不同階段的細節時，心理一定會想：數學家就是喜歡做這樣的分類。我向你們保證，提出這三個階段和數學家無關，而是課本的無能讓我不得不指出實際教學中所犯的錯誤。當然，浪漫、精確和綜合運用，三階段各有側重，自始至終地彼此交替地佔據着主導地位，這種交替最終形成了不同的循環周期。

①哈姆雷特（Hamlet），莎士比亞著名悲劇的劇名和主人公。《哈姆雷特》是他最負盛名的劇本，在劇中，復仇的故事中交織着愛恨情愁，對於顛倒混亂的社會現實表現出深深的憂慮，呼喚理性、秩序和新的道德理想、社會理想，表達了對美好人性的追求嚮往、對現實中被慾望和罪惡玷污的人性的深刻批判。

儘管劇中充斥着各色丹麥人物名字，但故事中發生的一切恰恰描寫的就是當時英國的社會；整個故事滲透着屬於莎士比亞那個時代的精神，是莎士比亞人文主義和對現實生活批判精神最深刻的表達。

To be or not to be: that is the question（生，還是死，這是個問題），是《哈姆雷特》一句經典台詞。——譯者注

②荷馬（Homer），公元前八九世紀間的古希臘詩人，一般認為，荷馬出生在小亞細亞沿岸區，以兩部英雄史詩《伊利亞特》和《奧德賽》成為古希臘文化的源頭。他被認為是古希臘民族精神的塑造者，民族文化的奠基人，是一部「古代的百科全書」。——譯者注

③《奧德賽》（Odysseus），古希臘的兩部著名史詩之一，為盲詩人荷馬所編輯整理。《奧德賽》着重描寫了俄底修斯10年海上漂泊中最後40天的事情：俄底修斯歷盡艱險最後到達斯刻里亞島，受到國王菲埃克斯的隆重接待，酒席間應邀講述他遭遇風暴、獨目巨人、風袋、女妖和雷擊等海上經歷。後化裝乞丐返鄉，設計比武射殺了聚集在他宮中向他妻子逼婚的眾多貴族，並與忠貞不渝的妻子佩涅洛佩和勇敢的兒子忒勒馬科斯團圓。《奧德賽》以海上冒險和家庭生活為中心，描寫俄底修斯的不畏艱險和佩涅洛佩的堅貞，歌頌了智慧、勇敢和忠誠。——譯者注

④喬治·威廉·弗利德里希·黑格爾（Georg Wilhelm Friedrich Hegel，1770-1831），德國哲學家、古典唯心主義的集大成者，創立了歐洲哲學史上最龐大的客觀唯心主義體系，並極大地發展了辯證法，是馬克思主義哲學的來源之一。恩格斯說，「近代德國哲學在黑格爾的體系中達到了頂峰。」他的主要著作有：《精神現象學》、《邏輯學》、《哲學全書》和《法哲學原理》等。——譯者注

⑤在黑格爾那裡，辯證法是由正題、反題與合題組成的。所謂「正題」、「反題」、「合題」，其實是絕對精神在不同階段的表現形式。正題必然地派生出它的對立面——反題，並且和反題構成「對立」，最終二者都被揚棄而達到「統一」的合題。所以，辯證法就是絕對精神不斷流動、展開的一個歷史過程，它是動態的。任何事物，都是在「正一反一合」的辯證發展的過程中存在。

那麼，怎麼理解「正一反一合」呢？黑格爾曾經形象地打了個比方，一顆麥粒，一開始它只是一顆麥粒（正題），但它實際上已經包含了突破自己、否定自己的因素——這就是要長成一株麥苗。當它真的長成一株麥苗時，它就不再是一顆麥粒了，而是達到了麥粒的對立面（反題）。麥苗最後還是會成熟結種，自己死去而產生新的麥粒。新的麥粒既不是麥苗，也不同於原來作為種子的麥粒，而是兩者綜合的產物（合題）。——譯者注

⑥《魯濱孫漂流記》一書的主人公。此書英文原名：Robinson Crusoe，又譯作《魯賓遜漂流記》，直譯作魯賓遜·克魯索，是一本由丹尼爾·笛福59歲時所著的第一部小說，首次出版於1719年4月25日。這本小說被認為是第一本用英文以日記形式寫成的小說，享有英國第一部現實主義長篇小說的頭銜。

笛福在書中塑造了一個勇於面對自然挑戰的新型人物——魯濱孫·克魯索。他不屑守成，傾心開拓，三番五次地拋開小康家庭，出海闖天下。在遭遇海難流落到荒島上以後，他運用自己的頭腦和雙手，修建住所，種植糧食，馴養家畜，製造器具，縫紉衣服，把荒島改造成「世外桃源」，並且救了一個野人「星期五」。他在海外冒險多年，經歷千辛萬苦，終於得到了可觀的財富，回到了英國，完成了一個時代的英雄人物的創業歷程。為此，笛福博得了「英國和歐洲小說之父」的稱號。

《魯濱孫漂流記》給笛福帶來了巨大成功並幫他還清了部分債務。此後，他還陸續寫成了《莫爾·弗蘭德斯》、《傑克上校》及另外兩本寫魯濱孫的小說，但債主總是跟着他追債。在他生命的最後幾年中，笛福體弱多病，無人陪伴，債主不斷上門，孩子們也狠心地對他撒手不管。1731年4月26日，丹尼爾·笛福死去，享年71歲。──譯者注

⑦「蒙特梭利教育法」是瑪麗亞·蒙特梭利創立的教育體系，認為兒童具有創造潛力和個人主動精神，強調教育應使兒童的這種潛能得到自由的發展。

瑪麗亞·蒙特梭利（Maria Montessori，1870-1952）是意大利著名醫生、教育家、哲學家和慈善家，以其革命性的教育哲學與兒童教育方法聞名於世。

蒙特梭利於1870年8月31日出生於意大利安科納省的希亞拉瓦萊鎮，6歲開始在當地接受初等教育，12歲時全家搬遷至羅馬，以讓她接受更好的教育。1890年，她進入羅馬大學醫學院，是意大利第一位女醫學博士。畢業後成為羅馬大學附屬精神病診所的助理醫生，並在婦女和兒童醫院工作。1897年，她開始系統學習教育學課程，並轉向兒童教育研究。1907年1月，她創辦了第一所「兒童之家」，系統進行教育實驗，後相繼開設其他「兒童之家」，在意大利產生了很大反響。

1909年，蒙特梭利寫成了《運用於兒童之家的科學教育方法》一書；1912年這部著作在美國出版，並很快被譯成20多種文字在世界各地流傳。

1913年，蒙特梭利訪問美國，受到熱烈歡迎，美國著名教育家杜威出席儀式並致辭，稱她為「歷史上最偉大的女教育家」。──譯者注

第三章　自由和訓練的節奏

理想的漸次消失，證明瞭人類的努力遭受了挫折，非常悲哀。在古代學校裡，哲學家渴望的是傳授智慧；而在現代的大學裡，我們卑微的目標卻是教授各種科目。從古人追求神聖的智慧墮落到現代只為獲取各個學科的書本知識，這標誌着在漫長的時間裡教育的失敗，潰不成軍、一蹶不振。當然，我並不是說，在教育實踐中，古人比我們更成功。

你只要去讀讀盧奇安（Lucian）①的作品，看看他筆下對諸流派哲學家自命不凡的主張所進行的戲劇化的諷刺，我們或許能夠明白，古聖先賢在教育方面好像並未有太多值得炫耀的地方。我想強調的是，在歐洲文明曙光乍現的時候，人們一開始總是滿懷着種種美好的理想，這種理想本該促進教育向理想方向發展；但是，漸漸地，我們的理想淪落到和我們的實踐不相上下的地步了。

當理想下降到實踐的水平時，就會造成教育的停滯不前。特別是當我們把智力教育僅僅看作是大腦機械獲取知識的能力，或者是對實用性原理進行的系統化闡述，那麼教育就不會有任何進步。在盲目修訂教學大綱的過程中，我們試圖拋開時間不足的問題——但這是徒勞的——因為時間不足是難以避免的，然而我們還是有迴旋的餘地、有很大的能動性。我們必須接受這樣一個無法迴避的事實：上帝創造了世界，這個世界上有許多讓人渴望瞭解和學習的知識，但是絕對不是一個人就可以全部掌握的。羅列每個人應該掌握的學科毫無價值。學科太多了，所有的學科都有值得學習的理由。也許，這種知識的過剩狀態對我們來說是幸運的，或許正是因為對許多重要原理的無知，我們需要學習探索，所以才使這個世界變得趣味無窮。我懇請你們牢記：雖然智力教育的主要目的是傳授知識，但是智力教育還有另外一

個要素——「智慧」——古人稱之為「智慧」——雖然模糊但卻偉大，甚至更為重要。沒有一些基礎的知識，人不可能變得聰明；但是哪怕可以輕而易舉地獲取了知識，但是未必習得了智慧。

　　智慧是掌握知識的方法。它涉及知識的處理和遇到問題時對所需知識的選擇，以及運用知識從而使我們的直覺經驗更有價值。這種對知識的掌握和運用就是智慧，是可以獲得的最本質的自由。古人比我們更清楚地認識到——智慧高於知識。但是很遺憾，他們在教育實踐中、在追求智慧的過程中不幸犯了錯誤。他們草率行事，自以為是，他們認為智慧可以通過哲學家對着年輕人滔滔不絕地講演來傳授。因此，在那個時代的學校里，出現了一大批靠不住的哲學家。通往智慧的唯一途徑是在知識面前享有絕對的自由；通往知識的唯一途徑是對事實進行條分縷析的訓練。自由和訓練是教育的兩個要素，因此，我今天演講的題目是「自由和訓練的節奏」。

　　教育中自由和訓練的對立，並不像我們在對這兩個詞進行邏輯分析時所想象得那麼尖銳。孩子的心智是一個不斷發展的有機體。一方面，它並不是一個可以被人無情地塞滿各種陌生概念的匣子；另一方面，有序地獲取知識，對孩子正在發育的心智來說，則是天然的食品。因此，在一個理想的教育體系中，教育的目的應該是使自由選擇的訓練成為自動自發的結果，自由則因為訓練而得到豐富的機會。自由和訓練，這兩個原則並不對立，應該在孩子的生活中得到平衡，使之適應每個人個性的自然發展。這種在兒童身心發展過程中對自由和訓練的調節，就是我在其他場合所提到的「教育的節奏」。我確信，過去之所以有那麼多令人沮喪的失敗，原因就在於忽略了這種節奏的重要意義。我的主要看法是，在教育的開始和結束這兩個階段其主要的特徵是自由，但是中間會有自由居於次要地位的訓練階段。此外，我認為，並非只有「自由—訓練—自由」這一個大的循環周期，在智力發展的整個過程中，其實是由多個這樣的循環周期以及大周期中的

小周期所組成。如果把一個循環比作一個單獨的細胞或一塊磚，那麼智力發展的整個過程就是由這樣的細胞組成的有機體。在分析任何一個這樣的細胞時，我稱第一個自由階段為「浪漫階段」，稱中間的訓練階段為「精確階段」，稱最後的自由階段為「綜合運用階段」。

現在，我來詳加解釋。沒有興趣就沒有智力的發展。興趣是注意和理解的先決條件。你可以用體罰來引起興趣，或用一些愉快的活動來誘發興趣。沒有興趣就沒有進步。激發生命有機體朝着適合自己的方向發展，最自然的方式就是快樂。幼兒受媽媽和保姆的愛撫而使自己適應環境；我們用餐是因為我們喜歡美味佳餚；我們征服大自然，因為永不滿足的好奇心驅使我們去探索奧秘；我們喜歡運動，因為鍛鍊身體讓我們更有自信；我們痛恨危險的敵人時有着異教徒般的熱情。毫無疑問，痛苦是引發有機體行動的一種次要因素，這通常是在缺乏快樂的時候才會出現。快樂是一種激發生命力的既正常又健康的方式。我並不是說，我們可以沉溺於當前諸多娛樂的誘惑之中，我的意思是，我們應該尋求一種符合自然發展規律的模式，讓人在自然而然的快樂中張揚個性，只有這樣的發展才是令人滿意的。處於次要地位的嚴格訓練，必須以保證某些長遠利益為目的；要保持必要的興趣，就必須有一個適當的高些的目標。

我想說明的第二個基本觀點是：知識貧乏的確不幸，但是無關緊要。知識的重要性在於它的運用，在於我們對它的能動的掌握——也就是說，在於智慧。在談及知識時，把它和智慧割裂開來，好像知識給予了它的擁有者一種特殊的高貴，這似乎是一種慣例。像這樣推崇知識，我不贊成。一切取決於誰擁有知識以及他用知識做什麼。給個性增添價值的是這樣一種知識，它經過處理，可以改進直接經驗的各個方面。鑒於知識的能動性，教育中過分嚴格的訓練極其有害。積極而富有創新精神的思維習慣，只有在充分自由的環境下才能產生。不加區別的嚴格訓練會使心智遲鈍，反而實現不了自身的目標。如果你

與那些從中學和大學出來的年輕人有較多接觸的話，你很快就會注意到其中一些人心智遲鈍、缺乏活力，顯然，這些人所接受的所謂教育，就是由那些沉悶無趣的知識所組成的。英國社會那種陰鬱的氣氛，為教育的失敗推波助瀾。此外，那種單純傳授知識的方式操之過急，結果只能適得其反。人的心智拒絕接受這種填鴨式灌輸進來的知識。年輕人生來渴望發展，充滿激情，反感枯燥乏味且具強迫性的知識訓練。知識的訓練應該滿足一種對智慧的天然渴望，因為這種智慧給原始的經驗增添了價值。

　　現在，讓我們仔細考察一下這種人類心智自然求知的節奏。在一個陌生的環境中，心智的第一個過程是在一堆概念和經驗中開始有點兒散漫的活動。這是一個發現的過程，一個習慣於奇思妙想的過程，一個提出問題並尋求答案的過程，一個設計新體驗的過程，一個注意到新的探險活動會引起什麼後果的過程。這個過程既普通自然又十分有趣，我們可以注意到：八歲到十三歲之間的兒童專注於這樣令人激動的過程。在這個年齡段，好奇心佔據了主導地位——那些摧毀這種好奇心的蠢人都應該受到詛咒。毋庸置疑，這個發展階段需要得到幫助，甚至需要受到訓練。心智活動的環境必須經過仔細挑選，必須適合兒童的成長階段，必須適合個人的需要。從某種意義上來說，這個要求有點過分；但是從深層次來看，它順應了孩子內心需求。在教師的意識裡，孩子是被送到望遠鏡前來觀察星星的；在兒童的心目中，教師給了他璀璨星空的自由通路。假如不改變強加給兒童的種種習慣做法，即使是最愚笨的孩子，他的天性也會使他拒絕吸收外界的知識。必須記住，教育絕不是往行李箱塞滿物品的過程。這樣的比喻不完全恰當。當然，教育是一個具有自身特點的過程。與教育最相似的是生物有機體吸收食物的過程。眾所周知，在適當的環境下，美味可口的食物對健康是多麼必要。當你把你的靴子放進行李箱，它們會一直在那裡，直到你把它們拿出來的那一刻；但是，你給孩子餵錯食

物，情形就完全不同了。

這種最初的浪漫階段需要特殊的指引，畢竟，兒童是漫長人類文明史的繼承者，讓他在冰川時期的知識迷宮裡遊蕩是很荒謬的。因此，適當地指出重要的事實，闡明簡化的概念，提示普通常見的名稱，這些都能加強學生學習的動力。在教育的任何階段，都不能沒有訓練，都不能沒有自由；但是在浪漫階段，重點必須放在自由方面，允許兒童自己觀察，自己想象，自己行動。我的觀點是，對正在成長的兒童，如果在浪漫階段的自然發展尚未結束時，就對他們進行精確訓練，必然會妨礙他們對概念的理解和吸收。撇開了浪漫，就無所謂理解力了。我始終認為，過去的教育是那麼失敗，其原因就是對浪漫應有的地位沒有進行仔細的研究。沒有浪漫的冒險，你得到的不過是一堆枯燥無味的知識；但是，如果你不僅輕視概念，而且還不具備與概念相關的知識，那就糟糕透頂了。

但是，如果浪漫階段引導得當的話，就會出現另一種結果。兒童對缺乏經驗而引發的新鮮感逐漸消失；對客觀事實和理論基本有了一定的認知；重要的是，他們已經能夠對直接經驗進行獨立思考——包括思想和行動的多次探險。因此，他們也可以理解精確知識所帶來的啓發。

這種啓發就像常識一樣，涉及的都是熟悉的知識。現在是向前推進、正確認識各個學科並銘記其顯著特徵的時候了。這就是精確階段。在傳統的教育體制中，無論中學還是大學，這一階段是唯一集中學習的階段。你不得不被迫學習一些課程，對教育的主題卻不可多說。這個關鍵發展階段常常被過度地延長，其結果就是生產出了大量的書呆子；只有極少數的學生，他們天生的興趣沒有被毗濕奴的車輪②碾碎。的確，人們經常企圖教給學生更多的客觀知識和精確的理論，這些往往超出他們在這個階段所能接受的範圍。如果他們真能夠吸收這些知識，那會很有用。我們——我說的是中學的校長和大學的

教授們——往往容易忘記我們在一個成年人的教育過程中只是起着次要的作用；學生們在以後的生活中終究要獨立學習。成長切忌急於求成，學習不能超過其特定的範圍。笨拙的執業醫生很容易損毀一個敏感的有機體。儘管之前已經多番告誡，但是，盲目地去瞭解基本細節和重要且正確的概括，或是尋求一種簡單技術的掌握方法，這樣的事情還是會發生。要想在現代社會中表現得有價值，你必須充分掌握最好的練習方法，這是一個無法迴避的事實。要寫詩，你必須要學習韻律；要造橋，你必須要瞭解材料的強度。甚至如希伯來③的先知們都學習了書寫，可能在當時，書寫需要付出極大的努力。未經教育技藝的精雕細琢，就奢望有所成就——用《祈禱書》④裡的話來說——是一種徒然的、天真的、虛構的事情。

在精確階段，浪漫退居幕後。支配這一階段的是這樣一個無法迴避的事實：正確的方式和錯誤的方式同時存在，另外還存在着許多有待瞭解的真理。但是，浪漫精神並不是消失不見了，教學的藝術就是在完成明確指定的學業的過程中培養出浪漫精神。浪漫精神必須得到培養，因為浪漫是我們孜孜以求的和諧智慧中的必要組成部分；因為浪漫，理解才能保持活力，生命才會吸收工作產生的果實。在實踐中發現自由和訓練之間的平衡，這種平衡能使求知獲得最大的收穫，這是真正的關鍵。我一直堅持的節奏性准則，可以應用於一切學科，適用於所有學生，除此之外，我不相信有任何抽象的准則可以這樣。這種節奏性准則就是：在成長的早期，應該注重自由；在稍後的中間階段，重點放在對精確知識的掌握上。我確信，如果浪漫階段得到了適當的安排，那麼第二階段的訓練就不會有什麼問題，孩子知道如何學習，渴望把事情做好，我們對他們所做的一切大可放心。此外，我認為，唯一具有重要意義的訓練是自我訓練——這種訓練只有通過充分享有自由才能獲得。但是，教育中有非常多微妙的問題需要考慮——在生活中必須養成這樣的習慣：愉快地完成必須做的工作。如果這些

工作符合學生發展階段的自然需要，如果這些工作能夠使學生充分發揮自身的能力，如果學生們的努力能夠收到預期的效果，如果學生們在完成這些工作的過程中享有合理的自由，那麼，結果就會令人相當滿意。

出色的教師如何才能使他的學生保持活力四射的浪漫，難就難在他花了很長的時間去闡述理論，卻花了很短的時間去實踐。維吉爾優美的詩文，可以通過朗誦時字正腔圓的發音而產生的悅耳的效果來表達；數學論證的簡約美，最有效的方法是通過列舉一般原理來闡述複雜事實展現。在這個階段，教師責任重大。老實說，除了少數具有天賦的教師以外，我認為，既帶領全班學生有序進行精確學習，同時又不減損學生某種程度的興趣，這是難以做到的。首創精神和訓練都是需要的，但是訓練往往又會扼殺首創精神，這是兩難選擇，讓人頭疼。

承認這一點，並不意味着可以原諒那種令人難以忍受的無知，即不知道如何來緩解這個不幸的事實。理論上不一定非要這樣，因為在處理各個學生的具體情況時並沒有一個完美的方法。我們過去使用的方法扼殺了學習的興趣；我們現在討論的是，如何降低這種不幸所帶來的危害。我只是想提出一個忠告：教育是一個複雜的課題，沒有任何一個簡單的公式，可以一勞永逸地完全解決這個複雜的課題。

不過，在這方面，有一個實際的問題被人們大大忽略了。浪漫興趣的範圍很大，且沒有清晰的輪廓，不能用任何明確的界限來確定，只可意會，難以言傳。但是精確知識的範圍，像在任何普通教育體系中所要求的那樣，可以而且必須進行明確界定。若將範圍定得太寬，則會扼殺學生學習的興趣，致使課程目標落空；若將範圍定得太窄，學生就難以有效地掌握知識。確實，在不同課程中，每一門科目所要求掌握的精確知識都必須經過最充分的調查後才能確定。遺憾的是，這一點到目前為止也沒有完全有效地做到。例如，對於那些準備從事

科學工作的男孩子——也是我最感興趣的一類學生——在學習古典課程的時候，哪些拉丁詞彙是他們應該學習掌握的？哪些語法規則和結構是他們必須瞭解的？為什麼不能一勞永逸地把這些東西確定下來，然後每一次練習就把這些東西牢牢記住，同時瞭解它們在拉丁語、法語和英語中的派生詞。隨後，對於其他在閱讀教材中出現的句法和詞彙，則以最簡便的方式提供最充分的信息。某種徹底的確定性在教育中是必需的。我確信，成功教師的秘訣是他十分清楚學生需要精確學習的知識範圍，他不讓學生記一些不相關的次要的知識。成功的秘訣就是速度，速度的秘訣是專注。但是，就精確知識而言，秘訣就是速度，速度，還是速度。迅速地學習知識，然後加以應用。如果你能得心應手地應用知識，你便牢牢地掌握它了。

我們現在來討論這種節奏性循環周期中的第三個階段，即綜合運用階段。在這一階段，出現了一種回歸浪漫的情形。學生對一些確定的知識有了一定的瞭解，養成了學習的習慣，對一般規律和規則的系統闡述和詳細例證也基本明白。這時，學生想要使用他的新武器了。他是一個活生生的人，他想展現他學習知識後的效果。他重新回到浪漫階段中開始散漫的冒險之中，然而不同的是，此時他的心智已經受過嚴格的訓練，而他本人也非烏合之眾了。從這個意義上講，教育應該在研究中開始，在研究中結束。畢竟，教育從整體上說，是為了使受教育者做好準備，去迎接現實生活中的種種經歷，用相關的思想和適當的行動去應付每時每刻發生的情況。教育如果不以激發首創精神開始，不以促進這種精神而結束，那麼它一定是錯誤的。因為教育的全部目的——就是使人具有活躍的智慧。

我在數所大學任教，痛感學生思維的僵化，這是對精確知識漫無目的的積累且又不加以利用所導致的結果。一位大學教授應該展現他本人的真實個性——以一個正在思考並積極利用他作為知識海洋中略知一二的無知者的身份出現。在某種意義上，隨着智慧增長，知識

將減少：因為知識的細節消失在原理之中。在生活中，哪怕是業餘愛好，你都可以學到很多重要的知識和細節；養成積極應用某個原理的習慣，才是真正地擁有智慧。精確階段是通過掌握精確的知識細節進而領悟原理的階段；綜合運用階段是拋棄細節而積極使用原理的階段，這時知識細節退卻到下意識的習慣中去了。我們不用刻意地把二加二等於四掛在嘴邊，儘管我們曾經用心去記憶。我們靠的是學習初等算術所養成的習慣。綜合運用階段的本質是，脫離那種被訓練的被動狀態，進入到積極主動應用知識的自由狀態。當然，在這個階段，精確知識將會繼續增長，而且比以往任何時候都更為活躍，因為心靈已經感受到了「精確」所帶來的力量，並對獲得一般原理和豐富例證均可以作出適當的反應。但是，知識的增長逐漸變為無意識的了，而成為積極思想探險中的小插曲。

關於智力發展節奏三個階段的闡述就到此為止了。一般來說，教育的全過程都受這三重節奏支配。浪漫階段一直延續到十三、十四歲；十四到十八歲，是精確階段；十八到二十二歲，是綜合運用階段。但這些僅是一般情形，只是描繪心智發展的大致輪廓。沒有一個學生在學習各個科目時，能夠同時完成這三個階段的發展。比如，當語言學習開始啓動它的精確階段，即開始掌握詞彙和語法的時候，科學學習應該處在浪漫階段。語言的浪漫階段開始於嬰幼兒的牙牙學語時期，這樣語言學習在後面就隨之進入到精確階段；相對而言，科學學習較為滯後。如果在比較小的年紀反復灌輸精確的科學知識，反而會扼殺學生的首創精神和求知興趣，從而使得學生逃避能夠豐富他們心智的科學主題。因此，在語言學習的精確階段開始之後，科學學習的浪漫階段還要持續若干年。

在各個階段的發展中，在每天、每周、每學期的學習過程中，都有若干較小的漩渦，這些漩渦本身就包含着三重節奏循環。學生大體瞭解某個模糊的議題，掌握了相關的細節，最後按照相關的知識將

整個科目歸納在一起。學生能夠持續進步、信心滿滿，前提是他們能夠持續不斷地被興趣所激發，不斷地獲得某些技能，不斷地為成功所激勵。總的來說，在最近的三十年裡，英國的中學一直在向大學輸送大批令人失望的年輕人，這些人就像被接種了預防智力熱情蔓延的疫苗，拒絕任何智慧火花的迸發。大學的教育進一步強化了中學的教育，進一步加劇了這種失敗。結果，年輕人的熱情轉向了其他方面，於是，老大帝國真的變老了，有教養的英國不再容易接受新觀念了。國家的偉大成就（戰爭除外），如果能夠表明是在學校的課堂上獲得的，而不是在操場上贏得的，那時候，我們才可以對我們的教育模式感到滿意。

至此，我一直在討論心智發展的教育問題，我的論點局限在一個很小的範圍裡。畢竟，我們的學生是充滿活力的，不能像拆遊戲拼板那樣，分離成一片片。在機械生產中，建設的能量來自它的外部，它將分離的各個部分組裝在一起。但是對於一個活生生的有機體來說，情形就大不一樣了，它依靠自身自我發展的衝動而成長。這種衝動可以從機體的外部進行激發和引導，也可能為外界的力量所扼殺。儘管外界的力量可以激發和引導這種衝動，但是，心智發展的創造性衝動來自內部，而且完全為個體所特有。教育是引導個體去領悟生活的藝術。我所說的生活的藝術，是指人在各種活動中最完美的實現，它表現了充滿活力的個體在面對現實環境時所具備的潛能。實現這種完美涉及一種藝術的鑒賞力，在個性的潛能方面，低級的服從高級的。無論是科學、藝術，還是宗教和道德，等等，都是從生物組織內部的這種價值感中產生的。每個個體都體現了一種生存的探險。生活的藝術就是引導這種探險。

偉大的宗教文明在它們最初的教義中都包含了這樣的內容：反對把道德作為反復灌輸的清規戒律。道德，就這個詞的消極意義上來說，是宗教的死敵。使徒保羅（Paul）⑤指責《律法書》（Law）⑥，

《福音書》⑦則激烈地反對法利賽人⑧。每一次宗教的盛行，都表現出強烈的對抗性——這種對抗性隨着宗教的衰落而得以緩解。注意發展的節奏規律，道德和宗教教育做得比任何教育領域都要成功。不管論述宗教教義的適當途徑是什麼，就宗教而言，堅持過早的精確階段對宗教意味着死亡。宗教的活力是通過發展的節奏規律來表現的，這種方法使得宗教精神在宗教教育的嚴峻考驗下仍然得以傳承。

教育中的宗教問題範圍太大，大到我無法在這段演講中進行討論。但是還是要提一下它，我不想讓人懷疑我在這裡提倡的原則要從狹義上去理解。生活較高層次中的節奏性發展的一般規律，包括最初的覺醒，其次的訓練，以及在較高層次上的收穫。我現在堅持的是**發展的本能來自於自身：發現是由我們自己完成的，訓練是自我訓練，收穫是我們自身首創精神的成果。**教師有着雙重作用。他以自己的人格和個性，使學生產生共鳴而激發出熱情；同時創造出具有更廣泛的知識、更堅定的目標的環境。他的作用就是為了避免浪費，而浪費在較低層次的生存階段是自然的進化方式。根本的動力，是對價值的認可，是對重要性的認知，無論在科學、道德還是宗教領域，概莫如此。讓個性和超越自我的東西融合，需要各種形式的疑惑、好奇、尊敬或崇拜，以及各種形式的強烈慾望。對價值的認可會給生命增添難以置信的力量；沒有它，生活將回復到較低層次的被動狀態中。這種力量的最深刻的表現就是美感，對於所實現的完美境地的審美感。這一想法不禁讓我想問：在現代教育中，我們是否對藝術的重要性給予了足夠的重視？！

我國公立學校特有的教育，以前是為那些來自富有的、有教養的家庭的男孩子們設計的。這些兒童到意大利、希臘和法國旅行，他們自己的家也常常佈置得優美典雅。這樣的條件沒有一個是現代國家的中小學教育所具備的，甚至對於我們擴大了的公立學校系統中的大多數兒童來說也不具備。在精神生活中，如果你忽視像藝術這樣的偉

大因素的話，那麼你肯定會蒙受若干損失。我們的審美情趣使我們對價值有生動的理解。如果你傷害了這種理解，你就會削弱整個精神領悟系統的力量。在教育中要享受自由的權利，必然包含了這樣一個結果──必須注重健全的個性發展。你決不能武斷地拒絕這種迫切的要求。在經濟不景氣的年月裡，我們常會聽許多關於教育的議論：努力沒有效果，是否可以減少努力。致力於發展一種純粹的智力，必將導致巨大的失敗。這恰恰是我國學校正在做的事情。我們的所作所為或許足以使人興奮，但絕不足以令人滿意。

歷史告訴我們，藝術的全面繁榮是國家通往文明之路的首要行動。但是，即便是如此簡單明確的事實，我們卻總是向廣大民眾關上藝術的大門。很多簡單通俗而受人喜愛的藝術，無需耗費多少資源就可讓民眾欣賞，但是我們卻沒有做到，真是愚蠢至極。這樣一種喚起強烈願望又使之落空的教育將會導致失敗和不滿，我們已經見怪不怪了。通過某些重大的改革，或許可以消除艱苦繁重的勞動和就業的不安全感。但是，大幅度地提高平均收入基本上就難有可能，類似的空想卻難行得通。不過，我們還是需要盡最大努力，利用學校培養新人：他們熱愛音樂，喜歡戲劇，醉心於造型和色彩的美。我們也能夠在普通民眾的生活中提供滿足這些情感的方式。如果考慮最簡便的方式，你們會發現：物質資源的緊缺微不足道。當你們做到了這些，當你們的國民廣泛地欣賞藝術所能給予的東西──歡樂和恐懼時，他們更容易接受教育或教誨──來自於牧師宣揚對上帝的愛，預言家宣傳的義不容辭的責任，政治家召喚愛國主義。

從中世紀進入到文藝復興時代這般壯麗的生活中，莎士比亞──這個美麗的國家培養出來的英國人寫下了很多戲劇，接着，有了一個深切呼喚浪漫精神的跨越海洋的新世界。今天，我們面對的是集中在城市、成長於科學時代的人。我一直擔憂：如果我們不能用新方法迎接新時代，維持和提升國人精神生活的水準，那麼遲早，那些落空的

願望會轉化為狂野的爆發，我們將重蹈俄國的覆轍⑨。歷史學家將為英國寫下這樣的墓誌銘：由於其統治階級精神上缺乏遠見，由於他們單調的功利主義傾向，以及他們像法利賽人一樣沉溺於渺小的治國之術，大英帝國不可避免地衰亡了。

---

①盧奇安（Lucian，約公元120-180），古希臘修辭學家和諷刺作家。出生在羅馬帝國統治下的敘利亞境內的薩莫薩塔城。他的父親是一個貧苦的手工業者。他年輕時曾被送去學習雕刻，後來致力於研究演說術，曾在小亞細亞、希臘、意大利等地周遊和講學。在演說術方面取得相當的成就之後，他對這種職業感到失望，轉而研究哲學。約公元165年以後，他在雅典居住過一段時間，晚年移居埃及的亞歷山大城，曾任本城的法官。他以描述到月球旅行的《信史》（周作人譯名《真實的故事》）及一系列對話集聞名，其作品富於機智和嘲諷，對當時哲學、文學和知識界生活等多有深刻的批判。

主要代表作品《真實的故事》。在《真實的故事》中，盧奇安越過大西洋去旅遊，經歷了一連串令人難以置信的歷險，如人被吹到月亮上、在大鯨魚的肚子里生活了近兩年等。他在一開頭寫這個故事的時候說，那些喜歡講天花亂墜的故事的人不真誠，明明是假的事卻要說成是真的，但他說「我覺得奇怪的倒是，他們寫這麼些謊話，怎麼不怕別人識破。於是我的虛榮心也翻上來了，總想也留點東西給後世，講故事的自由總不能單單我沒份兒吧」，他於是就開始「老老實實講假話」了，他讓「讀者大可不必相信」，這顯然是把自己的責任降到最低的表現，就像給小孩子講童話但還殘忍地告訴他一切都是假的那麼殘忍。想想吧，假如不知道是假的故事，月亮國和太陽國打仗還是挺有趣的。《真實的故事》在基督教一統歐洲大陸前都是禁書。文藝復興以後，很多人的創作都受到他的影響：托馬斯·莫爾、埃拉斯穆斯、拉伯雷、伏爾泰、斯威夫特、菲爾丁，甚至西班牙塞萬提斯以及後來的魔幻現實主義也能看到盧奇安的那些影子。英國作家斯威夫特的《格列佛遊記》直接受它的影響。

盧奇安的作品反映了二世紀奴隸制社會開始瓦解時期奴隸主思想意識的崩潰。他的散文風格輕快，並愛引用古希臘文學、歷史、哲學中的辭句，也染上修辭的習尚。周作人曾翻譯其作品，如《盧奇安對話集》共選三十篇（人民文學出版社，1991 年）。——譯者注

②毗濕奴（Juggernaut），印度教主神之一Vishnu的化身。傳說印度教徒每年用車載着此神像遊行，許多人相信被神像車碾死即可升天，不惜投身車下。該節日每年都會舉行大型遊行，其中包括奎師那勳爵的偶像旅行車。數百名奉獻者用繩索拉動馬車，形成了巨大的動力，勢不可擋。——譯者注

③希伯來，漢語「希伯來」，譯自英語Hebrew。在猶太人的語言裡，這個詞的正確發音應該是「Ivri」，意為「渡過」。最早的猶太人被稱為「希伯來人」，意為「渡過河而來的人」。根據《聖經》和其他史料記載，猶太人族長亞伯拉罕率領其族人從兩河流域的烏爾城（Ur）渡過幼發拉底河和約旦河，來到當時被稱為「迦南」（Canaan）的巴勒斯坦，此後，這些古猶太人被稱為「希伯來人」（見《聖經·創世紀》第14章13節）。——譯者注

④《祈禱書》是一部借贊美上帝以展現資本主義沒落時期精神矛盾的長詩。作者里爾克（Rainer Maria Rilke，1875-1926），是二十世紀最有影響的德語詩人。他於1875年12月4日生於當時隸屬於奧匈帝國的古城布拉格（現屬於捷克）的鐵路職工家庭，大學攻讀哲學、藝術與文學史。1897年後，他懷着孤獨、寂寞的心情遍游歐洲各國。他會見過托爾斯泰，給大雕塑家羅丹當過秘書，並深受法國象徵派詩人波德萊爾等人的影響。第一次世界大戰時，他曾應徵入伍，1919年後遷居瑞士。1926年12月29日，死於瑞士的瓦爾蒙。里爾克平生留下的文字作品可謂浩沆無邊，題材涉及詩歌、小說、藝術隨筆、書信和日記等，其中最為重要的有：詩歌《圖像集》《祈禱書》《旗手克里斯托弗·里爾克的愛和死之歌》《新詩集》《新詩續集》《杜伊諾哀歌》《敫奧爾菲斯的十四行詩》等；小說《布拉格兩故事》《親愛的上帝及其他》《馬爾特手記》等。——譯者注

⑤保羅（天主教譯保祿，約3-67），猶太人，早期教會最具有影響力的傳教士之一，基督徒的第一代領導者之一，因為他首創向非猶太人轉播基督的福音，所以被奉為外邦人的使徒。在諸多參與基督教信仰傳播活動的使徒與傳教士之中，保羅通常被認為是在整個基督教歷史上最重要的兩個人之一，並且是史上最偉大的宗教領導者之一。新約聖經諸書約有一半是由他所寫，他保留下來的書信是現存最早的基督教文獻。他在整個羅馬帝國的早期基督教社群之中傳播耶穌基督的福音。——譯者注

⑥《律法書》（Law）即摩西五經（Pentateuch），又被稱為摩西五書，是《舊約》聖經最初的五部經典：《創世記》、《出埃及記》、《利未記》、《民數記》和《申命記》等。它是猶太教經典中最重要的部分；同時也是公元前6世紀以前唯一的一部希伯來法律匯編，並作為猶太國國家的法律規範。其主要思想是：神的創造、人的尊嚴與墮落、神的救贖、神的揀選、神的立約和神的律法等。——譯者注

⑦福音書（Gospel），福音的意思是「好消息」。福音書是以記述耶穌生平與復活事跡為主的文件、書信與書籍。在基督教傳統中，它通常意指《新約》聖經中的內容。更狹義的說法，則是專指四福音書：《馬太福音》、《馬可福音》、《路加福音》和《約翰福音》等。——譯者注

⑧法利賽人（Pharisees），一個猶太人宗派，曾在耶穌時代很流行，但過於強調摩西律法的細節而不注重道理。「法利賽」的意思是「分離」，指一些為保持純潔而與俗世保持距離的人。傳統猶太教的典範、今日猶太教所有教派的根本都受其影響。——譯者注

⑨第一次世界大戰爆發前夕，俄、英、法三國結成協約國集團。1917年，戰爭即將結束時，由於資產階級和無產階級運動，俄羅斯羅曼諾夫王朝的統治被撳垮，末代沙皇尼古拉二世退位，古老的羅曼諾夫王朝結束了在俄羅斯三百年的帝國統治。國家的統治由克倫斯基領導、由貴族與前貴族組成的臨時政府接手。

其後，俄羅斯經歷了被稱為「資產階級民主革命」的二月革命和被稱為「社會主義革命」的十月革命。

從後來發掘出來的文獻中可見，當時組成臨時政府的舊貴族認為，二月革命是他們有預謀地發動的一場逼使沙皇退位的政變：1917年2月，他們利用首都彼得格勒的食品供應危機，縱容煽動下層工人示威、士兵造反的活動，以此作為逼迫沙皇退位的理由。可是，在目標達成以後，貴族們卻無法控制住民眾引發的危機，反而讓布爾什維克有機可乘。因此，二月革命與其說是「資產階級民主革命」，不如說是沙皇與貴族、高級軍官及大工業家之間發生了嚴重的衝突引發的政變；貴族與高級軍官本期望以「民主立憲」的承諾控制住他們煽動起的民眾造反，然而事件的發展卻完全超出他們的掌控範疇，由他們引發的無政府狀態最後為布爾什維克所用，構成了十月革命爆發的基礎。——譯者注

第四章　技術教育及其與科學和文學的關係

這次演講的主題是技術教育。我希望考察它的本質，以及它與自由教育的關係。這樣的探索可以幫助我們認識一個國家技術訓練體制的成功運行所需要的條件。在數學教師中，這也是一個十分激烈的討論熱點，因為大部分的技術課程都包括數學。

我們要想好我們心目中的理想模式，然後再進行討論，或許我們在不遠的將來可能會取得一定的成果，但是我們的期望值可以保守些。

首先，我們要在腦海裡勾勒出我們渴望實現的最佳目標，否則，現在我們馬上投入到這樣的討論中是不切實際的。然而，在預期近期可能做到的事情的時候，我們的期望要盡可能地審慎。

人們怕談理想，因此，一位現代劇作家①借一個瘋狂的神父之口描繪人類的理想狀態，讓我們首先來借用一下：

> 在我的夢想之中，有這樣一個國家，在那裡，國家就是教會，教會就是人民，三位一體，一體三位。那是這樣一個國家，工作就是娛樂，娛樂就是生活，三位一體，一體三位。那裡是一座教堂，祭司就是禮拜者，禮拜者就是受敬拜的人，三位一體，一體三位。那是神，眾神皆有人性，眾生皆有神性，三位一體，一體三位。總而言之，那是一個瘋人的夢想。

在這段話中，我注意到這樣的一句：「那是這樣一個國家，工作就是娛樂，娛樂就是生活。」這是技術教育的理想狀態。當我們用這句話來對照現實時，你會覺得完全不可思議。那些辛苦勞作的人們，那些雇主們，你所見到的，更多的是疲倦、不滿和精神冷漠。我不是

在做社會分析，我只是希望你們能夠明白：目前的社會現實與理想相去甚遠。當然，我們都同意，如果僱主按照「工作即娛樂」的原則經營他的工廠，那麼這個工廠不要一周就會倒閉。

無論在傳說還是在現實中，都有一個魔咒落在人類的身上：如果想要生活下去，就得靠自己的辛勤勞動。但是，理性和道德的直覺——覺察到了——在這種苦難中——蘊含了人類進步的基礎。早期本篤教派（Benedictine）②的僧侶們樂於勞作，因為他們相信，這樣做就能與基督同在。

去掉神學的華美外衣，基本的思想仍然清晰可見：工作應該充滿智慧和道德的想象，因而人們能夠克服工作帶來的所謂的枯燥乏味和勞累痛苦，使工作成為一種樂趣，享受工作。每個人都會根據自己的認知，更具體地重申這一抽象表述。只要不在具體細節中遺漏掉要點，你想怎麼表述就怎麼表述。但是不管你怎樣表達，「享受工作」始終是辛苦勞作的人們所懷有的唯一的真正願望；它就掌握在技術教師的手中，掌握在那些能控制他們活動範圍的人的手中，如此塑造國民，使國民以昔日僧侶的精神去從事日常勞作。

我們國家目前迫切需要大量的熟練工人、具有創造精神的人才和關注新思想發展的僱主。

要想取得令人贊嘆的成果，只有一種方法——而且是唯一的方法——那就是——培養出享受工作的工人、科技人員和僱主。基於一般人性的認知，不妨設想一下：一個整天疲於奔命、厭倦、無奈的工人，無論他多麼地手巧，能生產出大量一流的產品嗎？他會限定自己的產量，馬馬虎虎地對待工作，老練地逃避監管；他抗拒適應新方法，最終他會成為不滿的焦點，腦子裡充滿了不切實際的革命念頭，對現實工作的職業環境缺乏體諒理解；等等。在我們的社會特別是動蕩不安的時期，推行廣泛的技術教育，如果不顧本篤教派的理想，會增加某些野蠻動亂的機會。最終，整個社會將受到報應。

其次，有創造天賦的人才進行充滿活力的工作時，需要愉快的精神活動作為一種條件。「需要是發明之母」是一句愚蠢的諺語。「需要只是無足輕重的託辭」才更接近於事實。現代發明增多，其基礎是科學，而科學幾乎完全是愉快的智力探究的產物。

第三種人是僱主，他們有事業心。我們會發現，真正重要的人還是那些成功的企業家，他們的生意遍布全球，躋身富裕階層。商業難免起伏興衰。但是如果整個商業處於衰退期，那麼指望貿易一枝獨秀就很愚蠢。如果這些人認為做生意只不過是一種稀松平常的謀生手段的話，他們就不會有激勵而變得機警敏捷。他們已經做得很好了，他們目前的經營就是一種足以使他們堅持下去的動力。雖然新方法難免效果難料，但他們樂於採用新方法。他們真正的心思在生活的另一面，在成就夢想。對金錢的渴望，導致的是吝嗇而不是進取心。有些人為了創辦醫院一類的慈善機構（目標十分高尚），繼續做着厭煩的工作；但是，如果廠商們能夠樂於從事他們的工作，那麼人類就會更有希望。

最後，只要大量僱主和一般人認為，他們從事的是向社會公眾無情地榨取金錢的工作，那麼工業的和平安定就無從談起。應該從更廣闊的視野來構想人們所從事的工作和因此所提供的公共服務機會，只有這樣，才能建立和諧合作的基礎。

從以上討論中所得出的結論是，對僱主和一般人來說，都必須以一種自由精神來看待技術教育——這種教育會處處滿足國家的實際需要，把它看作是一種運用原理和提供服務的真正的知識啓蒙。在這種教育中，幾何學和詩歌就像硬幣的正反面一樣不可或缺。

柏拉圖（Plato）③這樣神話般的人物可以作為現代自由教育的代表，就像聖本篤④可以作為技術教育的代表一樣。我們不必擔心自己是否有資格來恰如其分地表達兩位聖者的真實思想。他們在這裡是作為兩種不同觀念的象徵性人物。我們是根據柏拉圖現在所能代表的文

化類型來考慮問題的。

　　從本質上來說，自由教育是一種培養思維能力和審美鑒賞力的教育。它通過教授思想深刻的名著、富含想象力的文學作品和藝術傑作來進行。它所關注的作用是運用能力。這是一種需要休閒感覺的貴族式教育。這種柏拉圖式的理想對歐洲文明做出了不朽的貢獻。它促進了藝術發展，培養了那種代表科學之源的無偏見的求知精神，它在世俗物質力量面前保持了一種要求思想自由的精神的尊嚴。雖然柏拉圖沒有像聖本篤那樣為難自己，使自己成為奴隸勞作時的同伴；但是他理所當然地成為人類思想的先驅。他所代表的文化類型是自由貴族的特殊的鼓舞力量，歐洲就是從這個自由貴族階級那裡得到了今天它所擁有的有序自由。幾個世紀以來，從教皇尼古拉五世⑤到耶穌會學校，從耶穌會會士⑥到現代英國公學的校長們，這種教育理想一直得到神職人員的全力支持。

　　對某些人來說，這是一種非常好的教育。它符合他們的思想方式及其所處的生活環境。但是，教育所要求的遠不止這些。人們斷定整個教育是適當抑或欠缺的，要看它與這種獨一無二的教育相似的程度。

　　這種教育的本質，就是大量地瀏覽最優秀的文學作品。它培養出來的理想人才，應該熟悉迄今為止人類寫下的最優秀的作品，掌握世界上的主要語種，探究過各民族的興衰史，瞭解表達人類情感的最優美的詩篇，閱讀過最偉大的戲劇和小說。同時，他還瞭解主要的哲學流派，認真閱讀過某些具有鮮明風格的哲學著作。

　　顯然，如果要大致完成這樣的計劃，終其一生，他都將不可能有任何時間去做其他事情。順便提一下，盧奇安的劇本對白裡有這樣一個計算，當一個人在證明可以實踐當下某種倫理道德制度之前，他要花上一百五十年去驗證這種制度是否可信。

　　這樣的理想並不適合人類。所謂廣泛的文化修養決不是這樣的

雄心勃勃的計劃：完全掌握各種不同文明的各種不同的文學作品，從亞洲到歐洲的，從歐洲到美洲的。只需精選出一部分以供學習就足夠了；但是，正如我們所知道的，選出的必須是最優秀的部分。我始終對這種選擇表示懷疑：選擇希臘的色諾芬⑦而遺漏中國的孔夫子，雖然我從來沒有徹底讀過他們的原著。雄心勃勃的自由教育計劃確實應該壓縮，必須限定在研究兩種重要語言中所包含的某些文學作品的範圍內。

但是，對人類精神的表達並不局限於文學，還有其他的藝術，還有科學。教育應該超越對他人思想的被動接受，必須加強創造力。遺憾的是，創造力不是單一的，它包括思想上的創造力，行動上的創造力，藝術想象的創造力，即便是這三種類型，又各有更多的分支。

學習領域如此寬廣，而個人的時光轉瞬即逝，人生亦不甚完全，所以，古典學者、科學家和校長等，都同樣是無知之人。

有一種奇怪的幻覺，認為無才便是德。這種觀點的唯一收穫是愈加愚昧無知。不讀莎士比亞的作品，也不讀牛頓⑧和達爾文⑨的著作，那麼，在學習柏拉圖作品的過程中也會難有所得。近些年來自由教育的成就沒有變得更糟糕，主要得益於人們已經發現了這種教育的要求。

我的觀點是，沒有一門學科可以說已經達到了一種完美無缺的境地。即使將其次要因素完全剔除後亦是如此。柏拉圖式文化堅持無偏見的智力欣賞，這是一種心理學上的錯誤。我們的行為和我們在一系列事件轉換中所處的位置，存在着一種不可避免的因果關係，這是根本問題。試圖使智力或審美與這些根本問題進行分離的教育本身，就是文明的衰退。文化教育本質上應該是為了行動，應該使工人從盲目的辛苦勞頓中解脫出來。藝術豐富着我們的心靈，它的存在使我們感受這個世界的美妙。

對科學的好奇心不帶偏見，這是一種激情，它對一系列事件之

間的關聯持有序的理智的看法。這種求知的目標是為了思想和行為的緊密結合。在理論科學中，更是常常忽略這種不可或缺的行動介入。科學家不只是希望瞭解世界，他們渴望發現世界。他們不是為了瞭解而去發現，而是為了發現才去瞭解。藝術和科學會給辛苦勞作帶來愉悅，這是成功實現目標所帶來的快樂。同樣，藝術家和科學家也享受着這種快樂。

把技術教育和自由教育對立起來是錯誤的。沒有自由的技術教育不可能完美，沒有技術的自由教育不可能令人滿意。也就是說，所有的教育都是同時傳授技術和智慧。用更通俗的話來說，教育應該培養學生既能充分瞭解又能善於行動。這種實踐和理論的結合是相輔相成的。紙上得來終覺淺，紙上談兵，沒有多大意義。創造性的衝動需要迅速轉化為實踐，對兒童來說更是如此。幾何學和力學，輔以車間工場裡的實踐活動，就可以實現這樣的目標，否則，數學教育就成了一堆空洞無物的廢話。

在國家的教育體系中，有三種主要的教育形式，即，文學課程、科學課程和技術課程。不過，這些課程中的每一門課程都應該包括另外兩門。我的意思是，教育的每一種形式都應該向學生傳授技術、科學、各種一般的知識概念和審美鑑賞力，學生所受到的任意一種訓練，都必須與其他兩方面的訓練相輔相成相得益彰。即便是最有天賦的學生，由於人生時間有限，也不可能在每個方面都全面發展。因此，學習必須有所側重。在某些情況下，訓練為某種藝術或工藝所必須，這時最直接的審美訓練自然歸屬於技術課程的範圍。這樣的訓練對於自由教育和科學教育也非常重要。

文學課程的教學方法是研習語言，即，學習我們向他人表達心理狀態的方法。在這門課程中，應該獲得的技術是語言的表達；需要掌握的科學是語言結構的研究，還要分析語言和所傳達的心理狀態之間的關係。此外，語言和感情表達的精巧聯繫，書面語和口語所需要的

感覺器官的高度協調發展，成功運用語言喚起強烈的美感。最後，這個世界的智慧就被那些文學名作保存下來了。

這種課程具有同質的優點。所有不同的部分互相協調，互為補充。我們不用感到驚奇：這樣的一門課程一旦大體建立起來，就會成為一種唯一完美的教育形式。它的缺點是過分強調語言的重要性。誠然，語言表達的各種重要性如此突出，以至難以作出清醒的估計。最近幾代人親眼目睹了文學和文學表達形式的倒退，它們在智力生活中不再佔據唯一重要的地位。為了真正地認識自然改造自然，僅僅有文學才能是不夠的。

科學教育主要是一種訓練觀察自然現象的藝術，是認識和推論這些現象可能產生的後果有何規律的訓練，是對涉及一系列自然現象的法則進行演繹推理。但是，這裡就像自由教育中的情形一樣，我們遇到了時間短缺的限制。自然界中有如此之多的自然現象，每種現象後面都對應着一門科學，這種科學有其獨特的觀察方式，以及在觀察推論時要用到獨特的思維方式。在教育中，研究普遍的科學是不可能的，所能做的也就是學習兩三門相關的科學。因此，指責狹隘專業化的人，會極力反對任何一種基本上屬於科學性質的教育。顯然，這種指責是有事實依據的，值得我們思考：如何在科學教育的範圍內，發揚這種教育的長處，避免狹隘專業化的危險。

這樣的討論必須考慮到技術教育。技術教育是一種利用知識進行物質產品生產的技能方面的訓練。這種訓練強調手工技能、手和眼協調能力以及在控制生產過程中的判斷力。而判斷力需要具備自然變化過程的知識，因為製造過程要運用這些知識。因此，在技術訓練中，某些方面的科學知識教育是必要的。如果你輕視科學方面，你就會認為，那是科學家的事情；如果你重視它，你就會多多少少把它傳授給工人們以及——更重要的是——傳授給企業的中高層。

從智力方面來說，技術教育並不僅僅和科學知識相關，它也可能

是屬於對藝術家或某些藝術課程的工匠學徒的教育。在後者，就需要培養與之相關的審美鑒賞力。

　　柏拉圖式文化中有一個害處，它完全忽略了技術教育是理想人生得以完全發展的組成部分。這種忽略起因於兩種極為糟糕的對立，即，心智和身體的對立，思想和行動的對立。我在這裡要插一句——僅僅是為了避免批評——我非常清楚希臘人極為看重形體美和體育運動。但是，他們的價值觀是扭曲的——這是奴隸制帶來的必然結果。

　　我始終信奉這樣一條教育原理：在教學中，一旦你忘記了你的學生是有血有肉的，那麼你就會遭遇悲慘的失敗。這正是文藝復興之後柏拉圖式課程的失敗之處。但是，沒有任何東西能夠阻止人們接近自然。所以，在英國的教育中，自然被驅逐出了教室以後，她又以熱愛體育運動的形式回到了人們的生活中⑩。

　　智力活動和人體之間的聯繫，分佈於人體的各種感官中，但主要集中在眼睛、耳朵、口和手。感官和思想互相協調，大腦活動和身體的創造性活動之間也有一種相互的影響。在這種相互反應的過程中，手的作用尤其重要。究竟是人手創造了大腦，還是大腦創造了人手，這是一個可以討論的話題。但是手和大腦之間的聯繫一定是緊密的、相互的。這種關係根深蒂固，沒有因為數百年來某些特殊家庭廢棄手工勞動而普遍衰退。

　　不事手工技藝是貴族大腦慵懶的一個原因，這種大腦的慵懶只有通過運動來減輕，因為運動時腦力活動會減少到最低程度，手工活動不必十分精妙。經常的寫作和口頭表達，對於那些專業人員的思維能力來說，只是些微的刺激。那些偉大的讀者們，排斥其他活動，都不以頭腦敏銳而着稱。他們往往是膽怯守舊的思想者。毫無疑問，部分原因是他們背負的過多的知識壓制了他們的思維能力；另一部分原因就是因為缺乏來自手或口的富有創造性的活動所帶來的對大腦的刺激。

在評價技術教育的重要性的時候，我們必須突破把學習僅僅同書本知識學習相結合的框框。通過直接經驗獲得的知識是智慧生活的首要基礎。在很大程度上，通過書本學習得到的通常是第二手信息，因此，書本知識永遠不具有那種親身實踐的價值。

我們的目標是把我們生活中的直接事件看作是我們的一般概念的實證。學術界往往提供給我們一些二手信息，這些二手信息又是從其他的二手信息中總結出來的。學術界這種二手信息的性質，是其平庸無能的原因之一。這些知識平淡乏味，因為其沒有經受事實的嚴格檢驗。弗蘭西斯·培根⑪最重要的影響並不在於他提出的一種獨特的歸納推理的理論，而在於他領導了對於二手信息的反叛。

科學教育的特點應該是，將思維建立在直接的觀察上；技術教育的特點是，它遵循我們內心深處的自然本能，把思維轉換成手工技藝，把手工活動轉化為思維。

科學所喚起的思想是一種邏輯思維。邏輯可分為兩種：發現的邏輯和被發現的邏輯。

發現的邏輯在於，權衡各種可能性，拋棄不相關的細節，推測事件發生的一般規律，以及通過設計適當的實驗來檢驗假設。這是歸納的邏輯。

被發現的邏輯是對特殊事件的推論演繹，在一定的條件下，這些特殊事件會遵循假定的自然規律而發生。於是，當這些自然規律被發現或假定時，是否利用它們就完全取決於演繹邏輯。沒有演繹邏輯，科學就毫無用處。它只會成為一種從特殊上升到一般的無聊的遊戲，除非之後我們把這個程序顛倒過來，再從一般下降為特殊，上升和下降就像雅各布的梯子⑫上的天使。當牛頓憑直覺發現了萬有引力定律的時候，他立即開始計算地球對表面上的蘋果的引力以及地球對月球的引力。我們可以順便提出，沒有演繹邏輯就沒有歸納邏輯。所以，牛頓所做的大量計算工作，是他對這個偉大的定律進行歸納證實的必

不可少的步驟。

數學不過是演繹推理藝術中比較複雜的部分，尤其在涉及數、量和空間的時候。

在科學教育的過程中，應該傳授思維的藝術：即，形成清晰概念並適用於直接經驗的藝術，憑直覺領悟一般真理的藝術，檢驗各種推測的藝術，以及通過推理將一般真理應用於某些具有特殊意義的特殊情況的藝術。此外，科學表達的能力也是必需的，以便能從一堆亂麻般的概念中清晰地闡明有關的問題，並對重點給予足夠的關注。

當對一門科學或一小類的科學進行了這種充分的教授，並對思維的一般藝術給予了適當的關注，那麼，我們在糾正科學的狹隘專門化方面就取得了很大的進展。建立在一兩門個別學科基礎之上的那種科學教育，其糟糕之處在於——教師受考試制度的影響，往往只向學生灌輸這些特定學科的狹隘知識——也必然會如此。重要的是，要不斷提示方法的一般性，並將這種一般性與特別應用的特殊性進行對比。一個人如果只瞭解自己所學的那門科學，把它作為這門科學特有的一套固定程序，那麼，他實際上並不懂那門科學。他缺乏豐富的思想，不具備迅速抓住不同概念之間的關係的能力。他會一無所得，在實際使用中也會反應遲鈍、笨手笨腳。

在特殊中表現出一般，非常難以做到，尤其是對於年紀較輕的學生。教育的藝術決非易事。克服教育的困難，特別是初級教育中的困難，值得最有天分的天才為之努力。教育是人類靈魂的訓練。

數學的本質是不斷地拋棄較特殊的概念，尋求較一般的概念；拋棄特殊的方法，尋求一般的方法。循序漸進地灌輸這種從特殊到一般的概念，數學，如果教授得法，是最有力的工具。我們用方程式表達一個特殊問題的條件，但是這個方程式適用於不同學科中數以百計的其他問題。一般的總是強有力的推理，因為演繹推理的說服力是抽象方式的特性。

　　這裡，我們還要特別小心。如果我們用數學僅僅是牢記一般原理，我們就會毀了數學教育。一般概念是聯繫特殊結果的手段。畢竟，具體特殊的問題才是重要的。所以，在處理數學問題時，你的結果越具體越好；而涉及到方法時，則是越一般越好。推理的基本過程是將特殊的東西一般化，將一般的東西特殊化。沒有一般化就沒有推理，沒有具體化則毫無意義。

　　具體化是技術教育的力量所在。我要提醒你們，缺乏高度一般性的原理未必必然是具體的事實。比如，X+Y=Y 比 2+2=4 這個代數原理更為一般。但是 2+2=4 本身就是一個缺乏任何具體成分的高度概括的命題。要想獲得具體的命題，就必須對涉及特殊客體的原理有直覺的認識；比如，如果你對蘋果有直接的感知或直覺的印象，「這兩個蘋果加上那些蘋果，一共是四個蘋果」就是一個具體的命題。

　　認識的目的是為了應用，而不是將其作為空泛沒有意義的公式；為了獲得對原理的充分認識，就必須進行技術教育，除此別無他法。僅僅做消極的觀察是不夠的。只有在創造中，才會對生產出來的物品特性有生動而鮮明的理解。如果你想瞭解什麼東西，那麼親自動手，這是一個可靠的原則。你的才能富有活力，你的思維栩栩如生。你的概念獲得了現實感，這種現實感來自於你親眼目睹了這些概念和原理的適用範圍。

　　在初等教育中，這條原則很久以前就被用於實踐。教師通過剪裁和分類這樣一些簡單的手工操作，來教孩子熟悉形狀和顏色。這樣雖然很好，但不是我想要表達的全部。那是你思考之前的實際體驗，是為了產生概念而先於思維的體驗，這是一種很好的訓練。但是，技術教育所涉及的遠甚於此——它是你在進行思考時的創造性的體驗，是實現你的想法的體驗，是教你協調行動和思維的體驗，是引導你把思維和預見、把預見和成就結合起來的體驗。技術教育提供理論並訓練敏銳的洞察力來判斷理論將在何處失去作用。

　　不應把技術教育看作是完美的柏拉圖文化的一種殘缺的替代物：即，看作是一種由於受生活條件所限而不幸不得不接受的有缺陷的訓練。任何人所能獲得的都不過是不完整的知識和不完整的能力訓練。不過，我們有三條主要的道路：文學教育、科學教育和技術教育——沿着這些道路，我們就能滿懷希望地朝向智力與個性的最佳平衡前進。其中的任意一種都不能孤立地進行，否則會導致智力活動和性格方面的慘重損失。但是，如果這三種方式機械地混合在一起，也會產生糟糕的結果：形成一大堆支離破碎的知識，永遠互不關聯，或得不到運用。我們已經注意到，傳統的文學教育的優點之一，就是它的所有部分都是相互協調的。教育需要關注的問題就是要保持原有的側重點，不論是文學的、科學的或技術的側重點；在不損害彼此協調的情況下，在每一種教育中融入其他兩種教育的內容。

　　確定技術教育的問題要注意兩個年齡：一個是13歲，這時小學教育已經結束了；另一個是17歲，這時作為壓縮在學校課程範圍之內的技術教育結束了。我注意到，在初級技術學校里，培養技工以三年期的課程較為普遍。另一方面，培養海軍軍官和一般的指揮階層，可能需要更長的時間以完成系統的課程。我們要考慮這樣一個管理課程的原則：這種課程可以讓17歲的青年人掌握對社會有用的技術。

　　學生的手工技能訓練應該從13歲開始，並與他們的其他課業保持適當的比例，而且應當逐年增加，最終達到較大比例。最重要的是，這種訓練不能過於專業化。工場的加工技術及其竅門，如果只適合某一特殊的工作，應該在商業性的工場教授，而不應該構成學校課程的基本內容。一個受過適當訓練的工人一學就會。在所有的教育中，失敗的主要原因就是平庸陳舊。技術教育是吸引孩子、向他們傳授一門高度專業化的手工技能制度，如果我們這樣認為的話，那麼技術教育注定失敗。國家需要勞動力的合理流動，不僅僅是從一個地方流動到另一個地方，而是在一個合理的相關職能的範圍內，從一個特殊工種

轉到另一個特殊工種。我知道自己現在身處微妙，我並不主張人們在專門從事一種工作時，應該不時地去做其他的工作。這是一個與教育家無關的企業組織問題。我只是堅持這樣的原則：獲得對不同要求的適應能力，會對勞動者有利、對僱主有利，對國家也有利，所以，訓練比起最終的專業化應該更廣泛一些。

在考慮課程的智力方面，我們必須遵循各門學科學習的協調性原則。一般來說，與手工技能訓練最直接相關的智力性的學習，是一些自然科學的某些學科。實際上，會涉及不止一門學科；即使不是這樣，也不可能把科學學習局限在一種單一的狹隘的思維路線之中。不過，如果我們不過於細緻地進行分類，那麼大體可將技術學習按照所涉及的主要學科來劃分。這樣我們就有六種門類：（1）幾何技術；（2）機械技術；（3）物理技術；（4）化學技術；（5）生物技術；（6）商業和社會服務技術。

這樣的分類意味着，除了某些從屬的學科以外，在大多數的職業訓練中，還需要學習某種特殊的科學課程。比如，我們可以把木工工藝、五金工藝和許多其他藝術性手工藝歸到幾何技術中。同樣，農業屬於一種生物技術。烹飪業如果包括提供飲食服務，可能會介於生物、物理和化學諸學科之間，儘管我還不是十分肯定。

與商業和社會服務相關的科學，部分會是代數（*其中包括算術和統計學*），另一部分是地理和歷史。但是，這部分學科在它們的密切關聯性方面還是有點不同。不管怎麼樣，根據科學對技術學習進行準確的分類，是一件很細緻的事情。基本的要點是，經過一定的思考，有可能找到可以說明大部分職業的科學課程。而且，這個問題也很好理解，在英國的許多技術學校和初級工藝學校都得到了很好的解決。

現在從科學轉到文學，在考察技術教育的智力成分時，我們注意到，許多學習介於兩種學科之間，比如歷史和地理。假使學到的是恰當的歷史和恰當的地理的話，那麼這兩門學科在教育中都有必要。描

述性地介紹一般結果的書籍和在不同學科中的思維系列，都屬於這個範疇。這類書籍部分是在描述歷史，部分是對已經產生的主要概念的闡述。它們在教育中的價值取決於它們對智力發展的激勵作用。決不能用什麼科學的奇跡來誇大它們的作用，它們必須要有廣闊的視野。

　　遺憾的是，在教育中，除了語法學習之外，文學內容很少被考慮。形成這種局面的歷史原因是，在現代柏拉圖式課程形成的時候，拉丁語和希臘語是開啓偉大的文學大門的唯一鑰匙。但在文學和語法之間沒有必然的聯繫。早在亞歷山大⑬的語法學家們出現之前，希臘文學的偉大時代就已經過去了。當今存活着的各色人等中，研究古典文學藝術的學者與伯里克利時代⑭的希臘人相比差得太多了。

　　純粹的文學知識並不重要，唯一重要的是，如何學習這些知識。相關的事實不足為道。文學之所以存在，只有為了表達和拓展我們生活的那個充滿想象的世界，表達和拓展我們內心所存在的那個王國。因此，技術教育中涉及的文學，應該致力於讓學生享受文學帶來的樂趣。他們從中學到了什麼並不重要，他們從文學欣賞中感受到樂趣才是至關重要的。在英國那些了不起的大學的直接管理之下，學校的孩子需要應付關於莎士比亞戲劇的考試，他們從文學欣賞中獲得的樂趣受到了某種程度的損害，應該起訴這些大學犯有謀殺靈魂之罪。

　　有兩種形式的智力享受：創造的享受和休閒的享樂。它們不是嚴格分離的。職業的變換，也許就能使上述兩種快樂同時出現，從而帶來快樂的最大化。文學欣賞確實是一種創造。那些寫下的美麗詞句，它的音樂感，它引發的聯想，都不過是刺激因素而已。除了我們自己，任何人、任何天才都不能使我們的生活生動活潑起來；但是，文學或許可以，它所喚起的圖景，彷彿我們自己生活在其中。所以，除了那些從事文學工作的人，對於其他人，文學也是一種休閒。從事任何職業的人，在其工作時間，某些方面往往受到抑制，而文學，能夠使那些受到抑制的方面得以放鬆。藝術和文學一樣，對於生活有同樣

的效果。

　　無須任何幫助就能獲得休閒的樂趣，這種樂趣不過就是停止工作而已。這種單純的休息是健康的必要條件。過度工作的危險眾所周知。在人們需要放鬆休息的大部分時間裡，大自然賦予我們的不是快樂，而是大腦陷於一片空白的睡眠。創造的快樂是成功的努力帶來的結果，它需要幫助才能獲得。這種快樂對高節奏的工作和有獨創性的成就來說必不可少。

　　讓那些沒有經過休息而重新獲得活力的工人加快生產節奏，這樣的經濟政策極其危險。就算取得暫時的成功，也是以犧牲全體國民的利益為代價的；因為，之後，那些手工工人疲憊不堪，無法再繼續工作，為了維持他們的漫長生活，政府將不得不對他們進行資助，而資助的代價是全民承擔。爆發性的努力和完全的放鬆，這樣大起大落式的替換同樣有害。完全的放鬆期如果不被嚴厲縮短，那麼就會成為退化的前奏；正常的休息是變換活動方式，滿足天性的需要。遊戲可以提供這樣的活動。這種休閒方式的效果很好，因為它和工作無關；但是，遊戲過度常會使人感到空虛。

　　正因如此，文學和藝術在一個健康而組織有序的國家中，應該起着十分重要的作用。它們對經濟生產帶來的貢獻，僅次於睡眠和吃飯。我現在不是在談論一個藝術家的培養問題，而是在談論如何運用藝術作為健康生活的條件。藝術之於人類社會就像陽光之於自然界。

　　在幫助提升藝術享受水準方面，當我們擯棄了「知識是要來索取的」的觀念，那麼，就不會有特別的困難或不必支付特別的費用了。可以定期讓所有的學童到附近的劇院去看戲，在那裡上演的適合學生看的戲劇都可以得到補貼。音樂會和電影也可同樣如此。圖畫對於孩子們的吸引力比較難確定，但是不妨試試，因為用情趣盎然的圖畫來表現孩子讀過的景致或學過的概念，或許會有一定的吸引力。學生在藝術上的努力應該得到鼓勵。最重要的是，要培養學生朗讀的藝術：

艾迪生⑮關於英國鄉紳柯弗利的隨筆，就是可讀性極強的散文典範。

在賦予生命活力方面，藝術和文學並不只是起到了一種間接的作用，它們還給予我們洞察力。世界的廣闊性，遠遠超出了我們有着各種精妙的反應和情感的波動的肉體感官之所能及。洞察力是具備控制力和指導能力的先決條件。各民族之間的競爭，最終將取決於工場而不是戰場，勝利將屬於在利於成長的條件下工作、受過訓練並精力充沛的主人。藝術——這是其中不可或缺的、根本的條件！

如果時間允許的話，我還想談一些其他的問題：比如，應該在所有的教育中加入一門外語。根據我的親身觀察，這對於工匠的孩子來說是可能的。但是，關於我們在進行國民教育時所需要遵循的原則，我已經講得夠多的了。

最後，我還是回到本篤教派的思想，他們通過把知識、勞動力和道德力量聯合起來，為人類拯救了正在消失的古代世界文明。我們的危險在於把現實看作是邪惡的王國，認為在這個王國中只能逐出理想的目標，才可能獲得成功。我認為這種觀念是一種謬誤，已經被實踐經驗直接否定了。在教育中，這種觀念表現為對技術教育的輕視。我們的祖先，在漫長的黑暗世紀中，將崇高的理想體現於傑出的組織結構中，從而拯救自己。不要被動地去模仿，要大膽地運用我們的創造力量，這是我們今天的任務！

---

①參見：蕭伯納（George Bernard Shaw，1856-1950）：《英國佬的另一個島》（John Bull's Other Island）。——原注

②本篤教派（Benedictine），天主教的一個隱修會，公元529年由貴族出身的意大利人本篤在意大利中部卡西諾山所創，遵循中世紀初流行於意大利和高盧的隱修活動。會規要求祈禱不忘工作，視遊手好閒為罪惡。其規章成為西歐和北歐隱修的主要規章。本篤會隱修院的象徵是十字架及耕地的犁。——譯者注

③柏拉圖（Plato，約前427-前347），古希臘偉大的哲學家，也是全部西方哲學乃至整個西方文化最偉大的哲學家和思想家之一，他和老師蘇格拉底、學生亞里士多德並稱為古希臘三大哲學家。另有其他概念包括：柏拉圖主義、柏拉圖式愛情、經濟學圖表等含義。柏拉圖是西方教育史上第一個提出完整的學前教育思想並建立了完整教育體系的人。他的名言有：

不知道自己的無知，乃是雙倍的無知。

教育是約束和指導青少年，培養他們正當的理智。每個人最初所受教育的方向容易決定以後行為的性質，感召的力量是不小的。

子女教育是社會的基礎。

初期教育應是一種娛樂，這樣才更容易發現一個人天生的愛好。

我們應該盡量使孩子們開始聽到的一些故事必定是有道德影響的最好的一課。

無論你從什麼時候開始，重要的是開始後就不要停止；無論你從什麼時候結束，重要的是結束後就不要悔恨。

只要有信心，人永遠不會挫敗。——譯者注

④聖本篤（St. Benedict，480-547），又譯聖本狄尼克，意大利天主教教士、聖徒，本篤會的創建者；天主教隱修制度的創始人，被譽為西方修道院制度的創立者，1220年被封為聖徒，是天主教會重要聖人之一。當今教宗本篤十六世的聖號即來源於他。他經常與《元素論》作者聖安東尼奧一起供奉，侍候於聖保羅左右。左手持十字架，右手持《修院聖規》，神情悲憫，呈慈悲相。

1964年10月24日，教宗保祿六世往訪本篤會時宣佈他為歐洲的主保，贊揚聖本篤「是和平統一的使者，西方文明的大師，尤其是信仰的先鋒和西歐隱修生活的始祖」。贊揚了他對天主教和歐洲文化的偉大貢獻。——譯者注

⑤教皇尼古拉五世（1357-1455），被稱譽為文藝復興教皇，他即位時心裡就有三個願望：成為一個好教皇；重建羅馬；恢復古典文學、藝術和知識。在位期間：1447-1455年。——譯者注

⑥耶穌會會士（The Jesuits)），創立於1534年的天主教男修會耶穌會的成員，主要從事各級教育工作或在非天主教地區從事傳教工作。

中國耶穌會的開創者是意大利人利瑪竇。他於萬曆十一年（1583）入居廣東省肇慶。在耶穌會遠東巡視員范禮安領導下，為耶穌會在華傳教需要，他制訂了一整套入鄉隨俗的「調和策略」，主要內容包括：結交中國士大夫和中國朝廷；傳播西方科學技術和其他人文科學；遵行儒家習俗，尤其贊同中國教徒實行祭祖祭孔禮儀。

他們結交的士大夫，如徐光啓、沈德符、李贄、袁宏道、袁中道和楊廷筠等均是萬曆、天啓、崇禎朝的重要人物與知名之士。在中國學者與文人幫助下，耶穌會士翻譯、撰寫了許多種有關天文、歷算、地理學、物理學以及語言學的著作，把西方科學技術和人文科學傳播到中國。其影響顯著者，數學有利瑪竇口授、徐光啓筆譯的《幾何原本》；天文學有徐光啓督改、耶穌會士鄧玉函、龍華民、羅雅各布和湯若望參加修撰的《崇禎曆書》（一百三十七卷）；地理學有利瑪竇編著的各種版本的世界地圖和艾儒略的《職方外紀》；物理學有鄧玉函口授、王徵繪譯的《奇器圖說》；語言學有利瑪竇《西字奇跡》（今改名《明末羅馬字注音文章》）和金尼閣《西儒耳目資》等。——譯者注

⑦色諾芬（Xenophon，約430-354 BC），古希臘歷史學家、作家，雅典人，蘇格拉底的弟子。他的散文受到古代文論家的推崇，至近代仍享有盛譽。公元前401年參加希臘僱傭軍助小居魯士（Kurush，約424-前401）爭奪波斯王位，未遂，次年率軍而返。前396年投身斯巴達，被母邦判處終身放逐。著有《遠征記》、《希臘史》（修昔底德

《伯羅尼撒戰爭史》之續編，敘事始於前411年，止於前362年）、《居魯士的教育》、《經濟論》以及《回憶蘇格拉底》等。——譯者注

⑧艾薩克·牛頓爵士（Sir Isaac Newton，1642年12月25日-1727 年3月31日），人類歷史上出現過的最偉大、最有影響力的科學家，同時也是物理學家、數學家和哲學家，晚年醉心於煉金術和神學。他在1687年7月5日發表的不朽著作《自然哲學的數學原理》裡，用數學方法闡明了宇宙中最基本的法則——萬有引力定律和三大運動定律。這四條定律構成了一個統一的體系，被認為是「人類智慧史上最偉大的一個成就」，由此奠定了之後三個世紀中物理界的科學觀點，並成為現代工程學的基礎。

著有《自然哲學的數學原理》、《光學》、《二項式定理》和《微積分》等。牛頓為人類建立起「理性主義」的旗幟，開啟工業革命的大門。牛頓逝世後被安葬於威斯敏斯特大教堂，成為在此長眠的第一個科學家。名言：如果說我比別人看得更遠些，那是因為我站在了巨人的肩上。——譯者注

⑨查爾斯·羅伯特·達爾文（Charles Robert Darwin，1809年2月12日-1882 年4月19日），英國生物學家，生物進化論的奠基人。他以博物學家的身份，參加了英國派遣的環球航行，做了五年的科學考察，在動植物和地質方面進行了大量的觀察和採集，經過綜合探討，形成了生物進化的概念。1859年出版了震動當時學術界的《物種起源》。除了生物學外，他的理論對人類學、心理學及哲學的發展都有不容忽視的影響。名言：就我記得的我在學校時期的性格來說，其中對我後來發生影響的就是：我有強烈的多樣的趣味，沉溺於自己感興趣的東西，深喜瞭解任何複雜的問題和事物。——譯者注

⑩像本書第一章提到的拉格比公學（Rugby School），就是英式橄欖球運動的發源地。——譯者注

⑪弗朗西斯·培根（Francis Bacon，1561-1626），偉大的哲學家、科學家和思想家，近代英國思想史上最重要的代表人物之一，也是近代人類思想史上具有里程碑意義的傑出人物之一，現代實驗科學的先驅。著有：《新工具》、《學術的進步》、《新大西島》、《亨利七世本紀》和《人生論》等。他提出了「知識就是力量」的著名論斷，創立了科學歸納法，鼓勵人們以科學的方法認識自然和改造自然。

在應用科學方面，培根感興趣的主要是工匠的技術和工業生產過程，被稱作「工業科學的哲學家」。

培根還是一位散文家，他在1624年出版的《人生論》（Essays），文筆非常優美，是值得一讀的佳作。

他的名言有：

讀史使人明智，讀詩使人聰慧，學習數學使人精密，物理學使人深刻，倫理學使人高尚，邏輯修辭使人善辯。

求知可以改進人性，而經驗又可以改進知識本身。人的天性猶如野生的花草，求知學習好比修剪移栽。學問雖能指引方向，但往往流於淺泛，必須依靠經驗才能扎下根基。

習慣是人生的主宰，人們應當努力求得好的習慣。最好的習慣應該在青少年時代就開始培養，我們把這稱作教育；實際上教育就是為了培養早期習慣。

一切幸福都絕非沒有憂慮和煩惱，而一切逆境也都絕非沒有慰藉與希望。——譯者注

⑫雅各布的梯子（Jacob's Ladder），典出《舊約·創世紀》，又稱「天梯」，喻指通向神聖和幸福的途徑。

雅各布夢見一個梯子立在地上，梯子的頭頂着天，有神的使者在梯子上，上去下來。

耶和華站在梯子以上，說：「我是耶和華，你祖亞伯拉罕的神，也是艾薩克的神，我要將你現在所躺臥之地賜給你和你的後裔。你的後裔必像地上的塵埃那樣多，必向東西南北開展，地上萬族必因你和你的後裔得福。我也與你同在，你無論往哪裡去，我必保佑你，

領你歸回這地，總不離棄你，直到我成全了向你所應許的。」

　　雅各布睡醒了，說：「耶和華真在這裡，我竟不知道！」就懼怕，說：「這地方何等可畏！這不是別的，乃是神的殿，也是天的門。」

　　上帝在哪裡？遠在天邊，近在眼前！

　　耶和華真在這裡！何等令人震驚的發現！

　　照理，雅各布早就瞭解耶和華上帝無所不知。但朦朧中，總認為他可能只是父親艾薩克的神。

　　照理，雅各布早就明白耶和華上帝無所不能。但感覺上，總認為他不過是以往歷史中的神。

　　照理，雅各布早就知道耶和華上帝無所不在。但意識裡，總認為他似乎高不可攀，遙不可及……

　　皆因，雅各布自己從來沒有親身的經歷！

　　如今，他真知確信了，因為親耳聽到上帝對他講話，證據不再是二手資料。

　　現在，他驚恐害怕了，因為親眼看見上帝向他顯現，敬畏之情發自內心深處。

　　雅各布與神相遇了！

　　父母的信仰不能代替孩子的信仰；

　　別人的經驗不能代替自己的經驗。

　　耶和華真在這裡！但願這是你自己的發現。

　　因耶穌的話，信的人就更多了。便對婦人說：「現在我們信，不是因為你的話，是我們親自聽見了，知道這真是救世主。」——譯者注

　　⑬亞歷山大（Alexandria），埃及北部城市，曾是古代世界主要的學術中心和最偉大的城市之一。始建於公元前332年，按其奠基人亞歷山大大帝命名，作為當時馬其頓帝國埃及行省的總督所在地。亞歷山大大帝死後，埃及總督托勒密在這裡建立了托勒密王朝，加冕為托勒密一世（救星）。亞歷山大成為埃及王國的首都，並很快就成為古希臘文化中最大的城市。在西方古代史中其規模和財富僅次於羅馬。但埃及的伊斯蘭教統治者在奠定了開羅為埃及的新首都後，亞歷山大港的地位不斷下降。在奧斯曼帝國末期它幾乎已淪為一個小漁村。

　　亞歷山大是古代歐洲與東方貿易的中心和文化交流的樞紐，是一個古希臘文化的中心，也是當時世界上最大的猶太人城市。開始的托勒密統治者維護城市的發展，並使得其大學成為希臘最好的大學。同時，這些統治者將其居民分為希臘人、猶太人和埃及人。亞歷山大港早期的居民之一就有數學家歐幾里得。從托勒密四世開始，城市內各個民族之間的矛盾開始加劇。古代亞歷山大港著名的還有亞歷山大燈塔（世界七大奇跡之一）和亞歷山大圖書館。——譯者注

　　⑭伯里克利時代（Periclean times），是指古希臘的一個歷史時期，其始於波希戰爭的終結，終於伯里克利離世或伯羅奔尼撒戰爭結束，大約由前480年至前404年。

　　伯里克利支持文學藝術，給雅典帶來之後再也未曾有過的輝煌；他還主持大量公共項目以改善公民生活。雅典的奴隸主民主政治發展到高峰，公民大會是國家的最高權力機關，五百人會議是最高的行政機構，陪審法庭是最高的司法和監察機構。所有這些，使得雅典進入黃金時代，亦為古希臘的全盛時期，故被稱為伯里克利時代。

　　伯里克利時代是希臘古典文化高度繁榮的時代。希臘世界著名的學者文人和藝術大師都薈萃於雅典，聚集在伯里克利的阿那克薩戈拉周圍，授課講學，尋求真善美，探索宇宙的奧秘和人生的真諦。傑出的哲學家阿那克薩戈拉、雕塑家菲狄亞斯和悲劇家索福克勒斯與伯里克利過從尤密。伯里克利的妻子米利都人阿斯帕西亞，才華出眾，智慧過

人，受到蘇格拉底的推崇，不少哲學家和藝術家成為她的座上賓，很多雅典人甚至一些婦女來向她求教。伯里克利年輕時即主辦戲劇演出，主政期間又採取了給貧苦公民以觀劇津貼、舉行節日音樂競賽和修築奏樂館等措施。

從公元前447年起，伯里克利大規模修建雅典衛城。他動用同盟金庫貯存，先後興建帕特農神廟、雅典衛城正門、赫淮斯托斯神廟、蘇尼昂海神廟、埃列赫特伊昂神廟，以及附屬於這些建築的各種塑像、浮雕等精美絕倫、千古不朽的造型藝術傑作。

伯里克利為發揚光大希臘古典文化作出了卓越的貢獻。他的文化政策是與其政治、經濟和對外政策緊密相連的。無論是修建公共工程還是舉辦節日演出，其目的全是為了鞏固民主政治，改善廣大公民的物質文化生活，促進工商業的發展，以及樹立雅典的光輝形象來吸引希臘各邦的景仰和嚮往。

在雅典人紀念死去的戰爭英雄的一次集會上，伯里克利作了演講：

「我們的國體之所以被稱作民主，是因為權力不是被少數人而是被所有人民所掌握。當私人糾紛產生時，所有人在法律面前一律平等。正像我們的政治生活是自由而開放的那樣，日常生活中我們的人與人之間的關係也是如此……在這裡，每一個個人不但對他自己的私事感興趣，也對整個社稷的大事感興趣。」

伯里克利（Pericles，約前495-429）古希臘民主政治的傑出代表，古代世界最著名的政治家之一。他出身於雅典的名門貴族，他的性格也是真正的貴族式的，有良好的文化、音樂和哲學教養，思想十分開放。──譯者注

⑮約瑟夫·艾迪生（Joseph Addison，1672年5月1日-1719年6月17日），英國散文家、詩人、劇作家和政治活動家，英國期刊文學的創始人之一。

約瑟夫·艾迪生與他的長期搭檔理德·斯蒂爾在發展短篇詼諧散文方面成就斐然，此類散文在現代雜誌中多有轉載。艾迪生曾闡述自己的想法「用智慧來激活道德，用道德來諧調智慧」。

艾迪生與斯蒂爾合作發表的作品使他聲名遠揚，這些作品發表在期刊《藝術家》和《旁觀者》上。通過這些作品，他逐漸將期刊散文完善成為一種文學形式。斯蒂爾創辦並主編的《藝術家》（1709-1711），艾迪生為該雜誌撰寫了42篇文章。之後艾迪生與斯蒂爾協力推出《旁觀者》（1711-1712），並為該雜誌撰寫了274篇散文。該期刊的辦刊宗旨在於教化新興的中產階級；散文主題從女士應該佩戴什麼樣的帽子到怎樣欣賞彌爾頓的《失樂園》等，包含甚廣。

其中，關於羅傑·德·柯弗利（Roger de Coverley）的散文最受歡迎，這是在《旁觀者》雜誌上發表的一系列提倡提高道德修養和文學欣賞的文章中的一個鄉紳，艾迪生對這個人物勾勒精推細敲，賦予他深度和活力，柯弗利是斯蒂爾最早以「旁觀者俱樂部」會員身份介紹的一個人物。

艾迪生通過普及哲學家約翰·洛克的理念，使人們對民歌的興趣再度燃燒，而且薰陶了平民階層。艾迪生在《旁觀者》中寫道，「對於我自己，我一心認為是我本人把哲學從壁櫥和圖書館以及大學院校中解放了出來，使其扎根在俱樂部、集會場、茶桌旁和咖啡屋」。

艾迪生的散文非常優美，對社會和政治醜惡進行委婉奚落，文筆優雅，思想見解深刻，這使其成為英國文學奧古斯都時期最棒的社會幽默作家，被譽為英語散文大師。1719年6月17日，艾迪生逝世，他被安葬在威斯敏斯特教堂（英國名人墓地）。──譯者注

第五章 古典文化在教育中的地位

古典文化①在這個國家的未來，不是由它給一個優秀的學者帶來的樂趣所決定的，也不是為學者的業餘愛好而進行這方面的訓練來決定的。以古典文學和古典哲學為主要基礎的教育，使受教育者得到快樂和品質的錘鍊，已經為幾個世紀以來的經驗所證明。今天的古典文化學者對古典文化的熱愛，已經不如他們的先輩了；但是，古典文化所面臨的危險，不是由於這個原因引起的。

過去，古典文化在整個高等教育領域佔有絕對優勢，根本沒有其他科目可以與之媲美。因此，所有的學生在他們的整個校園生活中，都沉湎於古典文化中；在大學裡，只有對於數學的嚴密訓練，才能對古典文化所佔據的統治地位形成一定的挑戰。這樣的狀態導致了如下的後果：（1）僅僅出於教學的需要，就產生了對古典文化學者的大量需求；（2）在學術生活的各個方面都瀰漫着古典主義的氣息，古典文化的造詣成了能力的代名詞；（3）任何一個有望在這方面有點發展的孩子，都開始自覺不自覺地培養自己在古典文化方面的興趣。

然而，這一切都一去不復返了。漢普迪·鄧普迪②只要待在牆頭上，那麼他還是一個完好的雞蛋；如果他摔下來了，那麼誰也不能讓他恢復原狀了。現在的學校裡，還有很多其他的學科，每一種學科都牽涉到普遍感興趣的課題，這些課題間又存在着複雜的關係；每個學科也都展現出天才以其豐富的想象力和哲學家般的敏銳洞察力，在學科發展過程中建立豐功偉績。現代生活中的每一個部分都是一門有學問的專業，需要一門或幾門學科作為其專門技能的基礎。人生苦短，而大腦可以接受新事物的可塑性時期更短暫了。因此，即使所有的孩子都適合接受古典文化的教育，也完全不可能保持這樣一種教育制度，即把古典文化學者所接受的充分訓練作為掌握其他學科的必要

條件。

　　作為「研究古典文學在教育中的地位首相委員會」的一名成員，我很不幸地聽到許多徒勞的哀嘆，這些哀嘆是由目睹現代家長更趨於唯利是圖而發出的。我不相信今天來自不同階層的家長比他們的前輩更加唯利是圖。當古典文化是通向成功的必經之路時，它就成為最受歡迎的學科。風水輪流轉，古典文學陷入到了危險的境地。亞里士多德㊹說過，「豐厚的收入是知識生活令人滿意的附屬」。我很想知道，今天我們偉大的公立學校的校長，對作為一名父親的亞里士多德所說的這句話作何感想。根據我對亞里士多德有限的瞭解，我猜想，一場辯論必不可少，而亞里士多德將完勝。我力求全面地審視古典文化在教育系統中所面臨的危險。我所得出的結論是：在今後幾年中，古典文化的命運將由英國的中學做出決定。三十年內，不管願意與否，那些偉大的公立學校都將不得不跟着出牌。

　　將來18歲離校的學生，90%將不再會去閱讀原版的古典著作。那些更早離開學校的學生，百分比估計將會從90%上升到99%。基於這樣的事實，應該採取什麼樣的步驟呢？我曾聽到和讀到過很多動聽的闡述，說明古典文化對那些坐在沙發裡閱讀柏拉圖和維吉爾的學者是多麼有價值。但是之後，這些人就再也不會坐在沙發裡或者是在其他情形下閱讀古典著作了。我們必須要為古典文化打一場保衛戰，這事關90%的學生。如果古典文化被清掃出這個時期的課程表，那麼剩下的10%學生更不會去關注古典文化了。在任何一所學校裡，都不會再有古典文學的老師去教這門課了。問題很嚴峻。

　　但是，如果斷言古典文學面臨着來自學術界或那些關注教育和效率關係的工業界領袖的非議，那就大錯特錯了。就這個主題，我參加過公開或私下的討論，最近一次，是在一所相當現代化的大學裡的一個很重要的委員會上進行的，那是一次簡短而熱烈的討論。來自科學學科的三位代表極力強調古典文化價值的重要性，他們推崇古典文

應該作為科學家學習的基礎學科。我之所以提及這件事情，因為我的
經歷便是很好的例證。

我們必須牢記，整個智力教育的問題要受到時間有限的制約。如
果瑪士撒拉④不是一位受過良好教育的人，那麼一定是他自己的過錯
或是教育他的老師的過錯。我們的任務是，如何利用中學階段的五年
時間。在這段時間裡，要盡可能地讓古典文化比其他科目更快地豐富
學生的智力品性，將古典文化教育和其他科目一起排在這個時期的課
程表上；只有這樣，古典文化教育才能從根本上得到保護。

在古典文化的學習中，我們通過對語言全面而透徹的學習，來發
展我們在邏輯、哲學、歷史和文學的審美情趣等方面的心智。語言的
學習——拉丁語或希臘語——則是促進這個最終目標的一種輔助性手
段。當目標達到之後，除非學生有機會和有選擇權對這種語言進行進
一步的學習和研究，語言學習也就完成了它的使命。存在着某些不同
智力的學生，其中最優秀的一些尤其如此，其對語言的分析不是達到
文化修養目標的手段。對他們來說，一隻蝴蝶或一台蒸汽機，比一句
拉丁語的句子更有廣泛的標誌性意義。對於那些有着生動的領悟能力
和創造性思維的天才來說，更是如此。對這些人來說，那些指定的用
文字表達的句子總是在傳遞錯誤的東西，在用無關緊要的細枝末節來
干擾他們的思維。

但是，總的來說，正常的途徑是對語言的分析。對學生來說，它
是最普通的學習古典文化的方法；對老師而言，它顯然也是最容易完
成的工作。

在這點上，我必須捫心自問。我的另一個自我會問：如果你想讓
孩子學習邏輯這門課，你為什麼不直接去教他們邏輯呢？

這難道不是一個顯而易見的步驟嗎？我用一位偉人的話來回
答這個問題，這個偉人就是不久前去世的奧多學校⑤的前校長桑德
森⑥，他的逝世對我們來說是無法估量的損失。他說：他們通過接觸

來學習。這句話的意義直擊教育實踐中的核心問題。教育必須從精確的事實開始，對個人的領悟力來說，是具體而確切的，然後逐漸地過渡到一般概念。要避免的可怕的夢魘就是：灌輸與個人經歷毫不相關的一般陳述。

現在，應用這一原則來確定一種最佳方法，以幫助孩子形成思維的哲學分析。我將以更普通的方式來論述這個問題：使孩子思維清晰、表述有條理的最好方法是什麼？邏輯學的書籍上的一般陳述和孩子在生活中所認識的東西沒有任何相關的地方。這些一般陳述屬於教育成熟階段的內容——大學或接近於大學。你必須從分析熟悉的英語句子着手。但是，這個語法學習的過程在其初級階段結束以後繼續延長的話，就會極其枯燥。此外，它還有一個缺陷是，它的分析只是在英語的語言分析的範圍內進行，而沒有闡明英語詞彙和短語的複雜含義，以及心理認知過程的習慣。你下一步要做的，是教孩子一門外語。這時，你有一種極大的優勢：擺脫了令人厭惡的純粹為了練習而練習的形式主義；這時，分析成為一種自主的行為，學生的注意力集中到如何運用這種語言來表達他想要表達的東西，或去理解他人說話的意思，或是想讀懂作家寫下的作品。每一種語言都體現了一種確定的心理智力形式，兩種語言必然會向學生展示兩種形式之間的某種差異。常識告訴我們，你應該盡早地讓孩子開始學習法語。如果你家境富裕，可以配備一名會講法語的保育員兼家庭女教師。不那麼幸運的孩子，只能在他們十二歲左右進入中學時開始學習法語。直接教學法或許可以用上，通過這種方法，孩子整堂課都置身於法語之中，學會用法語思考，不受英語和法語在詞彙及詞義上區別的干擾。甚至連一般水準的孩子也會學得很好，並且獲得操縱和理解簡單法語句子的能力。就像我之前所說的那樣，收穫是巨大的；此外，還掌握了今後人生中很有用的一個工具。語感形成了，語感是潛意識裡對語言作為一種有確定結構的工具的鑒賞力。

只有到了這個時候，開始學習拉丁語才是對智力發展最好的促進。拉丁語的元素展示出語言作為一種結構特別清晰具體的一面。如果你的智力已經發展到了這個層次，那麼你就能發現這個事實。對英語和法語的學習來說，你可能不會遇到這種情況。一句簡明的優美的英語可以被直譯成一句鬆散的法語，反過來，一句優美的法語也可以被翻譯成一句粗糙的英語。文學翻譯上鬆散的法語和優美的法語之間的差別，本該寫明白，但是，這種差別對於智力發展的那個階段來說，常常是相當微妙，且總是不大容易解釋清楚。這兩種語言在表達上都顯示出同樣的現代性。但是，對於英語和拉丁語來說，語言結構的差異顯而易見，但還不至於構成無法逾越的障礙。

按照學校老師的說法，拉丁語是一門非常受歡迎的課。記得在我還是一個學生的時候，我就很喜歡拉丁語。我相信，拉丁語之所以那麼受歡迎，是伴隨拉丁語的學習而體驗到的啓蒙感所造成的，你正在試圖弄清楚某些事情。拉丁語的詞彙，不知道為什麼，以不同於英語或法語詞彙的形式附着在句子中間，並帶有奇特古怪的不同的內涵。當然，在某種意義上，拉丁語是一種比英語更為粗陋的語言，如同一個未經分解的單元，它是一種更近似於句子的形式。

這就引出了我的下一個觀點，在我列出的拉丁語給我們帶來的諸多饋贈排序中，我把哲學放在邏輯學和歷史之間。以它和拉丁語的聯繫來說，這是個合適的位置。拉丁語喚起的哲學本能，在邏輯學和歷史之間穿梭，使它們變得更加豐富。把英語翻譯成拉丁語，或把拉丁語翻成英語，在這個翻譯的過程中，對思維的分析使學生得到對哲學邏輯所必需的初次體驗。如果你日後的工作是思辨性質的，那麼，感謝上帝，你已經在青少年時期的五年時間裡，每周寫一篇拉丁語散文，每天翻譯一些拉丁著作。任何一門學科的入門，都是一個通過接觸來學習的過程。對於大多數人來說，語言是對思維活動最直接的刺激，他們理解力的啓蒙都是從簡單的英語語法到法語，從法語到拉丁

語，其間穿插着幾何學和代數學的內容。我不用提醒諸位，對於我堅持的這個一般原則，我可以引用柏拉圖的權威理論來論證。

現在，我們從思維的哲學轉到歷史的哲學。我恐怕還是要重提桑德森的那句名言——他們通過接觸來學習。那麼，孩子究竟怎樣通過接觸學習歷史呢？那些原始文獻、憲章綱領，法律條文和外交信函，對他們來說如天書一般，都是些莫名其妙的話。一場足球賽或許就是學習了馬拉松戰役⑦的一種模糊反應。但是那也只是說明，不管哪個時代哪種環境下，人類生活都有共同的特性。而且，所有這些我們灌輸給學生的外交和政治的材料，都是一種非常淺薄的歷史見解。真正需要的是，我們應該對觀念、思想、審美以及種族衝突的不斷變化有一種本能的把握，因為這些衝突影響着動蕩的人類歷史。現在，羅馬帝國好像是一個瓶頸口，通過這個瓶頸口，陳年佳釀變成了現在的生活。就歐洲文明而言，打開歷史之門的鑰匙，就是理解羅馬精神和羅馬帝國的活動。

拉丁語，這種羅馬的語言用文學的形式體現了羅馬的觀念，從中我們得到了最簡單的素材，通過接觸這些素材，我們就能判斷人類事務的變化發展趨勢。單單語言之間的明顯聯繫，如法語、英語對拉丁語的聯繫，本身就體現了一種歷史的哲學。考慮到英語和法語的不同之處：英語完全中斷了與不列顛過去文明的聯繫，慢慢地回歸到源於地中海的涵義典雅的詞彙和短語上；而法語，在顯而易見的猛烈震動影響下，我們仍然看到了發展的連續性。我並不想就這個問題做自命不凡的、高深莫測的演講。事實本身不證自明。法語和拉丁語的初級知識，加上英語作為母語的條件，給予我們對歐洲的遊牧民族的傳說賦予不可或缺的現實感。歐洲就誕生於這種傳說產生的過程中。語言體現了使用它的這個種族的精神生活。每個短語和詞彙都包含了人們在犁地、居家和建設城市時的某些習慣性思維。從這個意義上來說，在不同語言之間，詞彙和詞組不會有真正的同義詞。我以上所說

的不過是對這個主題的一種鋪陳渲染，以及強調它的迫切重要性。英語、法語和拉丁語，就像一個三角形，其中的兩個頂點，英語和法語，體現了兩種主要的現代智力形成的不同表達方式。它們和第三個頂點——拉丁語的聯繫，體現了從過去地中海文明衍生而來的選擇過程。這是最根本的語言文化的一個三角形，其中包含了過去與現在的鮮明對比。它跨越時間和空間。通過「接觸」學習邏輯的哲學和歷史的哲學，最容易的方式是掌握法語和拉丁語，這些就是我們證明上面主張的依據。除了這些深刻的經驗之談外，你的思維分析和行為記錄只不過是虛張聲勢罷了。這種教育的途徑對大多數學生來說不簡單、不容易。對於絕大多數學生來說，他們的側重點是不同的。但是，我確信，這種方法能夠給絕大部分的學生帶來最大化的成功幾率。它的優點還在於：它經受住了實踐的檢驗。我認為，應該對現行的教育實踐進行大幅度的修正，使之適合當前的需要。但是，總的來說，這種文學教育的基礎，包括對傳統的透徹理解，包括能認識到這條途徑的大多數經驗豐富的優秀教師。

讀者或許已經注意到，我對燦爛的羅馬文學只字未提。當然，拉丁語的教學必須輔以學生對拉丁文學作品的閱讀來進行。拉丁文學擁有充滿活力的作家隊伍，這些作家在各個不同的方面成功地展示了羅馬精神生活，包括羅馬人對希臘思想的鑒賞。羅馬文學的特點之一是它比較缺少傑出的天才作家。羅馬文學的作家很少持超然的態度，他們表現自己民族的特點，但是很少涉及和其他種族的差異。除去盧克萊修⑧以外，你總是能感受到他們在寫作時所受到的限制。塔西佗⑨表達了羅馬元老院頑固派的觀點，但是由於沒有看到羅馬行省當局的成就，因而他的作品只能反映出希臘自由民在取代羅馬貴族。羅馬帝國和創造它的羅馬精神吸收了羅馬人的天才智慧。當對這個世界發生的大事失去了應有的關注的時候，羅馬文學幾乎找不到通達文學天堂的道路。天堂裡的語言會是中文、希臘語、法語、德語、意大利語和

英語等，天堂的聖人們愉快地討論着這些對永恆生活的精緻描述。他們將對希伯來文學中與已經消失的惡魔作鬥爭時所表現出的道德熱情心生厭倦，對羅馬作家把古羅馬廣場錯當成有生命的上帝的腳凳⑩心生厭倦。

我們教授拉丁文，並不奢望那些被閱讀的原著，成為學生的終身伴侶。英國文學更為偉大：它更為豐富，更為深邃，更為精妙。如果你具有哲學家的鑒賞力和品位，你會為西塞羅⑪而放棄培根、霍布斯⑫、洛克⑬、伯克利⑭、休謨⑮和穆勒⑯嗎？不會的，除非你對近代史的興趣讓你轉而關注馬丁·塔珀⑰。也許你特別想瞭解對人類迥異的生存狀態的反省，以及人物對環境的反應。你願意用莎士比亞和其他的英語作家去交換泰倫提烏斯⑱，普勞圖斯⑲和特立馬喬的宴會⑳嗎？還有我們的幽默作家，謝里丹㉑和狄更斯㉒等。有誰在閱讀拉丁作品時像讀他們的作品那樣開懷大笑？西塞羅是個大演說家，他曾在羅馬帝國的輝煌舞台上展示才華。英國也有充滿想象力地去闡述政策的政治活動家。我不想再列舉詩歌和歷史方面的名單，以免讓你們厭煩，我只是希望證實我對下述觀點的懷疑：拉丁文學完美地表現了人類生活的全部要素。拉丁文學不會讓人笑，也幾乎不會讓人哭。

你不能把拉丁文學和它所處的時代背景割裂開來看。希臘和英國創造出來文學，能表達人類一般情感，從這樣一種意義上來說，拉丁文學不是一種文學。拉丁語有一個主題——羅馬——羅馬是歐洲的母親——偉大的巴比倫，《啓示錄》的作者描述了它類似一個娼妓的命運㉓：

她遠遠地站着，對她將要承受的折磨感到無比恐懼，口中念念有詞，唉，唉，偉大的巴比倫城，強大的城啊！一個小時內你就要受到審判。世界上的商人們將為她哭泣，為她哀悼，因為沒有人會再買他們的商品。

那些金銀製品，稀有的寶石，珍珠，最好的亞麻布，紫袍，絲綢，大紅布，各樣香木，各種象牙器皿，用最珍貴的木材、黃銅、鐵和大理石製成的各種器皿。

還有桂皮，香料，油膏，乳香，酒，油脂，精制麵粉，小麥，野獸，綿羊，駿馬，戰車，奴隸，還有人的靈魂。

這是羅馬文明呈現在早期的基督教徒面前的方式。但是，基督教本身就是遠古文明世界的一部分，這個文明世界正是由羅馬傳遞到歐洲的。我們繼承的是東地中海文明的兩個方面。

拉丁文學的作用，就在於它反映了古羅馬的情況。當你的想象力可以為英國文學和法國文學增加羅馬文化的背景時，那麼你就打下了堅實的文化基礎。對羅馬文化的理解可以帶回到地中海文明，而羅馬正是地中海文明最後的篇章。這種理解自動地展現了歐洲的地理環境，以及海洋、河流、山川和平原的功能。在青年人的教育中，這種學習的好處是具體形象、激勵行動和偉大崇高。他們的目標是偉大的，他們的德行是偉大的，他們的惡行也是駭人聽聞的。他們手牽繮繩，驅動戰車，拯救罪惡，立下功績。如果不能經常目睹偉大崇高，那麼道德教育就無從談起。如果不能成就偉大，那麼做什麼和結果怎麼樣都無關緊要。現在，對偉大崇高的判斷是一種直覺，而不是爭論的結果。青年在宗教信仰的轉換過程中，懷有一種自己是一條可憐蟲而非男子漢的感覺，這是可以理解的；只要還保持對偉大崇高的堅定信念，這種堅定信念足以證明上帝的永恆懲戒是正當的。對偉大崇高的認識是道德感的基石。我們正處於一個民主時代的開端，究竟是在高層次上還是在低層次上實現人類的平等，還有待確認。沒有一個時代比現在更需要青年把握對羅馬的理解：羅馬本身是一部偉大的戲劇，它反映的問題要比它本身更為重要。我們現在已經沉浸在對文學作品的審美這樣一個主題中。就是在這裡，古典文化的教學傳統需要

進行強有力的改革，以適應新的形勢。造就完美的古典文化學者困擾着古典文化教學。舊傳統堅定不移地把學習的最初階段讓給了語言的學習，然後希望依靠流行的文學氛圍來保證對文學的喜愛。在19世紀的後期，其他學科侵佔了可利用的時間，結果常常把時間浪費在失敗的語言學習上。我常常想，正是這種失敗感，使得從英國的那些偉大學校裡出來的學生，表現出一種可悲的智力熱情的缺乏。為了取得明確的令人滿意的結果，學校開設的古典文化課程必須經過仔細的計劃安排。雄心勃勃的學術理想之路，總是伴隨着太多的失敗。

對待每一項藝術工作，我們必須恰當地關注兩個因素：尺度和速度。如果你用一個顯微鏡來觀察羅馬的聖彼得教堂㉔，那麼對它的建築師是不公平的；如果你以一天五行的速度來閱讀《奧德賽》㉕，那麼這部偉大的史詩也會變得枯燥無味。現在，擺在我們面前的問題就是如此。我們現在教的學生，他們的拉丁語永遠不會好到可以使他們快速閱讀的程度，需要啓發想象的地方還很多，而且必須以全部的歷史為背景。仔細地研究尺度和速度的問題，研究我們工作的不同部分的相互作用，這些似乎才是根本的問題。我還沒有發現一部作品，能夠從學生的心理角度來探討這個問題。它是一個共濟會㉖的秘密嗎？

我經常注意到，知名學者聚會，如果引出關於翻譯的話題，他們的情緒和感情表現，就像對着舉止優雅的人談論一個骯髒的性話題一樣。作為一名數學家，我不擔心丟了學者的面子。所以，我來談談這個問題。

按照我之前展開的整個思維路線進一步分析下去，正確欣賞拉丁詞彙的意義，欣賞概念在語法結構中的連接方式，欣賞有着明顯側重點的拉丁語句子的完整用法，便構成了我所認為的學習拉丁語的根本價值所在。因此，任何教學上的含糊不清，忽視了語言的精緻美好，都會導致我呈現給你們的整個理想目標的覆滅。運用翻譯來使學生盡可能快地擺脫拉丁語，或是避免分心去考慮結構等問題，這種做法是

錯誤的。精確、明確、獨立的分析能力，是在整個語言學習中獲得的主要收穫。

　　但是，我們仍然面臨嚴峻的速度問題，並且要在短短的四五年時間內學完全部課程。每一首詩都要在一定的時間內讀完。語氣的對比、形象化的比喻、情緒的轉換等，都必須與人的思想中的節奏變化相一致。這些都有它們的周期，不能超越一定的限度：你可以選出世界上最優秀的詩歌，但是，假如你用蝸牛般的速度慢慢地細讀，它就會從一件藝術品淪為一堆廢物。想象一下，孩子在專注於功課時的大腦活動：讀到「此時」，然後停了下來，查一查字典，然後繼續讀下去──「一隻鷹」，然後又查一下字典，接下來又對句子的結構感到驚嘆，如此這般，這般如此。那樣能有助於他認識羅馬嗎？當然，常識告訴我們，你可以盡可能地找到最好的譯本，這些譯本完美地保持了原著的魅力和生氣，然後以恰當的速度大聲朗讀，還要加上一些有助於理解的說明。然後，你開始加大對拉丁語的批評，感到它把一件活生生的藝術品奉為神聖。

　　但是有人會提出異議，認為遺憾的是翻譯總不如原著。翻譯當然不如原文，這就是為什麼學生必須掌握拉丁原文的理由。一旦原文掌握了，就可以定它一個適當的速度。我主張，按適當的速度對以翻譯形式給出的詩文整體做一個最初的認識，再按適當的速度對以原文形式出現的全部詩文價值做最後的評價。華茲華斯[20]曾談到那些持「謀殺是為了解剖」觀點的科學家。和他們相比，過去的古典學者才是真正的謀殺者。美感是急切而熱烈的，應該受到應有的尊重。但是，我想再進一步，用來傳達羅馬圖景的拉丁文學比學生能夠從原文中學到的更多。

　　學生們應該不局限於他們所學到的拉丁文學作品，而應該多讀一點維吉爾、盧克萊修，多讀一點歷史，多讀一點西塞羅。在研讀一位作家時，所選擇的拉丁作品應該能夠充分展示他的精神世界──雖然沒有用自己的母語、自己的話來表達更為有力。不過，如果一點也不

去閱讀作家的原文的話，那是一個極大的錯誤。

　　評價尺度的困難主要與古典歷史的描述有關。展現在青年學子們面前的每一事物都必須立足於特定的和個別的情形。然而，我們想要闡述所有歷史階段的一般特徵。我們必須讓學生從接觸中學習。我們能夠通過直觀演示來展現生活方式。各種建築物圖片、各種雕像模型、花瓶的圖片或者說明宗教神話或家庭生活場景的壁畫。這樣，我們就能把羅馬和以前東地中海文明作比較，和後來的中世紀作比較。一定要讓孩子們弄明白，人們是如何改變其衣着外貌、住處、技術、藝術以及宗教信仰等等。我們要學習動物學家的做法，他們手頭上有着整套的動物製作標本，他們通過示範典型的例子來教學。我們必須以同樣的方式，來展現歷史上羅馬的情形。

　　人類的生活是建立在技術、科學、藝術和宗教之上的。這四者相互間都有內在的聯繫，且源於人類的整個智慧。但是在科學和技術之間，藝術和宗教之間，有着特別密切的聯繫。沒有這四個根本因素，根本無法理解任何一種社會組織結構。一個現代的蒸汽機能夠完成古代一千個奴隸才能完成的工作。劫掠奴隸是古代帝國生存的關鍵。一台現代的印刷機則是現代民主政治的得力助手。**現代智慧發展的關鍵，是科學的持續進步帶來思想的轉變和技術的發展。**

　　在古代，美索不達米亞㉘和埃及，能夠以灌溉為生。但是羅馬帝國的存在，靠的是世人迄今所看到的最廣泛的技術運用：它的道路，它的橋梁，它的溝渠，它的隧道，它的排水管，它的宏偉建築，它的有組織的商船隊，它的軍事科學，它的冶金術，以及它的農業。這是羅馬文明得以拓展和統一的秘密。我經常在疑惑，為什麼羅馬的工程師們沒有發明蒸汽機。他們隨時隨地可以把它造出來——如果這樣，世界歷史將會多麼不同啊。我把原因歸於他們當年生活在溫暖的氣候中，沒有引進茶和咖啡。在十八世紀，成千上萬的人坐在火堆旁，看着他們的水壺沸騰。當然，我們都知道，亞歷山大里亞的希耶羅（Hiero）㉙曾經發明過一些小東西——當時最需要的，是一種對於蒸汽推動力量的深刻印象——羅馬的工程師們在注視水壺被燒開的過程

中——可惜，他們錯過去了。

人類歷史必然與技術進步有着適當的關聯。在最近的一百年中，先進的科學和發達的技術緊密結合，開創了人類的新紀元。

同樣，大約在公元前1000年，當寫作的藝術流行開來的時候，第一個偉大的文學時代隨之開啓了。在它最初的朦朧起源階段，這種藝術已經在傳統的僧侶經文、正式的官方文件記錄和編年史中使用。如果認為在過去一開始就能預見一種新發明的影響力度，那就大錯特錯了。即便是在現在，我們受過良好的訓練，在對各種新構想的可能性進行思考時，情況也不是這樣。但是在過去，由於不同的思維傾向，新事物緩慢地滲透到社會體系中。相應地，作為個人思想創造的一種激勵，寫作在東地中海的沿海地區慢慢地被掌握。當希臘人和希伯來人完全掌握了這種寫作術的時候，文明掀開了新的篇章。雖然希伯來精神的一般影響被延遲了一千年，直到基督教的誕生。但是，就是在那個時候，希伯來的先知們開始記錄他們的內心思想，而這時希臘文明正在開始成型。

我想說明的是，在大量論述理解羅馬的背景和前景所必需的歷史的時候，符合我們歷史傳統的對政治事件的連續性記載完全不存在。甚至文字的說明在一定程度上也不為人所知了。我們必須利用模型、圖片、圖解和圖表，來展現技術發展的典型例子以及它對目前生活方式的影響。藝術也是這樣，它是實用與宗教的巧妙結合，兩者都反映了想象力的現實的內在的生命，而且正是通過這種反映改變着內在的生命。孩子們可以通過模型、圖片甚至博物館裡的展品，來瞭解過往時代的藝術。探討過去的歷史，絕不能從一般性的陳述入手，而必須從具體的事例入手，這些事例展現了從一個時代到另一個時代、從一種生活方式到另一種生活方式、從一個種族到另一個種族的緩慢的連續的發展歷程。

當我們開始討論東地中海的文學和文明的時候，我們必須同樣從具體的事例入手。只要你意識到這一點，沒有任何東西可以替代第一手的知識，古典文化重要性的所有要求都落腳在這個基礎之上。由

於希臘和羅馬是歐洲文明的創立者，所以歷史知識首先就是關於希臘人和羅馬人思想的第一手資料。因此，為了把對羅馬的理解置於其本來的背景中，我極力主張學生應該直接閱讀一些希臘文學的範文。當然，肯定是翻譯作品。但是，我寧願選擇希臘人原文的譯文，也不要由一個英國人所寫的關於希臘人的空話——無論他寫得有多好。掌握了一些希臘的直接知識以後，便可以開始閱讀一些關於希臘的書了。

　　我所說的這種閱讀，指的是閱讀用韻文翻譯的《奧德賽》，一些希羅多德㉚的作品，一些由吉爾伯特·默里㉛翻譯的戲劇裡的合唱句，普魯塔克㉜寫的傳記作品，特別是關於阿基米得㉝在馬克盧斯㉞執政時的那部分生活，還有歐幾里得《幾何原本》㉟中的一些定義、公理和一兩個命題——但要讀希思㊱翻譯的那種準確的學者式譯文。在所有的這些閱讀中，對作者的心靈依託的環境要有足夠的說明。羅馬在歐洲處於一個了不起的地位，源於這樣一個事實，即它給我們留下了一份雙重的遺產。它吸收了希伯來的宗教思想，融合了希臘文明，傳給歐洲。羅馬本身就代表了各種紛繁活躍的元素的組織和聯合。羅馬法體現了羅馬之所以偉大的秘密，那就是在帝國鋼鐵般的結構中，通過對人性隱私權的斯多葛（Stoics）㊲式的尊重。歐洲總是因為它所繼承的遺產中的多種多樣的爆炸性的特質而四分五裂，又總是因為它從來不能擺脫繼承自羅馬的那種統一性的影響而趨於聯合。歐洲的歷史就是控制希伯來人和希臘人的羅馬的歷史，同時伴隨着它們各自的衝突，即緣於完全不同的宗教信仰、科學、藝術、物質欲和支配欲等的衝突，這些衝突之間劍拔弩張，勢不兩立。對羅馬的深刻認識，就是對文明統一性的深刻認識。

---

①西方學術界通常將古代希臘、羅馬稱之為古典時代或古典世界，並將古代希臘、羅馬文化界定為古典文化。「古典」一詞源於拉丁文classicus，意思是「第一流的」、「最上乘的」。實際上，當羅馬人在全面吸收古希臘文化時就曾賦予它以典範的含義。

　　因此，所謂的西方古典文化，便是由希臘人開創並在羅馬人那裡得到發揚光大的一種文化傳統或文化體系，它以其典範楷模和啓迪之功而成為近現代西方文化發展的源泉和動力。——譯者注

　　②漢普迪·鄧普迪（Humpty Dumpty），童謠中的矮胖子，蛋的化身，他從牆上跌下來摔得粉碎。此處指一經損壞便無法復原的東西。原文為：Humpty Dumpty was a good egg so long as he was on the top of the wall, but you can never set him up again.

Humpty Dumpty

Humpty Dumpty sat on a wall,

Humpty Dumpty had a great fall;

All the king's horses and all the king's men

Couldn't put Humpty together again.

歌詞大意：

蛋頭先生

蛋頭先生坐牆頭，

栽了一個大跟鬥。

國王呀，齊兵馬，

破鏡難圓沒辦法。

　　蛋頭先生（Humpty Dumpty）是《鵝媽媽童謠》中的人物。隱喻出在政治上登上高位的人本質不過是個空虛的蛋，從高位墜下後，必將支離破碎，權勢和財富都拯救不了他的命運。

　　這首Humpty Dumpty是世界上最有名的英文童謠之一，在英語系國家家喻戶曉。在18世紀的時候，這首兒歌其實是個謎語，謎底就是「蛋」。當今由於謎底盡人皆知，已經沒有人把它當作謎語來看，變成了一首普通的兒歌。Humpty Dumpty在英語俚語也變成了「又矮又胖的人」之意。

　　Humpty Dumpty 的形象深入人心，他是英國作家劉易斯·卡羅爾（Lewis Carroll）《愛麗絲漫遊奇境記》（Through the Looking-Glass, and What Alice Found There）中的一個角色。

　　在電影《碟中諜3》中，湯姆·克魯斯在梵蒂岡任務中，爬上牆頭那一段，說了這麼一句話：Humpty Dumpty sat on a wall, 就是這首兒歌的開頭。在電視劇《越獄》第二季中，Bellick審訊越獄失敗的胖子時就叫他Humpty Dumpty。

　　科學家們用Humpty Dumpty 的故事來演示熱力學第二定律（或稱「熵增定律」）：在自然過程中，一個孤立系統的總混亂度（即「熵」，entropy）永不自動減少，熵在可逆過程中不變，在不可逆過程中增加。——雞蛋從牆上掉下摔碎了以後，就幾乎不可能回到原先那個熵值更低的完好狀態了，破鏡難圓也是這個道理。

　　「Humpty Dumpty」這個詞的發音很有趣，念起來彷彿是牙牙學語的小娃娃的口氣。當H和D大寫時，Humpty Dumpty指的就是兒歌裡的這個角色的名字，它是一隻在很多英語兒童讀物中出現過的蛋，整天坐在牆頭，一不小心跌下來就碎掉了。而當H和D小寫時，在兩個詞的當中加上一個連接符，humpty-dumpty這個詞就有了另一個意思：矮矮胖胖的、有點笨拙的人。早在十八世紀，這個發音有趣的詞就被用來形容矮胖的人了，

後來人們為這個詞編寫了謎語和兒歌，又對應矮胖者的形象畫出了那只傻乎乎的大胖蛋。——譯者注

③亞里士多德（Aristotle，前384年4月23日-前322年3月7日），世界古代史上最偉大的哲學家、科學家和教育家之一，柏拉圖稱之為「學園之靈」。他是柏拉圖的學生、亞歷山大大帝的老師，他和柏拉圖、蘇格拉底（柏拉圖的老師）一起被譽為西方哲學的奠基者。

公元前335年，他在雅典辦了一所叫呂克昂的學校。在這個學校裡，老師和學生們習慣在花園中邊散步邊討論問題，得名為「逍遙派」。

作為一位百科全書式的科學家，他對古希臘人已知的各個學科的知識進行了整理，並提出了自己的創造性見解。他對哲學的幾乎每個分支學科都做出了貢獻。他的寫作涉及邏輯學、形而上學、神學、倫理學、心理學、政治學、修辭學、教育學、詩學、風俗以及雅典法律。亞里士多德的思想對西方文化的根本傾向和內容產生了深遠的影響。

「吾愛吾師，吾更愛真理」這句名言鮮明地表達了他對智慧和真理的熱愛和追求。

他的主要名言還有——

遵照道德准則生活就是幸福的生活。

事業是理念和實踐的生動統一。

教育的根是苦的，但其果實是甜的。

在科學上進步而道義上落後的人，不是前進，而是後退。

習慣實際上已經成為天性的一部分。事實上，習慣有些像天性，因為「經常」和「總是」之間的差別是不大的，天性屬於「總是」的範疇，而習慣則屬於「經常」的範疇。

德可以分為兩種：一種是智慧的德，另一種是行為的德；前者是從學習中得來的，後者是從實踐中得來的。

對上級謙恭是本分，對平輩謙遜是和善，對下級謙遜是高貴，對所有人謙遜是安全。

智慧不僅僅存在於知識之中，而且還存在於運用知識的能力中。——譯者注

④瑪土撒拉（Methuselah）是《聖經·創世紀》中的人物，猶太族長，活了969歲，據說是世界上最長壽的人。他是以諾之子，《創世記》中亞當與夏娃在該隱之後所生的賽特的後裔。瑪士撒拉是拉麥的父親，諾亞（築方舟保存了地球各類動物的諾亞）的祖父。他的子孫包括亞伯拉罕、雅各布和大衛。——譯者注

⑤奧多中學（Oundle School），位於英國北安普敦郡內的一所中學，創辦於1556年，1990年首次接納女學生。學校致力於培養具有自律能力、社會責任感、自我發展和領導能力的全方位發展的復合型人才，學校鼓勵相互尊重的學術氛圍，啟發學生成為自信、有知識並且對社會有所貢獻的人。在桑德森（F.W. Sanderson）任校長領導奧多期間（1892-1922），奧多聲名遠揚，穩居領先英國公立學校之一，三十年間在校生人數翻了兩番多。學校1930年受皇家冊封。——譯者注

⑥弗雷德里克·威廉·桑德森（Frederick William Sanderson，1857-1922年），英國中學教師，1889年為倫敦達利奇學院高級物理教師，1892-1922年任奧多學校校長。通過建立實驗室、天文台、圖書館、工場車間和實驗農場等龐大的建築計劃，並增設理工科，使學校大為改觀。他建立了奧多在科學和工程學術領域的聲譽。桑德森改組奧多學校的做法對英國中等教育的課程和教學法產生了重大影響。——譯者注

⑦馬拉松戰役（the Battle of Marathon），公元前490年秋季，希臘軍隊和波斯軍隊在希臘阿提卡東北部馬拉松平原上進行的一場決戰，雅典人在這次戰役中擊退了波斯大軍的入侵。為了把勝利的消息盡快傳達給首都人民，青年士兵菲力彼得斯從馬拉松一直跑回雅典，全程約42.195公里，途中從未停頓。當他以最快的速度從馬拉松跑到雅典中央

廣場，對着盼望的人們說了一聲「大家歡樂吧，我們勝利了」的消息後，就因為精疲力竭倒在地上犧牲了。為了紀念馬拉戰役的勝利和表彰菲力彼得斯的功績，1896年在雅典舉行的第一屆奧林匹克運動會上，增加了馬拉松賽跑項目。

在馬拉松戰役中，雅典人以少勝多，以弱勝強，終於打敗了敵人，取得了鼓舞全希臘人的勝利，對以後各個戰役有重要的意義。馬拉松戰役可以說是雅典，也可以說是整個希臘第一次依靠自己的力量擊退波斯的一場會戰，對於希臘文明在之後三個世紀中所達到的光輝無比的成就而言，馬拉松戰役無疑是這一成就的最初的台階。然而，對於希臘和波斯之間的戰爭而言，馬拉松戰役的勝敗並不具有決定性意義，因為，希波戰爭一直到前449年方才結束。——譯者注

⑧提圖斯·盧克萊修·卡魯斯（Titus Lucretius Carus，約前99-約前55），羅馬共和國末期的詩人和哲學家，以哲理長詩《物性論》著稱於世。他繼承古代原子學說，特別是闡述並發展了伊壁鳩魯的哲學觀點。認為物質的存在是永恆的，提出了「無物能由無中生，無物能歸於無」唯物主義觀點。——譯者注

⑨普布里烏斯·克奈里烏斯·塔西佗（Publius / Gaius Cornelius Tacitus，約55-前120），古代羅馬最偉大的歷史學家，曾擔任古羅馬元老院議員，主要著作有《歷史》和《編年史》，今僅存殘篇。他繼承並發展了李維的史學傳統和成就，在羅馬史學上的地位猶如修昔底德在希臘史學上的地位。

塔西佗在西方歷史學史上第一次明確地提出了「抽離自我，超然物外」的客觀主義寫史原則，這是塔西佗史學成就的最高體現，也標誌着西方史學在對史學本體的認識上達到了一個新的高度。——譯者注

⑩上帝的腳凳，語出《聖經·舊約·馬太福音》第5章，「不可輕易發誓！人不可指天起誓，因為天是上帝的寶座；不可指地起誓，因為地是上帝的腳凳；不可指着自己的頭顱起誓，因為人不能使自己的白髮變黑。凡事，是就是是，非就是非；再多說一句，就是出於惡魔。」

誓言是為了加強自己話語的可信度而發出的；但假如人人說話皆如季布一諾，又何必起誓？聖經記載上帝起誓，是為了讓人放心，因為人總是三心二意，故以己度神，不相信上帝話語的功效。——譯者注

⑪馬庫斯·圖留斯·西塞羅（Marcus Tullius Cicero，前106-前43），羅馬共和國晚期著名政治家、演說家、雄辯家、法學家和哲學家。西塞羅是羅馬最傑出的演說家、教育家，古典共和思想最優秀的代表，羅馬文學黃金時代的天才作家。

他的典雅的拉丁文體促進了拉丁文學的發展，從而影響了羅馬以及後來歐洲的教育。西塞羅的影響在啟蒙時代達到了頂峰，受其政治哲學影響者包括洛克、休謨、孟德斯鳩等哲學家。亞當斯、漢米爾頓等人也常在其作品中引用西塞羅的作品。

他在政治、法律思想方面的代表作是《論國家》和《論法律》。認為國家是人民的事務，是人們在正義的原則和求得共同福利的合作下所結成的集體。在哲學方面的創作有《論至善和至惡》，《論神性》等，他主張綜合各派的學說，他是第一個將古希臘哲學術語譯成拉丁文的人。在教育方面的創作有《論演說家》等，他談論一個演說家所必需的學問和應該具有的品格；他認為教育的最終目的是培養有文化修養的雄辯家，而訓練的方法是實地練習。

他的名言有：

有勇氣的人，心中必然充滿信念。

沒有誠實，哪來尊嚴。

如果一個人能對着天上的事物沉思，那麼在他面對人間的事物時，他的所說所想就會更加高尚。——譯者注

⑫霍布斯（Thomas Hobbes，1588-1679），英國政治家、思想家、哲學家，歐洲蒙運動時期的傑出人物，英國理性主義傳統的奠基人，是近代第一個在自然法基礎上系統發展了國家契約學說的啓蒙思想家。著有《論物體》、《利維坦》、《論人》、《論社會》和《對笛卡爾形而上學的沈思的第三組詰難》等。

霍布斯出生於英國威爾斯特郡一個鄉村牧師家庭，自幼聰穎好學，15歲進入牛津大學學習。畢業後不久，到一個大貴族家任家庭教師。在歐洲大陸旅遊多年，結識了許多科學家。曾經做過培根的秘書，深受培根思想的影響。英國資產階級革命期間，一度移居法國，克倫威爾執政時，經過十一年的流亡生活，返回英國。霍布斯的政治主張恰逢其時，他的名著《利維坦》很快便在倫敦出版了，提出了主權至上與不受限制的國家主義，深受克倫威爾贊賞，在《利維坦》中霍布斯將國家比喻為保障社會統治的實施和人們生命安全和健康的人工機器。這是他第一次公開在英國發表的著作，一般人得知霍布斯的大名就是通過這本書的。

培根晚年受貶後退隱鄉間，從事著述活動。大約1621—1625年間，霍布斯給他當過秘書。他們兩人經常在花園裡散步。霍布斯總是拿着紙和筆，隨時記錄下培根不時迸發出來的新的思想火花。培根常說，他特別喜歡霍布斯記錄他的思想，因為比起其他人來說，霍布斯更善於領會他的思想，他也更能明白霍布斯所記錄的東西。霍布斯還幫助培根把他的某些作品翻譯成拉丁文。霍布斯可謂是最好的秘書。

通過兩人的交往，霍布斯受到了培根哲學思想的熏陶。——譯者注

⑬約翰·洛克（John Locke，1632-1704），英國哲學家、經驗主義的開創人，同時也是第一個全面闡述憲政民主思想的人。洛克開創的經驗主義被後來的喬治·貝克萊以及大衛·休謨等人繼續發展，成為歐洲的兩大主流哲學思想。

洛克是第一個系統闡述憲政民主政治以及提倡人的「自然權利」的人，提出「天賦人權」學說來反對「君權神授」思想，他把在英國革命中提出的各種基本要求概括為自由權、生命權和財產權，並把它們說成是天賦人權。他的政治思想對後來的政治發展起到了極大的作用。洛克的自由主義被美國奉為神聖，成為民族理想。他的思想深深影響了托馬斯·傑弗遜等美國政治家，並且在美洲引發了一場轟轟烈烈的革命浪潮。洛克的影響在法國則更為激烈。伏爾泰是第一個將洛克等人的思想傳到法國去的人，法國後來的啓蒙運動乃至法國大革命都與洛克的思想不無關係。

《教育漫話》是他的教育代表作。在西方教育史上第一次將教育分為體育、德育、智育三部分，並作了詳細論述。它強調環境與教育的巨大作用，強調在體魄與德行方面進行刻苦鍛鍊。他的教育思想還包括「白板說」，認為人的心靈如同白板，觀念和知識都來自後天，並且得出結論，天賦的智力人人平等，「人類之所以千差萬別，便是由於教育之故。」主張取消封建等級教育，人人都可以接受教育。

洛克1632年出生於英國，從小受到嚴格的教育。1646年在威斯敏斯特學校接受傳統古典文學基礎訓練。後到牛津大學學習，並在那兒居住了15年。洛克終生未娶。

著有《論寬容》、《政府論》、《人類理解論》、《關於教育的思想》、《教育漫話》和《聖經中體現出來的基督教的合理性》等。——譯者注

⑭喬治·伯克利（George Berkeley，1685-1753），愛爾蘭哲學家、科學家和主教，通稱為伯克利主教，與約翰·洛克和大衛·休謨被認為是英國近代經驗主義哲學家的三位代表人物。著有《視覺新論》、《人類知識原理》等。美國加州的伯克利市和耶魯大學有一個本科寄宿學院以他的名字命名。——譯者注

⑮大衛·休謨（David Hume，1711-1776），蘇格蘭哲學家，出生在蘇格蘭的一個貴族家庭，曾經學過法律，並從事過商業活動。1734年，他第一次到法國，開始研究哲學，並從事著述。1763年，又去法國，擔任英國駐法國使館秘書，代理公使。1752年至1761

年，曾進行過英國史的編撰工作。他的主要著作有：《人性論》、《人類理解研究》、《道德原則研究》和《宗教的自然史》等。他與約翰·洛克和喬治·伯克利並稱英國三大經驗主義者。

完成《人性論》一書時，休謨年僅26歲。此書剛出版時並沒有獲得多少重視。休謨在記載到當時自己缺乏大眾重視時這樣寫道：「媒體對這本書的反應是一片死寂，甚至連對那些狂熱的讀者群都沒有半點交代。不過我本來就養成樂觀而開朗的個性，很快就從這樣的挫折里站了起來，並繼續在鄉下努力地進行研究。」他繼續寫下了《人性論摘要》一書，但沒有寫出自己的名字，他試着縮短並精簡他之前的冗長著作以吸引更多讀者，但即使經過這樣的努力，他依然沒有成功使《人性論》一書重獲重視。現代的學者們大多將《人性論》視為是休謨最重要的一本著作，也是哲學歷史上最重要的著作之一。——譯者注

⑯約翰·穆勒（John Stuart Mill，1806-1873），英國心理學家、哲學家、邏輯學家和經濟學家，古典自由主義最重要的代表人物之一，因其對個人自由的熱情辯護並以清晰的邏輯對自由主義原理作出了傑出闡釋，而被尊稱為「自由主義之聖」，有人將他的作品《論自由》的發表作為自由主義理論體系最後完成的標誌。他還是經濟學的古典學派的最後代表人物、心理化學理論的創始人，是公認的有史以來智商最高的人之一。除《論自由》外，他還著有《代議政治論》、《功用主義》、《邏輯學體系》、《政治經濟學原理》和《論婦女的從屬地位》等。——譯者注

⑰馬丁·塔珀（Martin Farquhar Tupper，1810-1889），英國作家、詩人。——譯者注

⑱泰倫提烏斯（Publius Terentius Afer，約前190-前159），古羅馬喜劇作家。

生於北非的迦太基，幼年來到羅馬，淪為奴隸。主人欣賞他的才智，讓他受到良好教育，解除了他的奴籍。

泰倫提烏斯共寫有6部詩體喜劇，全部保存下來，《安德羅斯女子》、《自責者》、《閹奴》、《福爾彌昂》、《兩兄弟》和《婆母》等。他的《兩兄弟》一劇主要談年輕人的教育問題，主張尊重年輕人的生活要求，但也反對過度放縱，在兩種思想的激烈鬥爭中，表現出一定的折衷傾向。

泰倫提烏斯的喜劇以其嚴肅、文雅的風格，更受貴族文人的歡迎。他的語言被奉為純正拉丁語的典範，對後世歐洲戲劇產生了巨大的影響。——譯者注

⑲普勞圖斯（Titus Maccius Plautus，約前254年-前184年），古羅馬劇作家，他的喜劇是現在仍保存完好的拉丁語文學最早的作品，音樂劇最早的先驅者之一。古代以他的名義流傳的劇本有130部，現存21部喜劇，代表作有《撒謊者》等。他的喜劇從平民觀點諷刺社會風習，特別針對當時淫亂、貪婪和寄生等現象，予以針砭。他出身於意大利中北部平民階層，早年來到羅馬，在劇場工作；後來經商失敗，在磨坊做工，並寫作劇本。——譯者注

⑳古羅馬詩人佩特羅尼烏斯（Petronius）的諷刺詩中的情節，特立馬喬（Trimalchio）是一個有錢而無風趣的暴發戶，「特立馬喬的宴會」，是針對這批暴發戶的一種譏笑。——譯者注

㉑理查德·布爾斯利·謝里丹（Richard Brinsley Sheridan，1751-1861），18世紀英國最有成就的喜劇家、政治家，出生於愛爾蘭，著有《造謠學校》、《批判家》等。歸葬於威斯敏斯特教堂「詩人角」。——譯者注

㉒查爾斯·狄更斯（Charles Dickens，1812-1870），英國小說家，出生於海軍小職員家庭，10歲時全家被迫遷入負債者監獄，11歲就承擔起繁重的家務勞動。

狄更斯曾在黑皮鞋油作坊當童工，15歲時在律師事務所當學徒，後來當上了民事訴訟法庭的審案記錄員，接着又擔任報社派駐議會的記者。他只上過幾年學，全靠刻苦自學和艱辛勞動成為知名作家。

狄更斯是高產作家，他憑藉勤奮和天賦創作出一大批經典著作，主要作品有《匹克威克外傳》、《霧都孤兒》、《雙城記》、《遠大前程》、《老古玩店》、《艱難時世》、《我們共同的朋友》和《大衛·科波菲爾》等。他的作品至今依然盛行，對英國文學發展有着深遠影響。他又是一位幽默大師，常常用妙趣橫生的語言在浪漫和現實中講述人間真相。他特別注意描寫生活在英國社會底層的「小人物」的生活遭遇，深刻地反映了當時英國複雜的社會現實，為英國批判現實主義文學的開拓和發展做出了卓越的貢獻。他的作品在藝術上以妙趣橫生的幽默、細緻入微的心理分析，以及現實主義描寫與浪漫主義氣氛的有機結合著稱。——譯者注

㉓見《新約全書·示錄》第十八章，巴比倫是聖城耶路撒冷的原型，被描繪成一個女人。人們認為巴比倫暗指先知時代古代世界的首都羅馬。——譯者注

㉔聖彼得教堂（Basilica di San Pietro in Vaticano），是羅馬基督教的中心教堂，世界第一大教堂，歐洲天主教徒的朝聖地與梵蒂岡羅馬教皇的教廷，位於梵蒂岡。它是世界著名的偉大建築，其名聲和在建築史上的成就是第一流的，被認為是人類智慧的結晶之一。

聖彼得大教堂以聖彼得為名，他是耶穌的門徒之長聖彼得，是耶穌的12個門徒之一。

彼得的名字就是耶穌所起，含義是「盤石」，意思是他將成為教會的基石。耶穌升天後，彼得以耶穌繼承人的身份傳道，公元64年，他在羅馬被尼祿皇帝殺害。彼得殉教後被後人尊為首任教皇，而之後的天主教皇都作為聖彼得的繼承人，被看成基督在世的代表。

聖彼得大教堂不愧為一座偉大的藝術殿堂，是人類歷史上不朽的建築藝術瑰寶，由文藝復興時代的建築名師布拉曼特設計，後由拉斐爾和米開朗琪羅主持施工和設計修改工程，修建這座大教堂用了120年的時間，許多藝術家貢獻了畢生的心血。——譯者注

㉕奧德賽（Odyssey），古希臘的兩部著名史詩之一（另一部是《伊利亞特》），為盲詩人荷馬（Homer）所編輯整理。描述希臘英雄奧德修斯在特洛伊戰爭中取勝及返航途中的歷險故事。《奧德賽》是歐洲敘事詩的典範，是西方文學的奠基之作。——譯者注

㉖共濟會（Freemasonry），全稱Free and Accepted Masons，是一種非宗教性質的兄弟會，基本宗旨為倡導博愛、自由、慈善，追求提升個人精神內在美德以促進人類社會完善。即是「How to make a good man better」（如何令一個好人更好）。

共濟會自稱起源於公元前4000年，1717年成立英格蘭第一個總會所，早期為石匠工會，有獨特儀式和標誌，後來發展成世界組織，成為權貴交流的俱樂部。會員包括眾多名人和政治家。入會申請者必須是男性、有神論者或有兩個共濟會會員推薦。

共濟會並非宗教，對入會申請者是否有宗教信仰或是什麼宗教背景並沒有要求，但申請者必須是有神論者，相信存在着一位神。

入會是加入共濟會的第一步。共濟會要求，會員不得向「世俗」（即非會員）洩露組織的秘密，會員要按慣例發一系列「毒誓」，發誓不會出賣共濟會的隱秘信息。這使其蒙上一層神秘的面紗，亦是諸多陰謀論的由頭。——譯者注

㉗威廉·華茲華斯（William Wordsworth，1770年4月7日-1850年4月23日），英國浪漫主義詩人，與雪萊、拜倫齊名，湖畔詩人的代表。其代表作有與塞繆爾·泰勒·柯勒律治合著的《抒情歌謠集》（Lyrical Ballads）、長詩《序曲》（Prelude）、《漫遊》（Excursion）。文藝復興以來最重要的英語詩人之一。

他提出「一切好詩都是強烈情感的自然流溢」（Poetry is the spontaneous overflow of powerful feelings），在詩藝上實現了劃時代的革新；開創了20世紀詩風的先河，被雪萊贊為「第一位現代詩人」，1843年被封為「桂冠詩人」，為繼莎士比亞、彌爾頓之後的一代大家。

華茲華斯的詩歌理論動搖了英國古典主義詩學的統治，有力地推動了英國詩歌的革新和浪漫主義運動的發展，因而，英美評論家將華茲華斯的《抒情歌謠集》稱為英國浪漫主義的宣言。

《我好似一朵流雲獨自漫遊》是華茲華斯抒情的代表作之一，他把自己比作一朵流雲，隨意飄蕩，富有想象的詩句暗示詩人有一種排遣孤獨、嚮往自由的心情。在他的回憶中，水仙花繽紛茂密，如繁星點點在微風中輕盈飄舞。——譯者注

㉘美索不達米亞，是古希臘對兩河流域的稱謂，meso意為中間，potamia為古希臘文中河流之意，轉化成為「（兩條）河流中間的地方」。這兩條河指的是幼發拉底河和底格里斯河，在兩河之間的美索不達米亞平原上產生和發展的古文明稱為兩河文明或美索不達米亞文明，它大體位於現今的伊拉克，其存在時間從前4000年到前2世紀，是人類最早的文明。

兩河流域是世界上文化發展最早的地區，為世界發明了第一種文字——楔形文字，建造了第一個城市，編制了第一種法律（有前言和後記及282條條文構成的《漢摩拉比法典》），發明了第一個制陶器的陶輪，制定了第一個七天的周期，第一個闡述了上帝以七天創造世界和大洪水的神話。至今為世界留下了大量的遠古文字記載材料（泥板）。——譯者注

㉙亞歷山大里亞的希耶羅（Hiero，10-70），古希臘數學家，居住於托勒密埃及時期的羅馬省。他也是一名活躍於其家鄉亞歷山大里亞的工程師，被認為是古代最偉大的實驗家，他的著作於希臘化時代（Hellenistic period）科學傳統方面享負盛譽。

希耶羅所發明的汽轉球，是有文獻記載以來的第一部蒸汽機，它比工業革命早兩千年製造。汽轉球主要是由一個空心的球和一個裝有水的密閉鍋子以兩個空心管子連接在一起，而在鍋底加熱使水沸騰然後變成水蒸氣然後由管子進入到球中，最後水蒸氣會由球體的兩旁噴出並使得球體轉動。

世界上第一部自動售賣機也是出於希耶羅之手，當在機器頂上的槽接受了投幣者的硬幣時，機器就會分配一定分量的聖水給投幣者。這項發明被收納在希耶羅的書《機械學與光學》的列表裡。希耶羅還發明了許多設備，如注射器、蒸氣風琴等。——譯者注

㉚希羅多德（Herodotus，約前484-前425），偉大的古希臘歷史學家，史學名著《歷史》一書的作者，西方文學的奠基人。他把旅行中的所聞所見，以及第一波斯帝國的歷史紀錄下來，著成《歷史》一書，成為西方文學史上第一部完整流傳下來的散文作品。《歷史》一書不僅具有重要的史料價值，而且具有高度的文學價值。更為重要的是，它開創了西方歷史寫作中的敘述體體裁，成為西方歷史著作的正宗。從古羅馬時代開始，希羅多德就被尊稱為「歷史之父」（pater historiae），這個名稱沿用至今。

他出身名門望族，父親是豪富的奴隸主，在當地頗有威望。叔父是著名詩人。富裕優越的環境使希羅多德自幼受到了良好的教育。他從少年時代起就勤奮好學，特別喜愛史詩。——譯者注

㉛吉爾伯特·默雷（Gilbert Murray，1866-1957），澳洲出生的英國古典學者和公共知識分子，古希臘語言和文化的傑出學者，英國古典文學學者，牛津大學教授，希臘學專家，在英語世界以翻譯評述古希臘戲劇聞名。他是古希臘戲劇大師埃斯庫羅斯、索福克勒斯、歐里庇得斯和阿里斯托芬斯的翻譯者，使他們的作品得以在當代舞台上重新流行。

默雷用押韻的詩句翻譯古希臘戲劇作品，再現古希臘詩歌的韻律。通過翻譯成韻律詩而不是空白詩句，他試圖恢復希臘詩歌的韻律特質。他還將人類學新興科學的見解應用於他的其他學術研究，從而拓寬了對荷馬和希臘宗教的較早形式的理解。

著有《希臘史詩的崛起》（1907年）和《希臘宗教的五個階段》等。——譯者注

㉜普魯塔克（Plutarch，約46-120），古希臘羅馬帝國時期的傳記作家，倫理學家，哲學

家。著有《希臘羅馬名人比較列傳》、《道德論叢》等。他的文筆典雅流暢，對16至19世紀歐洲作家和歐洲散文、傳記和歷史著作等發展曾產生巨大的影響。蒙田對他推崇備至，莎士比亞不少劇作都取材於他的記載。

他出身於希臘中部的貴族家庭。公元66年在雅典學習哲學，後去亞歷山大城進修。他還學習過修辭學、物理學、數學和其他自然科學。曾多次訪問羅馬，很受羅馬皇帝的賞識。

普魯塔克博覽群書，著述豐富；他的著作頗為完整地保存在拜佔庭的圖書館，論傳世作品的數量，他在古代作家中算數一數二。現存傳世之作包括50篇希臘、羅馬著名人物傳記的《傳記集》和由60餘篇雜文組成的《道德論集》。他撰寫歷史人物傳記的目的，並非記載歷史，而旨在說明人的性格如何決定命運。《道德論集》主要形式為對話或諷刺文章，涉及題材十分廣泛。——譯者注

㉝阿基米得（Archimedes，前287-前212），古希臘數學家、物理學家、發明家、工程師、天文學家。

阿基米得出生於西西里島的敘拉古，曾在亞歷山大城學習；到過亞歷山大里亞，據說他住在亞歷山大里亞時期發明了阿基米得式螺旋抽水機，今天在埃及仍舊使用着。

阿基米得流傳於世的數學著作有十餘種，多為希臘文手稿。第二次布匿戰爭時期，羅馬大軍圍攻敘拉古，阿基米得不幸死於羅馬士兵之手。相傳他的遺言是「別打擾我的圓圈」，指當時他被羅馬士兵打擾時正在研究的數學畫圖法中的圓圈。

阿基米得的幾何著作是希臘數學的頂峰。他把歐幾里得嚴格的推理方法與柏拉圖鮮艷的豐富想象和諧地結合在一起，達到了至善至美的境界，從而「使得往後由開普勒、卡瓦列利、費馬、牛頓、萊布尼茨等人繼續培育起來的微積分日趨完美」。阿基米得是數學與力學的集大成者，享有「力學之父」的美稱。

他通過大量實驗發現了槓桿原理，又用幾何演繹方法推出許多槓桿命題，給出嚴格的證明。他自己曾說：「給我一個支點和一根足夠長的槓桿，我就能撬動整個地球。」他還利用槓桿原理製造出一批投石機，凡是靠近城牆的敵人，都難逃他的飛石或標槍。這些武器弄得羅馬軍隊驚慌失措、人人害怕，連大將軍馬塞拉斯都苦笑地承認：「這是一場羅馬艦隊與阿基米得一人的戰爭」，「阿基米得是神話中的百手巨人」。

他發現了浮力定律（阿基米得原理）：物體在液體中所獲得的浮力，等於它所排出液體的重量。直到現代，人們還在利用這個原理計算物體比重和測定船舶載重量等。

阿基米得說過：「給我一個支點，我可以舉起整個地球。」他的主要名言語錄還有：

在對的時間遇上對的人，是一生幸福。在對的時間遇上錯的人，是一種悲哀。在錯的時間遇上對的人，是一聲嘆息。在錯的時間遇上錯的人，是一世荒唐！

放棄該放棄的是無奈，放棄不該放棄的是無能，不放棄該放棄的是無知，不放棄不該放棄的卻是執着！

如果能夠用享受寂寞的態度來考慮事情，在寂寞的沉澱中反省自己的人生，真實地面對自己，就可以在生活中找到更廣闊的天空，包括對理想的堅持、對生命的熱愛和一些生活的感悟！

有些機會因瞬間的猶豫擦肩而過，有些緣分因一時的任性滑落指間。許多感情疏遠淡漠，無力輓回，只源於一念之差；許多感謝羞於表達，深埋心底，成為一生之憾。

所以，當你舉棋不定時，不妨問問自己，這麼做，將來會後悔嗎？請用今天的努力讓明天沒有遺憾！——譯者注

㉞馬克盧斯（Marcus Claudius Marcellus，前268年-前208年。他於前222年、前215年、前210年和前208年任執政官。公元前222年他為山南羅盧勝利舉行凱旋式，慶祝該戰中以單打獨鬥斬殺了一個高盧大部族的首長，類似功績羅馬史上僅三人獲得，另外兩人其一是

羅馬傳說中的建城者，國王羅慕路斯，另一是前三巨頭克拉蘇之孫，執政官馬可斯·李錫尼烏斯·克拉蘇。之後與漢尼拔進行第二次布匿戰爭時，他表現突出，與費邊並列羅馬兩大支柱。

前211年，敘拉古倒向迦太基，西西里生變，他率領四個軍團長期圍攻敘拉古城，與阿基米得發明的各種城防機械對抗，經過多次失敗的攻城戰後，終於攻佔敘拉古，馬克盧斯本欲善待阿基米得，但阿基米得在亂軍中不幸意外被殺。

前208年，在一次對抗迦太基人的戰鬥中，他中了漢尼拔安排的的伏兵被殺。——譯者注

㉟歐幾里得（Euclid，約前330年-前275），古希臘數學家，被稱為「幾何學之父」。

他活躍於托勒密一世（前323-前283）時期的亞歷山大里亞，他最著名的著作《幾何原本》是歐洲數學的基礎，提出五大公設，被廣泛地認為是歷史上最成功的教科書。

他也寫了一些關於透視、圓錐曲線、球面幾何學及數論的作品，是幾何學的奠基人。歐幾里得還有另外五本著作流傳至今：《已知數》、《圓形的分割》、《反射光學》、《現象》和《光學》等，與《幾何原本》一樣，內容都包含定義及證明。

數學，尤其是幾何學，所涉及對象就是一般而抽象的東西。它們同生活中的實物有關，但是又不來自這些具體的事物，因此，學習幾何被認為是尋求真理的最有效的途徑。歐幾里得、柏拉圖甚至聲稱：「上帝就是幾何學家。」

《幾何原本》是一部在科學史上千古流芳的巨著。它不僅保存了許多古希臘早期的幾何學理論，而且通過歐幾里得開創性的系統整理和完整闡述，使這些遠古的數學思想發揚光大。它開創了古典數論的研究，在一系列公理、定義、公設的基礎上，創立了歐幾里得幾何學體系，成為用公理化方法建立起來的數學演繹體系的最早典範。

按照歐氏幾何學的體系，所有的定理都是從一些確定的、不需證明而礦然為真的基本命題即公理演繹出來的。在這種演繹推理中，對定理的每個證明必須或者以公理為前提，或者以先前就已被證明了的定理為前提，最後做出結論。這一方法後來成了用以建立任何知識體系的嚴格方式，人們不僅把它應用於數學中，也把它應用於科學，而且也應用於神學甚至哲學和倫理學中，對後世產生了深遠的影響。

歐幾里得是希臘亞歷山大大學的數學教授。著名的古希臘學者阿基米得，是他「學生的學生」——卡農是阿基米得的老師，而歐幾里得是卡農的老師。

歐幾里得不僅是一位學識淵博的數學家，同時還是一位教育家。在柏拉圖學派晚期導師普羅克洛斯的《幾何學發展概要》中，就記載著這樣一則故事，說的是數學在歐幾里得的推動下，逐漸成為人們生活中的一個時髦話題（這與當今社會截然相反），以至於當時亞歷山大國王托勒密一世也想趕這一時髦，學點兒幾何學。他問歐幾里得「學習幾何學有沒有什麼捷徑可走？」歐幾里得笑道：「抱歉，陛下！學習數學和學習一切科學一樣，是沒有什麼捷徑可走的。學習數學，人人都得獨立思考，就像種莊稼一樣，不耕耘是不會有收穫的。在這一方面，國王和普通老百姓是一樣的。」從此，「在幾何學裡，沒有專為國王鋪設的大道」這句話成為千古傳誦的學習箴言。

又有則故事。那時候，人們建造了高大的金字塔，可是誰也不知道金字塔究竟有多高。有人這麼說：「要想測量金字塔的高度，比登天還難！」這話傳到歐幾里得耳朵裡，他笑着告訴別人：「這有什麼難的呢？當你的影子跟你的身體一樣長的時候，你去量一下金字塔的影子有多長，那長度便等於金字塔的高度！」

來拜歐幾里得為師、學習幾何的人，越來越多。有的人是來湊熱鬧的，看到別人學幾何，他也學幾何。一位學生曾這樣問歐幾里得：「老師，學習幾何會使我得到什麼好處？」歐幾里得思索了一下，請僕人拿點錢給這位學生，冷冷地說道：「看來你拿不到錢，是不肯學習幾何學的！」——譯者注

㊱托馬斯·希思（Thomas Little Heath，1861-1940），世界數學史上的頂尖專家之一，希臘數學史的專家。

希思的英文版《歐幾里得原本卷》（The thirteen books of Euclid＇s Elements），是現行公認代表歐氏《原本》的權威著作，這部劃時代著作的意義與價值，在於它最早樹立了公理化演繹體系的典範。希思另著有《希臘數學史》（牛津大學出版社，1921年）。

希思在1912年當選為英國皇家學會（Royal Society）院士，並在其理事會中擔任了兩個任期。在《希臘數學史》出版後，他當選為1922-23年數學協會主席。1932年，他當選為英國科學院院士。——譯者注

㊲斯多葛學派（The Stoics），古希臘和羅馬帝國思想流派，哲學家芝諾於公元前3世紀早期創立，因在雅典集會廣場的廊苑（希臘語發音為斯多葛）聚眾講學而得名，是有極大影響的思想派別，被認為是自然法理論的真正奠基者。其代表人物有巴內斯、塞內卡、埃彼克泰特和馬可·奧勒留等。

斯多葛學派人士極富時代精神，思想非常開放。他們當中有許多人後來都成為活躍的政治家，其中最有名的是古羅馬唯一一位哲學家皇帝馬可·奧勒留（Marcus Aurelius，121-180），著有《沉思錄》，是學派晚期最著名的代表。他們在羅馬提倡希臘文化與希臘哲學，其中最出類拔萃的是集演講家、哲學家與政治家等各種頭銜於一身的西塞羅（Cicero，前106-前43），所謂「人本主義」（一種主張以個人為人類生活重心的哲學）就是由他創立的。若干年後，同為斯多葛學派的塞尼卡（Seneca，前4-65）表示：「對人類而言，人是神聖的。」這句話自此成為人本主義的口號。

斯多葛派有一格言：「依照自然而生活」，「自然」即宇宙運行的律則，受理性支配。人是自然的一部分，靈魂在自然中最偉大最高貴，理性也是人的主要特徵，成為人和禽獸的主要差別，「依照自然而生活」就是依照理性而行，使自然與人通為一。個體小「我」必須擴大自己，融合於整個大自然。小「我」的靈魂只有飛到高空，進入大自然的核心，才能成就最高度的充實和圓滿。靈魂喜愛在星辰之間翱翔，在那裡靈魂會得到豐富的營養，繼續成長，解除所有的束縛，回歸本源。

今天，仍用「斯多葛式的冷靜」（stoic calm）來形容那些不會感情用事的人。——譯者注

第六章　數學課程

　　現在的教育情況，如果不追溯到幾個世紀前中世紀學習傳統的中斷，就很難找到關於它的比較點。時至今日，相對於人類利益來說，傳統智力觀已經變得過於狹隘了，儘管它曾經成績斐然一執牛耳。人類利益的這種變化，其結果就要求教育的基礎也要作出相應的變化，以使學生適應在日後生活中在事實上影響他們心靈的那些思想。人類社會智力觀的任何根本性的重要變革，必然伴隨着一場教育的革命。既得利益或一些思想領袖自身的觀念局限，將影響到這場革命，讓它被拖上一代人的時間。但是，規律是不可抗拒的，要使教育生動活潑且富有成效，就必須予以指導，使學生瞭解那些觀念，並培養他們的能力，這些能力將有助於學生鑒賞他們所處時代的流行思想。

　　在真空狀態下，不可能產生一個成功的教育制度，也就是說，不可能有一個和現存智力環境毫無瓜葛的制度。教育必須是現代的，否則，會像所有有機體一樣，難逃消亡的命運。

　　但是，這個神聖的詞「現代」並不能真正解決我們的難題。我們所指的是，無論是在觀念的傳授上，還是在能力的培養中，要與「現代」的思想相關。從這個意義上來說，某些在昨天剛剛發現的東西未必能被稱為「現代」。它或許屬於在之前時代流行的某個過時的思想體系，更有可能的是，它太過於深奧難懂。當我們要求教育必須要與「現代」的思想相關的時候，我們指的是在受教育人群中廣泛流行的思想。在普通教育中教授深奧的課程並不合適，這個問題就是我今天下午想要演講的主題。

數學深奧嗎？

　　實際上，數學對於數學家來說，是一門相當棘手的科目。局外

人都傾向於譴責我們的科目過於深奧。讓我們馬上勇敢地處理棘手問題，並坦率承認，按照一般觀點，這正是深奧科目的典型例證。我所說的深奧，並不是指困難，而是其中涉及的概念都有非常特殊的用處，且很少影響思想。

這種深奧的傾向是一種特有的不幸，它很容易摧毀數學在自由主義教育中的功效。就這門科目的教育用途來說，我們必須承認，到目前為止，在普通的受教育人群中，數學水準還是處在一個令人悲哀的低水準上。對於擴大數學教育的範圍，我的渴望不亞於任何人。達到這一目的，不是單靠盲目地學習更多的數學知識。我們必須面對阻礙數學廣泛應用的真正困難。

這門科目深奧嗎？現在，從全局來看，我想是的。世界自有公論（Securus Judicat Orbis Terrarum）①——人類的一般判斷是可信的。

作為存在於大腦和學生的數學課本中的數學學科，它的確是深奧的。它從一般概念中推論出無數的特殊結果，每個結果比它的推論更為深奧。但是，我今天的任務，不是為數學作為一門深度研究的學科進行辯護。它完全可以不證自明。我想要說的重點是，讓這門學科對於學生而言，成為一種快樂的真正理由，也就是阻礙它作為一種有用的教育工具的原因，即，來自一般原理的互相影響的大量推論，它們的錯綜複雜性，它們與作為論點的概念之間明顯的距離，各種各樣的方法，它們純粹的抽象性質，這種抽象性質作為數學的禮物，帶來永恆的真理。

怎樣在普通教育中有用？

當然，數學的所有這些特性，對學生來說都是無價之寶；一直以來，它們吸引了一些最具敏感性的有識之士。我唯一的評價就是，除了一些被精心挑選出來的人以外，它們對教育的影響是不幸的。雖然很多細節無論與重要的概念抑或是與一般的思維都沒有明顯的關聯，

但是學生卻經常被各種各樣的細節所迷惑。進一步擴大獲得更多細節的這類訓練，是教育興趣所期望的最後的判斷尺度。

我們得出的結論是，**數學，若想在普通教育中有用，就必須經歷一個嚴格的選擇和適應的過程**。很明顯，我的意思不是說，無論我們在這門學科上投入多少時間，一般的學生都不會有所收穫。我的意思是說，無論我們的進步多麼有限，在任何階段都存在的這門學科的明確的自然的特徵，都必須被嚴格地排除。向青年展示這門科學，必須擯棄其深奧的一面。直面數學，它必須直接而簡練地探討一些具有深遠意義的一般概念。

在對數學教育的改革上，現在這一代的教師應該有理由為其成就感到自豪。數學教育已經顯示巨大的改革活力，並且在這麼短的時間內實現了遠超預期的目標。人們不是總能認識到，要對一門用公共考試制度加以認定確立的課程進行改革，這個任務是多麼艱難。

儘管如此，我們還是取得了巨大的進步，至少，舊的無效的傳統已被打破。我今天想指出，引導我們改革重建努力的指導思想是什麼。我已經用一句話來進行總結，那就是——**我們必須堅決把深奧性從這門學科的教育用途中根除。**

我們的教學課程，應該被設計得能夠簡單明瞭地對具有明顯重要性的概念進行舉例說明。所有的細小的題外話都應該被嚴格排除。我們所要實現的目標是：學生能夠通曉抽象思維，能夠認識到它是如何應用於特殊而具體的環境，應該知道怎樣在合乎邏輯的調查研究中使用一般的方法。對照這種教育理想，再也沒有什麼比盲目地增加我們課本中的定理更糟糕的事情了，而那些定理出現在課本中的唯一理由，就是讓學生去學習它們，然後老師可以針對這些定理巧妙出題考試。要學習的書本知識，應該是能夠解釋概念的非常重要的東西。舉的例子——要有盡可能多的例子，只要教師認為有必要——應該是對定理的直接說明，或是通過提煉特殊實例的方式，或是在具體現象中

應用的方式。這裡值得一提的是，如果在考試中出現的例子實際上需要更多的深奧的細節知識的話，那麼簡化書本知識其實毫無作用。這裡有一個被誤解的概念，認為習題能夠檢測能力和天賦，而書本知識能夠檢測學生死記硬背的本事。這不是我的經驗所得。只有那些為了獎學金而專門去死記硬背的學生，才可能成功地完成試題。適當地安排書本內容，而不是根據通常的不周到的計劃做些摘錄，是對能力的一種較好的檢測，再加上補充一點直接的例證。不過，這是考試對數學教學的不良影響而說的題外話。

數字、數量和空間的關係

作為數學基礎的那些主要概念其實一點兒也不深奧。它們是抽象的，但是在自由教育中，把數學包括進去的一個主要目的，就是訓練學生掌握抽象的概念。這門科學構成了最初的一大組抽象概念，這些概念很自然地以精確方式從腦子裡湧現出來。為了教育的目的，數學由數字關係、數量關係和空間關係所構成。這不是數學的一般定義，在我看來，數學是一門遠甚於一般的科學。但是，我們現在討論的是數學在教育中的應用。數學中的數字、數量和空間的關係是相互聯繫的。

在教育中，我們從特殊到一般。所以，孩子應該通過簡單的例題的練習來學習使用這些概念。我的觀點是，**學習數學的目的不是盲目堆積特殊數學定理，而是最終認識到，之前多年的學習說明了數字、數量和空間之間的關係，這些關係才是最為重要的**。這樣的訓練必須作為一切哲學思維的基礎。實際上，如果能夠正確地設想初等數學，就會正好能夠給予普通人以所能接受的方式接受哲學訓練。但是，無論如何，我們應該避免無意義的細節堆砌。只要你願意，就盡可能做些例題；讓孩子學上幾學期，或是幾年。但是這些例題必須能夠直接說明主要的概念。用這種方式——也只能以這種方式，才能避免致命的深奧性。

我現在所講的，不是特指那些打算成為職業數學家的人，或是那些因為職業的關係需要一定數學細節知識的人。我們在考慮的是，所有學生（包括以上的兩種學生）的自由教育。數學的一般用處，應該是簡單地研究一些一般定理，通過實例來給這些定理以有力的說明。這種研究應該被單獨考慮，在觀念上和之前談到過的職業化研究完全區別開來，而職業化研究需要做最充分的準備。這種學習的最後階段，應該是認識練習中已經闡明的一般定理。就我所指，目前數學學習的最後階段是證明與三角形相連的圓的某些特性。這些特性對數學家來說有無盡的興趣。但是，它們難道不是太深奧了嗎？這些定理和自由教育之間又有什麼確切聯繫？古典專業的學生學習所有語法的最終目的，是為了閱讀維吉爾和賀拉斯②——這些最偉大的人的最偉大的思想。難道，當我們為自己學科的教育做充分辯護的時候，我們能宣稱數學訓練的最終目的就是為了讓學生知道九點圓③的性質嗎？恕我直言：這太「掉價」了吧？！

這一代的數學教師已經在改革數學教學方面，做了很多勤勉努力的工作，沒有必要再為不能設計一門在學生腦海中留下比「歧例」（the ambiguous case）更為高貴的東西的課程而感到失望。

通過複習引導進一步發展

當初級課程結束的時候，怎樣才能通過最後的複習引導那些更聰明的學生進一步發展？毫無疑問，在一定程度上，它需要對整體所作的工作有一個一般的勘漏過程，不過分拘泥於細節，以突出最初應用的一般概念，以及這些概念在進一步的研究時存在的可能的重要性。解析幾何概念應該在物理實驗室裡找到直接的運用，在物理實驗室裡簡單的實驗力學課程也應該是系統學習過的。這裡的觀點具有雙重意義，物理概念和數學概念是相互說明的。

　　數學概念對力學規律的精確公式化表述是必不可少的。精確的自然法則，在一定程度上，經過我們的經驗的檢驗，因此，有關這些自然法則的概念和公式化表述這些法則時所使用的抽象思維，對學生而言，就變得非常明白無誤了。整個課程內容需要細緻地展開，同時給予充分的特別的說明，而且不能看作僅僅需要一些空洞的抽象說明。

　　但是，過分強調通過最後複習的方式，來直接說明之前學習的單純過程，那將是一個極大的錯誤。我的觀點是，**應該仔細甄選課程的最後目的，以便突出 ── 那些事實上作為在所有之前數學學習基礎的 ── 一般概念**。這一點完全可以通過明顯進入一個新課題的方式來完成。比如，量的概念和數的概念是所有正確思維的基礎。在前面的學習階段，它們沒有被截然分開；讓孩子學習代數，這是正確的，不會有太多的麻煩，也不會受到量的影響。但是，其中更為聰明的學生，在他們的課程結束之時，通過仔細思考量的基本特性就會大有收穫；一般來說，量的特性會引出數字度量（numerical　measurement）的問題。這個問題也有好處，就是實際上要去找一些必要的書籍查閱參考。歐幾里得的第五本書被業內資深人士公認為希臘數學的偉大成就之一。這本書正是探討了這個問題。這本書總是被忽略，這個事實更為典型地說明了傳統數學教育的無望而偏狹的特徵。它是說明概念的，所以就被排斥了。當然，對於更重要的命題的仔細挑選和對論點的仔細修正是必須的。不是整本書都要，而是只要其中體現基本概念的少數命題。這個主題對後進學生不適合，但是它肯定會讓那類更優秀的學生感興趣。有趣的討論範圍還很大，比如關於量的性質，在我們探討量的概念時，需要確定的測驗等。這種學習的過程完全不是空泛的，但是在每個階段都需要有確切的例證來說明，在這些例證中，量的特性是缺失的，或是模糊的，或是有疑問的，或是明顯的。溫度，熱度，電流，喜悅和痛苦，廣度和距離，等等，都可考慮進來。

另一個需要說明的概念是函數

函數中的分析與物理世界中的規律和幾何學中的曲線極其相似。孩子從開始學習代數起，在畫圖表的時候，就在學習函數與曲線之間的關係。最近幾年來，關於作圖一直在進行重要的改革。但是從現階段來看，這種改革不是走向極端，就是遠遠不足。僅僅學會畫圖表是不夠的。隱藏在圖表背後的思想——就像槍後面的那個人一樣——才是取得成效真正不可或缺的。現在，有一種趨勢就是，僅僅讓孩子們去學習畫曲線，這個問題現在還有待解決。

在學習簡單的代數函數和三角函數時，我們也開始研究物理規律的正確表達。曲線是表現這些規律的另一種方式。簡單的基本規律——比如說逆平方（the inverse square）和直接距離（the direct distance）——都應該在複習中省略，我們應該考慮如何用簡單的函數表達物理規律的那些重要且具體的實例。我不禁想，這個內容的最後複習不妨採取這樣的方式，即研究一些運用於簡單曲線中的微分學的主要概念。變率（a rate of change）的概念沒有什麼特別難懂的地方，區別X的數次冪，比如 x^2、x^3 等，也很容易實現；借助幾何的幫助，甚至正弦（sin）X 和餘弦（cos）X 也很容易區分。用孩子無法理解、將來也不會用到的定理去填鴨式地灌輸他們，這是怎樣的一種惡習！我們要徹底摒棄這樣的惡習，只有這樣，我們才會有足夠的時間，把孩子的注意力集中在一些真正重要的課題上。我們才能夠使他們通曉真正影響思維的概念。

在結束這個關於物理規律和數學函數的問題之前，有一些其他的問題還需要引起注意。精確的定律從來不是完全精確的觀察所驗證的，這個事實很容易說明，也能夠提供很多有說服力的例證。同樣，統計規律，即只有用大量數字獲得的平均數才能滿足的定律，也很容易研究和說明。實際上，統計方法以及它們在社會現象中應用的少量研究，就是一個關於代數概念的用途的最簡單的例子。

另一種可以歸納學生所學概念的方式是利用數學史，不能把數學史看作只不過是一串人名和日期的簡單集合，而應該看作是一般思維趨勢的闡述，這種闡述使得這些學科成為最初設計時的興趣目標。我在這裡只是想引起對它的重視，也許正是這門學科可以圓滿獲得我所期盼的結果。

邏輯方法訓練的主要手段

我們已經說明了兩個主題，即關於量和自然界規律的一般概念，這些概念應該成為自由教育中數學課程的學習目標。但是數學還有一個方面不能忽略。它是邏輯方法訓練的主要手段。

那麼，什麼是邏輯方法，一個人在邏輯的方法中怎樣才能得到訓練？

邏輯方法不僅僅是有效推理形式的單純知識，也不僅僅是貫徹這些推理時所必需的思想集中的訓練。如果它僅僅是這些，它仍然十分重要；因為在漫長的時代裡，人類智力的進化不是為了推理，而是為了提高在一日三餐的間隙捕得更多新鮮食物供給的藝術。所以，未經相當的訓練就能進行嚴密的推理，這樣的人太少了。

成為一個優秀的推理者，或者想用由構成這門藝術精華的知識去啟發普通人，僅僅有這一點遠遠不夠。推理的藝術在於不失時機地抓住主題，抓住那些說明整體情況的一般概念，並堅持不懈地整理在這些概念周圍的所有次要事實。除非通過長久的練習，認識到抓住重要概念到死也不鬆手的價值，否則，一個人不可能成為一個好的推理者。對於這種訓練，我認為幾何比代數更為合適。代數的思維領域更為模糊，而空間對世間萬物來說都是非常清楚的事情。於是，教育就成了簡化或抽象的過程，所有不相干的物質特性，比如顏色、味道和重量等，都被放在一邊。此外，定義，未經證明的假定的命題，都說明了對主題的基本事實和基本事實之間的關係──形成一個清晰的概

念的必要性。所有這些，都不過是這個主題的緒論。當我們開始深入學習，它的優點就開始增加。學習者不用一開始就面對任何符號，這些符號無論多麼簡單，它的規則都會干擾學習者的記憶。同樣，如果引導得當，推理從一開始就會被引導各個階段發展的明確概念所支配。於是，邏輯方法的本質就得到了即時的證明。

現在，讓我們暫時擱置由於普通學生的遲鈍而引起的局限性，以及其他學科造成的時間壓力，轉而來考慮一下幾何必須在自由教育中貢獻些什麼。我將簡要地說明這門學科的幾個學習階段，但並不意味着它們必須按照這個唯一的順序來進行學習。

第一個階段是全等（Congruence）的學習。我們對於全等的認識，實際上取決於我們的某種判斷，即，當事物的外在環境發生變化的時候，它們的內在特性是不變的。但是，不管全等是如何發生的，它在本質上就是兩個空間區域的點對點的相互聯繫，使所有對應的距離相等，所有對應的角相等。需要指出的是，長度相等、角相等，就是它們全等；至於所有相等的檢驗，比如用碼尺進行測量，只不過是為了讓全等的即時判斷更為容易的手段而已。我說這些話是想指出，除了與之相聯繫的推理之外，全等，不管是作為一個更廣泛、更深遠的概念的例子，還是就其自身而言，都是非常值得用心考慮的。全等所涉及的命題說明了三角形、平行四邊形和圓的基本特性，以及兩個平面之間的相互關係。把這部分經過證明的命題限制在一個最狹小的範圍內是令人滿意的，這個一方面可以通過假定多餘的公理性命題來做到，另一部分可以只介紹那些的確非常重要的命題。

第二個階段是相似性（similarity）的學習。這個可以歸併為三四個基礎命題。相似性是全等概念的拓展，和全等一樣，它是空間裡點和點之間一對一關聯性的另一個例子。對這門學科的進一步學習，最好是調查兩個相似的和處於相似位置的直線圖形的一兩個簡單特性。這門學科可以在平面圖和地圖中直接應用。但是，牢記這點很重要，

三角學的確是可以使主要定理得以有效應用的方法。

第三個階段是三角原理（the elements of trigonometry）的研究。這是對由循環（rotation）引出的周期性（periodicity）的研究，也是對保存在相似形的相互關係中的特性研究。代數分析以對數和量的研究為基礎，這裡，我們第一次介紹量的代數分析的用處。函數周期性的意義需要給予充分的說明。函數最簡單的特性是在解三角形時唯一需要的，也是在做測量時必不可少的。大量的公式本身是重要的，但是對於這種類型的研究則毫無用處。我們要把這些充斥着我們書本的公式嚴格排除出去，除非它們能被學生證明可以作為書本知識的直接例子。

排除公式的問題，通過考慮三角學這個例子就能得到最好的說明；雖然我完全可能發現有不幸的案例，但是，我判斷也會有誤。這門學科在教育中的一大部分優點，可以通過研究三角學的一個角，以及去掉多餘的正弦公式、餘弦公式及兩個角之和的公式來獲得。可以用圖表來表示函數，這樣三角形的解法就有了。因此，通過書本知識和例子，這門科學就能在學生的腦海裡留下這樣的印象：（1）條分縷析地體現了從全等和相似性中推論出的某些定理的直接效果；（2）能解答主要的測量問題；（3）研究了表達周期性和波動（wave motion）所需要的基本函數。

如果打算擴充這門課程，難免增加一些公式。但是要非常小心謹慎，排除學生專門研究他們在訓練中碰到的大量公式的傾向。這裡提到的「排除」，指的是學生在他們的教育中不應該花時間和精力獲得熟練推理的能力。教師發現，在全班面前做這樣的例題很有趣。但是，這樣的結果不屬於那些學生需要記住的東西。而且，我還要從三角學和以前學過的幾何課程中排除整個外接圓（circumscribed circle）和內切圓（inscribed circle）的主題。這個內容很好，但是我不理解它在一個初級的非專業課程中的功能是什麼。

因此，這門學科需要掌握的實際書本知識要被減少到可控的比例之內。有一天，我從一所美國大學得知，學生僅僅在三角學這一門課程上，需要用心記誦的公式和計算結果就多達九十個。我們現在的情況其實還沒有那麼糟糕。實際上，在三角學方面，我們已經非常接近我們所勾畫的有關初級課程的理想。

第四個階段是引入解析幾何（Analytic geometry）。在代數課程中對圖表的研究已經使用過那些基本概念，現在所要求的，是一個經過嚴格刪減過的用方程式的形式來表示直線、圓、三種類型的圓錐曲線（conic section）的課程。在此有兩點需要提醒。給我們的學生教授那些我們沒有證明的知識，是一件讓人嚮往的事情。比如說，在座標幾何學（Co-ordinate Geometry）中，化簡一般的二次方程可能已經超出了我們所考慮的絕大多數學生的能力。但是，由於我們已經詳盡研究了這種曲線的各種可能類型，所以，這並不妨礙我們解釋圓錐曲線的基本位置。

第二個需要提醒的是，完全不把幾何圓錐曲線（geometry conic）作為一門獨立的學科的主張。當然，在適當的時機，由於使用來自某個簡單圖形的推論，解析幾何的分析會受到啟發。但是，由於是從按焦點和準線性質來定義的圓錐曲線發展而來的，因此，幾何圓錐曲線有着明顯的缺陷。它的深奧性是沒有辦法解決的。圓錐曲線的基本定義是SP=e.PM，這個階段 的這門課程中，這個定義極其不適當。它過於深奧，沒有明顯的重要意義。究竟為什麼要研究這些曲線，且研究得比那些數目不定的其他公式所確定的內容還要更多？但是，當我們開始研究笛卡爾方法④的時候，一次方程和二次方程自然成為首先要考慮的內容。

在理想的幾何課程中，第五階段就應該是充分學習投影幾何（Project Geometry）的原理了。這裡的基礎是交比（cross ratio）和投影（projection）的一般概念。投影是我們在全等和相似性中已經學過

的一對一關聯性的更一般的例子。這裡，我們還是必須避免陷入到大量紛繁複雜的細枝末節中去。

投影幾何所說明的智力概念，對於論證一切能夠被證明具有同一性質的案例的相互關係時是重要的。投影幾何的重要教育思想是保留投射中的投射性質。交比只是作為要保留的基本測量方法才在課程中出現。需要考慮挑選極少的一些命題，來說明通過這個步驟實現的兩個關聯的方法。一個是簡化證明。這裡的「簡化」是心理的，而不是邏輯的——因為一般的例子從邏輯上來說是最簡單的。也就是說，通過分析對我們來說最熟悉或最容易思考的例子來進行證明。另一方法就是，一旦我們掌握發現這些案例或檢驗它們的標準，就馬上從耳熟能詳的一般真理中推理出特殊的例子。

圓錐曲線的投射定義，以及用一般二次方程曲線所獲得一致性的結果，都能進行簡單的說明，但是，它們都屬於學科的邊緣內容。這一類的題目可以傳遞某些資訊，但是證明需要完全廢止。

這裡構想的高度理想化的幾何課程——理想可能永遠不會實現——不是一門冗長的課程。在各個階段的書本知識中，實際的數學推理很少。但是要給予充分的解釋，通過例子來說明每個命題的重要性，這些例子不是已經解答，就是等待學生去解答；之所以進行這樣的選擇，是為了表明它所能適用的思維領域。通過這樣的課程，學生可以掌握分析主要的空間性質和研究它們時所使用的主要方法。

用這種精神來構想對數學原理的學習，將會形成一種邏輯方法的訓練；同時，還會獲得一種精確的概念，這些概念是對宇宙進行科學和哲學研究的基礎。在這一代教育者已經取得的輝煌成就的基礎上，繼續堅持數學教育的改革，使之能夠把這些更廣泛更具有哲理的精神包含進去，做到這一點容易嗎？坦率地說，竊以為單憑個人的努力去達到這個目標是很難的。由於我已經簡單說明過的許多原因，所有教育的改革都是非常難以取得成效的。

　　但是，如果這個理想的確能夠為廣大教師所接受，大家共同努力所造成的持續不斷的壓力，就能起到巨大的作用，最終帶來令人意想不到的改變。逐漸編寫必要的課本，逐步改革考試形式以弱化這門學科的技術色彩，然後，所有近期的經驗表明，大部分的教師，都已經做準備迎接任何一種具有實踐意義的方法，把數學學科從「是一種機械訓練」的指摘中解救出來。

---

① Securus Judicat Orbis Terrarum（世界自有公論），這是聖·奧古斯丁 (St. Augus-tine，354-430)的話。——譯者注

②賀拉斯（Quintus Horatius Flaccus，前65年12月8日-前8年11月27日），古羅馬奧古斯都時期的著名詩人、批評家、翻譯家，代表作有《詩藝》等。他是古羅馬文學「黃金時代」的代表人之一。

　　生於意大利南部阿普利亞邊境小鎮維努西亞（今維諾薩）。約公元前52-前50年左右到羅馬求學，後去雅典深造。公元前44年愷撒遇刺後，雅典成了共和派活動的中心，賀拉斯應募參加了共和派軍隊，並被委任為軍團指揮。公元前42年共和派軍隊被擊敗，他逃回意大利。在羅馬謀得一個財務錄事的小差事，同時寫作詩歌。他的詩才很快引起了著名詩人維吉爾的注意。

　　賀拉斯的美學思想見於寫給皮索父子的詩體長信《詩藝》。《書札》第一卷寫於公元前23-前20年，主要內容仍是生活哲理。第二卷全部與文藝批評有關，特別是其中第三首俗稱《詩藝》，成為歐洲古典文藝理論名篇。詩人從自己的豐富詩歌創作實踐出發，暢談藝術模仿、藝術與生活的關係、文藝的教育作用、詩人的修養等，對後世歐洲文藝理論很有影響。

　　賀拉斯認為詩的任務是秉承神旨指導人生。在模仿自然時允許虛構，但須合乎情理，切近真實，「虛構的目的在引人歡喜」，「寓教於樂，既勸諭讀者，又使他喜愛，才能符合眾望」。而詩人「應當日夜把玩希臘的範例」，應到生活和習俗中尋找真正的範本和吸取忠實於生活的語言，要發現人的類型和共性，並創造一些具有時代特徵的詞彙，可沿用傳統題材，描寫趨於定型的人物。

　　賀拉斯還認為，戲劇須保持結構一貫，人物的性格、年齡、語言相一致，從而構成一個有機整體以體現和諧。劇本的情節效果比道白效果更重要，以五幕、三演員最為相宜，還須避免凶殺和普通人的粗俗語言。按照上述目的和途徑，詩和戲劇才能實現其最高的品質，賀拉斯稱之為「適合」或「合式」（decorum）。

　　此外，賀拉斯還認為，天才不能偏重感情，判斷力（理性判斷）是寫作成功的開端和源泉，只有這樣，劇中才能產生光輝的思想，使觀眾喜愛和流連忘返。

　　賀拉斯的「寓教於樂」的觀點，以及對合式、類型、共性等論說，為十七世紀古典主義制定了基本原則，在西方古代美學思想史上佔重要地位，影響僅次於亞里士多德和柏拉圖。

作為翻譯家，受西塞羅的文學批評和理論的影響，用相當的篇幅談了創作中語言的使用和翻譯問題。綜合起來，主要有以下兩點：（1）翻譯必須堅持活譯，摒棄直譯；（2）本族語可通過譯借外來詞加以豐富。他在《詩藝》中說：「忠實原作的譯者不會逐詞死譯。」──譯者注

③九點圓，在任意的三角形中，三邊的中點、三條高的垂足、三條高的交點(垂心)與三角形頂點連線的中點，這九個點共圓，通常稱這個圓為九點圓（nine-point　circle），或歐拉圓、費爾巴哈圓。九點圓具有許多有趣的性質，如：

1. 三角形的九點圓的半徑是三角形的外接圓半徑之半；

2. 九點圓的圓心在歐拉線上，且恰為垂心與外心連線的中點；

3. 三角形的九點圓與三角形的內切圓，三個旁切圓均相切（費爾巴哈定理）；

4. 九點圓是一個垂心組（即一個三角形三個頂點和它的垂心，共四個點，每個點都是其它三點組成的三角形的垂心，共4個三角形）共有的九點圓，所以九點圓共與四個內切圓、十二個旁切圓相切。

5. 九點圓心(V)，重心(G)，垂心(H)，外心(O)四點共線，且 HG=2OG，OG=2VG，OH=2OV。──譯者注

④笛卡爾方法（Cartesian Methods），笛卡爾在其代表作《談談正確運用自己的理性在各門學問裡尋求真理的方法》（1637）（中國翻譯為《談談方法》，王太慶譯，商務印書館，2000年）一書中，他特別指出，「方法，對於探求事物真理是絕對必要的」。笛卡爾通過深邃的思考，總結出了四條培養心智的規則。他認為：「用不着制定大量的規條構成一部邏輯，單是下列四條，只要我有堅定持久的信心，無論何時何地決不違犯，也就夠了。」（1）懷疑原則：絕不承認任何事物為真，除非我明明白白知道它確實為真。（2）分析原則：將我們所要檢查的每一道難題，盡可能地分解成許多部分，以作為妥善解釋這些難題的要害。（3）建構原則：依照次序引導我們的思想，由最簡單的、最容易認識的對象開始，一步一步地上升到最複雜的知識。（4）全面原則：處處做周全無誤的核算與普遍不漏的檢查，直到足夠保證沒有遺漏任何一件為止。

勒內·笛卡爾（Rene Descartes，1596-1650），著名哲學家、科學家和數學家，堪稱17世紀及其後的歐洲哲學界和科學界最有影響力的巨匠之一，被譽為「近代科學的始祖」。笛卡爾最傑出的成就是在數學發展上創立了解析幾何學。在笛卡爾時代，代數還是一個比較新的學科，幾何學的思維還在數學家的頭腦中佔有統治地位。笛卡爾致力於代數和幾何聯繫起來的研究，於1637年，在創立了坐標系後，成功地創立了解析幾何學。他的這一成就為微積分的創立奠定了基礎。解析幾何直到現在仍是重要的數學方法之一。此外，現在使用的許多數學符號都是笛卡爾最先使用的，這包括已知數a，b，c以及未知數x，y，z等，還有指數的表示方法。他還發現了凸多面體邊、頂點、面之間的關係，後人稱為歐拉─笛卡爾公式。還有微積分中常見的笛卡爾葉形線也是他發現的。

笛卡爾的名言有：「讀傑出的書籍，有如和過去最傑出的人物促膝交談」，「讀一切好書，就是和許多高尚的人談話」，「我思故我在」，等等。──譯者注

第七章　大學及其作用

一

大學的快速擴張已然成為當前時代社會生活的一個顯著特徵。所有的國家都融入到這個趨勢之中了；美國更是如此，且居榮譽地位。但是，大學的發展甚至也有可能被好運帶來的禮物壓倒；由於缺乏大學對國家應起的基本作用的廣泛理解，大學用途的來源就可能遭到破壞，大學在機構數量、規模，以及組織的內在結構的複雜性的發展上，暴露出某種危險。這些關於重新考慮大學功能的評論，適用於所有的比較發達的國家，特別適用於美國。因為美國已經在這種發展趨勢中領先一步；在明智的引導下，這領先的一步將會被證明是迄今為止人類文明史上最值得慶幸的一步。

雖然任何一所大學的不同系科都有無數的特殊的問題，但是本章將只涉及最一般的原則。一般性需要例證說明，為此，我選擇了一所大學的商學院。商學院代表了大學活動中比較新穎的發展趨勢，這是我做出這個選擇所基於的一個事實。同時，它們也與現代國家中佔主導地位的社會活動有着更為特別緊密的關係，因此，用來說明大學教育活動會影響國民的生活方式，商學院會是很好的例子。在我有幸執教的哈佛大學，一所氣勢恢宏的商學院的地基也已經快竣工了。①

在這樣一所世界領先的著名學府裡，建立這樣規模的培訓學校，有一定的創新意義。這標誌着一個運動的高潮，多年來，這個運動使這樣的科系風靡全美大學。這是大學世界的一個新現象；單單它就能證明對大學教育的目的進行一般反省，同時也證明那個目的對於社會有機體福利的重要性。

我們絕不能誇大商學院的新穎之處，因為大學從來沒有局限於純粹抽象的學習中。歐洲最古老的大學之一、意大利的薩勒諾大學（Schola Medica Salernitana）②，是專門進行醫學教育的。在英國劍橋，1316年，特別建立了一所學院，培養「為國王服務的職員」。大學已經培養出神職人員、醫生、律師和工程師等。商業現在是高度智能化的行業，因此，它完全適合進入這個行列。但是，仍然有這樣一個與眾不同之處：適合一個商學院的課程，以及這樣一個學校應該提供的各種不同的活動，仍處於試驗階段。因此，結合這些學校的辦學模式，重提一般原則，就有特別重要的意義。不過，如果說我開始考慮細節，甚至考慮影響整個訓練平衡的政策，那也只是我的一種假定。因為我在這方面沒有特殊的知識，因此，我也無法提供建議。

二

大學既是實施教育的機構，也是進行研究的機構。但是，大學之所以存在的主要原因，既不是向學生傳授單純的知識，也不是單純地提供研究機會給科系的老師。

大學的這兩種功能可以以更經濟的方式來實現，而不需要大學這樣非常昂貴的教育機構。書本很便宜，學徒制的體系也很好理解。如果僅僅考慮傳授知識的話，在15世紀印刷術普及之後，那麼沒有一所大學有任何理由存在。然而，建立大學的主要推動力卻是在15世紀之後，在近代，發展勢頭更為迅猛。`

大學存在的理由是，它把年輕人和老年人聯合在一起，對學術展開充滿想象力的探索，從而在知識和生命熱情之間架起橋梁。大學傳授知識，但是它是以充滿想象力的方式來傳授。至少，這是它對社會

應起的作用。一所在這方面失敗的大學，就沒有存在下去的理由。充滿想象力的探索將會點燃令人激動的氣氛，這種氣氛會帶動知識的變化。事實不再是赤裸裸的事實，它被賦予了各種可能性；也不再是記憶的負擔：它像詩人一樣活躍我們的夢想，像建築是一樣構築我們的目標。

想象力是闡明事實的一種充滿創造力的方式，它不能脫離事實。想象力是這樣發揮作用的，它總結出運用於已存在的事實中的一般原則，然後對符合這些原則的各種可供選擇的可能性進行理智的考察。它使人們在面對新世界的時候，能夠構築出一個充滿智慧的視角，並通過展示令人滿意的效果而保持生命的熱情。

年輕人充滿想象力，如果這種想象力通過訓練得以加強的話，那麼這種想象力的能量就能夠在很大程度上保持終生。然而，人類的悲劇在於，有的人富有想象力但是缺乏經驗，有的人經驗豐富但是想象力貧乏。笨人憑想象力做事但缺乏知識，書呆子憑知識做事但缺乏想象力。大學的責任就是——把想象力和經驗完美地結合起來。

在人生充滿青春活力的階段，對想象力進行最初的訓練時，不能要求對直接行為承擔責任。當每天都需要保持一種有形的組織結構時，無偏見的思維習慣就不可能養成，而這種思維習慣正是從一般原則來認識各種不同的完美例證所憑借的。你必須自由地進行思考，不管是對是錯，自由地去欣賞未被危險因素干擾的大千世界的斑斕色彩。

這種對於大學一般作用的反省，商學院的特殊功能可以立即予以證明。我們必須坦率承認，這種學校的主要功能，是塑造擁有極高經商熱情的人。生活的熱情來自哪裡？會是直接以狹隘的物質享受為平庸的目的的產物嗎？這種觀點是對人性的侮辱。人類通過具有先驅性的直覺，及其他一些方式，證明這個謊言是何等地虛妄。

在現代複雜的社會結構中，生活的探險不能和智力的探險分離

開來。在相對簡單的環境裡，拓荒者能夠跟隨他的本能的熱切指引，從山頂一路狂奔到他視野的盡頭。但是在現代商業的複雜組織結構中，如果想要獲得成功的重組，就必須先進行分析和想象力重建方面的智力探險。世界越簡單，商業關係就越簡單，因為商業關係都是建立在人與人的直接接觸上，建立在所有物質境況面對面的比較上。現在，商業組織需要揣摩和抓住不同職業的人群的心理，這些人分散在城市、山脈和平原；還有那些分散在海洋上、礦井下和森林裡的人們。商業組織要求對熱帶和溫帶的情況有所瞭解。要求掌握各大組織間互相盤根錯節的利益關係，及對因某一因素的改變而引發的整個聯合體的反應。要充滿想象力地關注政治經濟的法律法規，不僅僅是抽象的，而且還要具備根據某個商業活動的特殊性去解釋這些法律法規的能力。對政府的習慣性做法以及在不同情況下這些習慣的變化要瞭然於胸。要用充滿想象力的視角去看任何人類組織的約束力，要用充滿同情的眼光去看人類天賦的局限性以及喚起服務忠誠度的條件。要掌握一些養生規律、疲勞規律和保持持久耐力的條件的知識。要富有想象地理解工廠的社會影響。要對科學對現代社會的作用有充分的概念。要懂得對別人說「不」或說「好」的原則，不是出於盲目的固執，而是基於對相關的可選擇的方案經過理智的評估後得出的堅定回答。

大學培養了我們文明社會知識分子的先鋒人物——神職人員、律師、政治家、醫生、科學家和文學家等。這些人一直是人類充滿理想的原因，這些理想引導人們去面對各個時代的困惑。朝聖先輩（Pilgrim Fathers）③離開英國，根據他們的宗教信仰的理想，建立了一個他們想要的社會制度；他們早期的活動之一，是在劍橋地區建立了哈佛大學④，以畢業於英格蘭劍橋大學的牧師約翰·哈佛之名命名，這所大學繼承了古老的源於英國的理想，我們祖輩中的很多人都曾在這裡受過教育。現代的商業行為需要有充滿智慧的想象力，就像以前

主要從事其他職業一樣；大學就是這樣的組織，它為歐洲民族不斷前進提供了這種智慧。

在中世紀早期，大學的起源模糊不清，也幾乎被忽視。它們是一個逐步自然的成長過程。但是，大學的存在是整個歐洲在諸多領域中取得持續不斷的快速發展的原因。作為媒介，大學實現了行動探險和思想探險的有效結合。這種組織的成功在之前是無法預言的。即使是在今天，人類事物還有諸多不夠完美的地方，有時還是很難理解大學是怎麼成功發揮作用的。當然，大學的作用中也有很多失敗的地方，但是，當我們用寬廣的歷史視角來看整個問題的時候，大學的成功還是不同尋常的而且幾乎是始終如一的。意大利、法國、德國、荷蘭、蘇格蘭、英國和美國的文化歷史見證了大學的影響力。談及文化歷史，我不是指那些學者的生活；我指的是這樣一些人的生命活動，他們給法國、德國以及其他國家留下了人類取得的成就印記，加上他們追求生活的熱情，這些成就了我們的愛國精神。我們非常驕傲能夠成為這樣一種社會的成員。

有一個巨大的困難妨礙着人類從事更高端的智力活動。在現代社會，這個困難甚至會演變成某種可能的不幸。在任何一個大的機構中，年輕人，即職場新人，一般會被安排在服從命令履行固定職責的工作崗位上。沒有一個大公司的老闆會讓年輕僱員到他的辦公室，然後安排給他公司裡最重要的工作。年輕人被要求按照固定程序工作，間或在進出辦公樓的時候見到老闆本人。這樣的工作是一種很好的訓練。它能傳授知識，可以鍛造可靠的品格，而且這是適合職業生涯初期的唯一工作，就是為了完成這樣的工作才僱用他們來的。對這種符合慣例的做法不會有什麼批評的聲音，但是卻可能導致一個不幸的後果——長時間地按照固定程序工作會鈍化想象力。

這樣做的結果就是，一個人隨後的職業生涯階段所必需的各種素質，在他開始踏入職場的時候就被撲滅了。相對於一般的事實而言，

這只是一個例子：職業所必需的優秀技術只能通過訓練來獲得，而這種訓練卻在毀壞指導技術成熟的大腦活力。這是教育中的關鍵事實，也是教育中存在的大部分困難的原因。

促進對構成這種職業基礎的各種一般原理進行充滿想象力的思考，這是一所大學在為腦力勞動的職業（比如現代商業或一種較古老的職業）做前期準備工作應該起到的作用。這樣，當學生進入到他們的技術學徒時期，這種把具體細節和一般原理相結合的想象力已經得到了鍛鍊。於是，這種固定的工作程序有了它的意義，也說明了那些給予它意義的原理。因此，一個受過適當訓練的人，就有希望獲得一種經過複雜事實和必要行為習慣所訓練的想象力，而不是一種由盲目的經驗所帶來的單調沉悶的工作。

因此，大學的恰當作用就是用充滿想象力的方式獲取知識。除了想象力的重要性之外，沒有任何其他理由來解釋：為什麼商人和其他專業人士，不能一點一點地蒐集事實，來解決他們所面對的特殊問題？！大學是充滿想象力的，否則，它就什麼也不是——至少毫無用處。

三

想象力彷彿一種傳染病。它不能用碼尺或磅秤稱量後，再由老師傳授給學生。它只能由那些用想象力裝點自己學問的教師來進行傳播。說到這一點，我只是在重復一個古老的言論。兩千多年前，我們的祖先把知識比喻成一個代代相傳的火炬。這個點燃的火炬就是我所說的想象力。大學組織的全部藝術，就在於供應一支用想象力點燃學問的教師隊伍。這是大學教育所有問題的重中之重。如果我們錯誤地認識這個問題，除非我們重視近期大學在學生數目和各種活動數量上

的快速增長——這當然值得我們驕傲——就會由於對這個問題的錯誤處理而產生錯誤的結果。

想象力和知識的融合通常需要一些閒暇，需要擺脫束縛之後的自由，需要從煩惱中解脫出來，需要各種不同的經歷，需要其他智者不同觀點和不同才識的激發。還需要強烈的求知慾以及自信心，這種自信心是由周圍社會在獲得知識進步方面所取得的成就而產生的自豪感。你不能一勞永逸地擁有想象力，然後無限期地將其保存在冰箱裡，定期按照一定的量來支出。有學問和充滿想象的生活是一種生存的方式，而不是一種商品。

給一支高效的教師隊伍提供條件，並促使他們使用這些條件，所以，教育與研究兩種功能在大學里交匯了。你想讓你的老師充滿想象力嗎？那麼，鼓勵他們去研究探索吧。你想讓你的研究者充滿想象力嗎？那麼，引導他們去支持在生命最充滿熱情和想象力的階段的年輕人去探索學習吧；恰逢此時，這些年輕人的智力開始進入成熟期訓練。讓你的研究人員對着那些思想活躍、具有可塑性和擁有世界的年輕心靈闡述自己吧；讓你的年輕學生通過接觸那些有天賦、有智力探險經驗的人，圓滿度過他們的智力獲取時期吧。

教育是對於生活探險的訓練，研究是智力的探險；大學應該是年輕人和老年人共同分享探險的理想之地。對於成功的教育來說，傳授的知識必須有一定的更新。要麼是知識本身的更新，要麼是知識在新時代新世界中新穎的應用。知識的保鮮有如魚的保鮮，不更新就會腐爛。你可能正在學習一些陳舊的知識種類，伴隨着一些過時的原理，但是儘管如此，要努力使這些知識對現實有即時的重要意義，就像剛從大海裡撈出來的魚一樣新鮮地呈現在學生的面前。

學者的作用是喚起生活中的智慧和美。如果沒有學者的神奇魔力，那些智慧和美可能就遺失在往昔的歲月裡。一個前進中的社會需要依靠這三類人：學者、發現者和發明者。它的進步也依賴這樣一個

事實，即，社會中的受教育人群由同時具有些許學識、發現能力和創造能力的人組成。我在這裡用的「發現」，指的是關於具有高度一般性的原理方面的知識進步；「發明」，指的是根據當前的需求，一般原理以某些特殊方式進行應用的知識進步。很明顯，這三類人是互相融合的。那些參與到實際事務中的人，只要他們對社會的進步作出了貢獻，也可以被稱為發明者。但是，任何一個獨立的個體在對社會作出的貢獻方面都有一定的局限性，同時也有自己特殊的需求。對一個國家來說，重要的是在它的所有進步元素之間有非常緊密的聯繫，這樣的話，研究可能影響市場，市場可能影響研究。**大學是把各種進步活動進行融合並使之成為有效促進社會進步的工具的主要媒介。**當然，它們不是唯一的媒介，但是今天的事實是，進步的國家通常就是那些大學空前繁榮的國度。

我們不必假定，一所大學的有創見的思想成果，只能以署名發表過的論文和著作的數量來衡量。人類思想成果的形式，正如它的思想內容一樣富有個性。對於某些思維最為活躍的人來說，寫作或寫下短小的文章，看起來似乎都是不可能的。在每一個教員群體中，你都會發現一些較為出色的老師不在發表論文或著作的名單當中。他們需要和學生面對面，以講座或個別交流的方式，來表達他們的創造性思想。這樣的人對人類的進步有無限的影響力；但是，當他們的學生一代過世以後，他們就長眠在那些無數的未被感謝過的人類的恩人之中了。幸運的是，其中一個人流芳百世，就是——蘇格拉底⑤。

因此，最大的錯誤就在於——根據署名發表的作品來衡量一位教師的價值。但是，目前就出現了陷入這種錯誤泥淖的趨勢；我們有必要堅決反對主管當局有損效率又對無私熱情所秉持的不公正的態度。

但是，當考慮了允許存在的所有因素以後，對一個教師群體總體效率的有效評價，就是作為一個整體，出版發表作品的方式可以按其對人類思想的貢獻，給予一定的配額比例。這樣的配額比例，應該以

思想的價值分量來評估，而不是作品的數量。

　　這裡的考察表明，對一所大學教師隊伍的管理和對一個商業組織的管理是截然不同的。教師的公眾意見和對大學辦學目標的共同熱情，形成了對發揮大學工作最高水平的唯一並有效的保障。大學的教師應該由一組學者組成，互相激勵，自由地決定他們各自不同的活動。你可以確保某些形式上的規範要求，比如說，課在給定的時間開始，教職員和學生必須準時出席。但是，本質問題不要受規章制度的制約。

　　公正對待教師的問題對事實影響不大。在工作時間和薪資的合法性之下，僱用一個人來提供合法的服務，這本身就是完全公正的。接受這個職位，意味着願意。

　　唯一的問題是，什麼樣的條件可以創建出一支成功大學所需的教師隊伍？危險在於，很容易培養出一支完全不合格的教師隊伍——那些高效率的學究式人物和笨蛋。十年樹木，百年樹人；子弟是否被誤，也不是立等可見。只有在大學阻礙了年輕人的前途多年之後，一般大眾才會察覺到老師之間的水平差異。

　　最高主管當局要實施獨特的管束，牢記不能根據人們熟悉的商業機構的規章和政策來管理大學，只有這樣，我們偉大民主國家的現代大學制度才能成功。商學院也不能脫離大學生活的這個規律。對於許多美國大學的校長們近期在公開場合發表的對這個問題的意見，我確實沒有什麼需要補充的了。但是，無論是在美國還是在其他國家，普通大眾中那一部分有影響力的公民是否會聽從他們的建議，就不得而知了。在教育方面，大學的全部意義就在於，把年輕人置於一幫富有想象力的學者的智力影響之下。經驗顯示，我們必須對——能夠產生這樣一幫教師的條件——加以適當的注意。

四

　　就歷史悠久和地位顯赫而言，歐洲首屈一指的兩所大學是法國的巴黎大學和英國的牛津大學。因為我對英國最瞭解，我就來談談英國的情況。牛津大學或許在很多方面犯過錯誤。但是，即使她有這些缺失，她在歷史的長河中，始終保持一種超然的價值，相形之下，所有的錯誤就像塵埃一樣，微不足道：這種價值就是幾個世紀以來，在牛津大學的漫長歷史中，她培養了一批又一批的充滿想象力的學者。就憑這一點，只要是熱愛文化的人，都會情不自禁地想到她。

　　但是對我來說，沒有必要去列舉一個跨越大西洋的例子。《獨立宣言》⑥的作者傑弗遜（Jefferson T.）先生⑦堪稱最偉大的美國人。他在各個方面所取得的輝煌成就，足以讓他躋身於人類歷史中為數不多的偉人之列。他創建了一所大學⑧，奉獻了他的部分天才，這座大學置身於能夠激發想象力的環境——建築之美，環境之美，以及其他任何可以激發學生想象力的設施和組織——之中。

　　在美國，還有很多其他的大學可以驗證我的觀點，但是，我最後一個例子想說的是哈佛大學——清教徒運動時期⑨的代表性大學。十七和十八世紀的美國新英格蘭的清教徒是最富有熱情和想象力的人，他們謹言慎行，但是，儘管如此，他們一直在被——自己對人類智慧想象出來的精神世界的真理的思考——所折磨。在那幾個世紀裡，信奉清教的教師一定是充滿想象力的，他們培養了很多名揚世界的偉人。在之後的歲月中，清教變得相對溫和了，在新英格蘭的文學黃金時代，愛默生⑩、洛威爾⑪和朗費羅⑫對哈佛產生了深遠的影響。隨之而來的是現代科學時代，我們在威廉·詹姆斯⑬的身上又看到了典型的富有想象力的學者氣質。

　　今天，商業進入了哈佛，這所大學要奉上的禮物就是古老的想象力，這代代相傳的智慧火炬。這是一件危險的禮物，它引起過很多滅頂的大火災。如果我們在面對那種危險時表現膽怯，那麼最好的辦法就是關閉大學。想象力經常是和那些具有商業才能的人聯繫在一起的天賦——比如希臘、佛羅倫薩和威尼斯，還有荷蘭的學術，英國的詩歌。商業和想象力同舟共濟，這是所有人都會為他們的國家所祈求的一個禮物，如果人們想要他們的國家重現雅典所取得過的那種輝煌：

　　　　她的公民，帝國精神
　　　　前見古人，後有來者

　　美國教育，引領世界；璀璨星空，遠大前程。

---

　　①哈佛商學院（HBS，Harvard Business School），世界最著名的商學院之一，早先名為「哈佛大學工商管理研究所：喬治·F.貝克基金會」，是常春藤聯盟商學院之一。學院1908年始於最早的一屆59個學生，最初坐落於美國馬薩諸塞州劍橋鎮。——譯者注

　　②薩勒諾大學（Schola Medica Salernitana），這裡指的是位於同一意大利南部城市的坎帕尼亞大區沿海城市薩勒諾的中世紀醫學院，現代薩勒諾大學（University of Salerno）另有所指。

　　學校始建於9世紀，最初位於修道院的藥房中，逐漸成為西歐最重要的醫學知識來源；1077年，君士坦丁非裔美國人薩勒諾的到來標誌著薩勒諾經典時期的開始，世界各地的人們（希望康復的患病者和學生）蜂擁而至學習醫學技術。11世紀初，學校成為醫學研究中心，猶太人阿非利加諾來到這裡，編譯希臘醫學家希波克拉底和阿拉伯的醫學著作，對醫學理論和醫療事業有很大的推動，於是醫學校名聲大振，有志學醫的青年聯合起來，和醫師訂立合同，規定學生納費和醫師傳藝的條件，進行知識交易。這便成為歐洲最早的醫科大學。1231年得到政府承認。12世紀以來，特別成為德國學生的目標。學校在十世紀和十三世紀之間獲得了最大的知名度。

　　「學校」基於對希臘—拉丁傳統的綜合，輔以阿拉伯和猶太文化的概念。該方法基於預防而非治療的實踐和文化，從而為醫學經驗方法開闢了道路。

　　醫學院的目的是讓完成了規定學習年限的學生接受嚴格的考試，以獲得學位，不僅要練習醫學而且要教醫學。醫學院是捍衛醫務人員利益和尊嚴的專業組織，也是藥品管理工作的組織。

大學頒發的學術頭銜逐漸獲得法律承認，學校逐漸形成一系列制度，並得到政府的認可，學校標準逐漸成為社會標準。

學校除了教授醫學（女性被接納為教師和學生）之外，還教授哲學、神學和法律，這就是為什麼有些人也將其視為有史以來第一所大學的原因。——譯者注

③朝聖先輩（Pilgrim Fathers），1620年到達北美大陸建立殖民地定居點的英國清教徒前輩移民。

歷史上，將在英國的新教徒——那些信奉加爾文教義、不滿英國國教教義的人稱為清教徒。由於英國的宗教迫害，大部分清教徒都逃亡到了美國，所以人們說起清教徒，一般指的就是美國的清教徒。

他們安排英格蘭投資者在北美建立一個新的殖民地。殖民地成立於1620年，成為北美第二個成功的英格蘭定居點（第一個是在1607年建立的詹姆斯敦），他們相信，新世界的新起點是他們唯一的機會。在為自己的群體尋求宗教自由的同時，他們對其他信仰表現出不寬容。朝聖先輩的故事成為美國歷史和文化的中心主題。——譯者注

④哈佛大學（Harvard University），為全美歷史最悠久的高等學府，1636年由馬薩諸塞州殖民地立法機關立案成立，是一所位於美國馬薩諸塞州波士頓劍橋城的私立研究型大學。1639年3月13日以一名畢業於英格蘭劍橋大學的牧師約翰·哈佛之名，命名為哈佛學院；1780年哈佛學院更名為哈佛大學。哈佛大學在世界上享有一流大學的聲譽、財富和學術影響力，被譽為美國政府的思想庫；其商學院的案例教學盛名遠播。在世界各報刊及研究機構的大學排行榜中，哈佛大學經常位居第一。——譯者注

⑤蘇格拉底（Socrates，前469-前399），古希臘著名思想家、哲學家和教育家，他和他的學生柏拉圖，以及柏拉圖的學生亞里士多德被並稱為「古希臘三賢」，更被後人廣泛認為是西方哲學的奠基者。沒有留下著作，其思想和生平記述於後來的學者（主要是他的學生柏拉圖）和同時代的劇作家阿里斯托芬的劇作中。柏拉圖的《對話》一書記載了蘇格拉底在倫理學領域的貢獻。

身為雅典的公民，據記載，蘇格拉底最後被雅典法庭以引進新的神和腐蝕雅典青年思想之罪名判處死刑。儘管他曾獲得逃亡的機會，但是蘇格拉底仍然選擇飲下毒堇汁而死，終年70歲；因為他認為逃亡只會進一步破壞雅典法律的權威，同時也是因為擔心他逃亡後雅典將再沒有好的導師可以教育人們了。

蘇格拉底終生從事教育工作，具有豐富的教育實踐經驗並有自己的教育理論。

教育目的是造就治國人才。他認為治國人才必須受過良好的教育，主張通過教育來培養治國人才。

關於教育的內容，他主張首先要培養人的美德，教人學會做人，成為有德行的人；其次要教人學習廣博而實用的知識；最後，他主張教人鍛鍊身體。他認為，健康的身體不是天生的，只有通過鍛鍊才能使人身體強壯。

在教學的方法上，蘇格拉底通過長期的教學實踐，形成了自己一套獨特的教學法，人們稱之為「蘇格拉底方法」，他本人則稱之為「產婆術」。他母親是產婆，他借此比喻他的教學方法。他母親的產婆術是為嬰兒接生，而他的「產婆術」教學法則是為思想接生，是要引導人們產生正確的思想。「蘇格拉底方法」自始至終是以師生問答的形式進行的，所以又叫「問答法」。蘇格拉底在教學生獲得某種概念時，不是把這種概念直接告訴學生，而是先向學生提出問題，讓學生回答，如果學生回答錯了，他也不直接糾正，而是提出另外的問題引導學生思考，從而一步一步得出正確的結論。它為啟發式教學奠定了基礎。蘇格拉底倡導的問答法對後世影響很大，直到今天，問答法仍然是一種重要的教學方法。

蘇格拉底的名言有：

別人為食而生存，我為生存而食。

教育不是灌輸，而是點燃火焰。

認識你自己。

想左右天下的人，須先能左右自己。

教育是把我們的內心勾引出來的工具和方法。

最有效的教育方法不是告訴人們答案，而是向他們提問。

要想向我學知識，你必須先有強烈的求知慾望，就像你有強烈的求生慾望一樣。

思想應當誕生在學生的心裡，教師僅僅應當像助產士那樣辦事。

每個人身上都有太陽，主要是如何讓它發光。

問題是接生婆，它能幫助新思想的誕生。

我不是給人知識，而是使知識自己產生的產婆。

最優秀的人就是你自己。

未經審視的生活是毫無價值的（一種未經考察的生活是不值得過的）。

好的婚姻僅給你帶來幸福，不好的婚姻則可使你成為一位哲學家。

我的母親是個助產婆，我要追隨她的腳步，我是個精神上的助產士，幫助別人產生他們自己的思想。——譯者注

⑥《獨立宣言》全稱是《北美十三國聯合一致的共同宣言》，為北美洲十三個英屬殖民地宣告自大不列顛王國獨立，並宣明此舉正當性之文告。1776年7月4日，宣言由第二次大陸會議於費城批准，當日茲後成為美國獨立紀念日。宣言之原件由大陸會議出席代表共同簽署，並永久展示於美國華盛頓特區之美國國家檔案和記錄管理局（National Archives and Records Administration）。此宣言為美國最重要的立國文書之一。

委員會的成員由馬薩諸塞的約翰·亞當斯、賓夕法尼亞的本傑明·富蘭克林、弗吉尼亞的托馬斯·傑弗遜、紐約的羅伯特·利文斯頓和康涅狄格的羅傑·謝爾曼組成，並被責成以起草合適的宣言。傑弗遜在起草宣言過程中發揮了重要作用。在宣言被大陸會議採納之前，大陸會議對傑弗遜的草稿作了重大改動，特別是在佐治亞州和南卡羅來納州代表們的堅持下，刪去了他對英王喬治三世允許在殖民地存在奴隸制和奴隸買賣的有力譴責。其中一個被移除的篇章涉及奴隸制度。

全美第二大歷史悠久的高等學府威廉瑪麗學院畢業的傑弗遜曾寫道，《獨立宣言》是「籲請世界的裁判」。自1776年以來，《獨立宣言》中所體現的原則就一直在全世界為人傳誦。美國的改革家們，不論是出於什麼動機，不論是為了廢除奴隸制，禁止種族隔離或是要提高婦女的權利，都要向公眾提到「人人生而平等」。不論在什麼地方，當人民向不民主的統治作鬥爭時，他們就要用傑弗遜的話來爭辯道，政府的「正當權力是經被統治者同意所授予的」。

《獨立宣言》由四部分組成：第一部分為前言，闡述了宣言的目的。第二部分高度概括了當時資產階級最激進的政治思想，即自然權利學說和主權在民思想。第三部分歷數英國壓迫北美殖民地人民的條條罪狀，說明殖民地人民是在忍無可忍的情況下被迫拿起武器的，力陳獨立的合法性和正義性。在宣言的最後一部分，美利堅莊嚴宣告獨立。

《宣言》的意義不在於是否創設了新思想，而是在於，它以官方文件形式把當時大家都瞭解的東西，作為原則加以肯定，以適應當時之需，且認為這是普適全人類的大原則。另外，儘管在美國歷史上，《宣言》被經典化、神聖化，但作為建國的核心文件，其適用性、彈性很強，每一句話都有很強的功能，可應用於諸多主題和場合，一切爭取

權利的人都可用它的語言，來表達自己的訴求。《宣言》已成為美國政治價值觀念的體現、象徵和標誌。——譯者注

⑦托馬斯·傑弗遜（Jefferson T. 1743年4月13日-1826年7月4日）美國建國先賢之一，美國政治家、思想家、教育家、科學家、音樂家、哲學家、建築師，他是美國獨立戰爭期間的主要領導人之一，《獨立宣言》起草人，第3任美國總統。他先後擔任了美國第一任國務卿，第二任副總統和第三任總統。他在任期間保護農業，發展民族資本主義工業。從法國手中購買路易斯安那州，使美國領土近乎增加了一倍。他一生追求智慧和真理，才華出眾，樂觀向上，受到人們的廣泛贊譽。

2006年，傑弗遜被美國的權威期刊《大西洋月刊》評為影響美國的100位人物第3位。

「一個明智而節儉的政府，應當防止人們彼此相殘，讓人們自由地從事他們自己的工作和不斷進步。」（引自傑弗遜首任總統就職演說）

傑弗遜是新聞自由的堅定擁護者，他曾說，「我們相信最終會證明，人是可以受理性和真理支配的。因此我們的第一個目標是給人打開所有通向真理的道路。迄今為止，找到的最好的辦法是新聞自由。」傑弗遜的新聞自由觀更多地着眼於從發揮報刊媒介監督政府、啓迪民智的作用。

美國人受賜於傑弗遜的實在太多了，他不只給了美國人《獨立宣言》、《人權法案》，還有美國歷史中民主的形成、在平等中覓取自由的原則、美國的貨幣制度、宗教自由的觀念和奴隸應該獲得自由的偉大思想；他還致力於最為實際的事業，拓展了美國的領土，發展了西部。

1826年7月4日，正好是他撰寫的《獨立宣言》發表50周年紀念日，傑弗遜逝世；他親自為自己撰寫了墓誌銘：「這裡埋葬着托馬斯·傑弗遜，他是獨立宣言的作者，弗吉尼亞州宗教信仰自由法案的作者，弗吉尼亞大學之父。」他甚至沒有提及自己曾經是美國的總統。

在他給孫子的忠告裡，他提到了以下10點生活的原則：

1.今天能做的事情絕對不要推到明天；

2.自己能做的事情絕對不要麻煩別人；

3.決不要花費還沒有到手的錢；

4.決不要貪圖便宜，購買你所不需要的東西；

5.絕對不要驕傲，那比飢餓和寒冷更有害；

6.不要貪食，吃得少一點不會使人懊悔；

7.不要做勉強的事情，只有心甘情願才能把事情做好；

8.對於不可能發生的事情不要庸人自擾；

9.凡事要講究方式方法；

10.當你氣惱時，先數到10再說話，如果還是氣憤，那就數到100。——譯者注

⑧指弗吉尼亞大學（The University of Virginia），簡稱為UVA，是由托馬斯·傑弗遜於美國弗吉尼亞州中西部的夏洛特鎮創建的一所公立研究型大學，是美國排名第二的公立大學，僅次於加利福尼亞大學伯克利分校（UC　Berkeley）。該校是北美地區唯一一所被聯合國教育科學文化組織列為世界遺產的高等院校。在美國歷史上，弗吉尼亞大學以其首創建築、天文和哲學等學術領域而著稱，同時它也是第一所將教育獨立於教會的高校。

傑弗遜對威廉瑪麗學院影響龐大的宗教勢力感到無奈，他想創立一所獨立於宗教的大學，而當時最好的哈佛、威廉瑪麗和耶魯這些學校都是由各個宗教派別影響，他認為，

母校的影響力過於強大，從而可能會帶領國家走向一個錯誤的方向。他的這種擔憂在1800年達到高峰，因此，傑弗遜聯繫了曾經一起在威廉瑪麗學院讀書的詹姆斯·門羅。在1788年，門羅已經買下了弗吉尼亞大學所處的土地。1817年，門羅恰好開始了他作為美國總統的第一個任期。在托馬斯·傑斐遜和詹姆斯·門羅的共同主持下，學校於1817年舉行了奠基儀式，於1819年獲得了弗吉尼亞州政府的大學辦學許可證。

弗吉尼亞大學的宗旨是：通過激發學生在瞭解自然界和人類社會過程中的持久的自由探索精神，豐富人類的思想寶庫。——譯者注

⑨清教徒運動，16世紀中葉，英格蘭國教會內部，以實現加爾文主義為目標的改革運動。主張清除國教會內殘留的天主教舊制和繁縟儀節，提倡「勤儉清潔」的簡樸生活。清教徒精神在宗教、社會、經濟、政治、文學和藝術教育等方面對英語世界產生了深遠影響。清教徒運動事實上也超出了教會改革的範疇，而發展成為一種特定的生活方式，如注意個人和家庭的宗教生活、遵守嚴格的道德准則、提倡勤勞樸素的生活、重視社會責任等。——譯者注

⑩拉爾夫·瓦爾多·愛默生（Ralph Waldo Emerson，1803-1882），美國思想家、文學家。他是美國文化精神的代表人物，美國總統林肯稱他為「美國的孔子」、「美國文明之父」。以愛默生思想為代表的超驗主義是美國思想史上一次重要的思想解放運動，被稱為「美國文藝復興」。超驗主義強調人與上帝間的直接交流和人性中的神性，具有強烈的批判精神。

「相信你自己的思想，相信你內心深處認為對你合適的東西對一切人都適用……」文學批評家勞倫斯·布爾在《愛默生傳》中說，愛默生與他的學說，是美國最重要的世俗宗教。

1803年5月6日出生於馬薩諸塞州波士頓附近的康考德村，1882年4月27日在波士頓逝世。他的生命幾乎橫貫19世紀的美國，他出生時候的美國熱鬧卻混沌，一些人意識到它代表着某種新力量的崛起，卻無人能夠清晰地表達出來。美國此時缺乏統一的政體，更沒有相對一致的意識形態。在他去世的時候，美國不但因為南北戰爭而統一，而且它的個性逐漸鮮明起來，除了物質力量引人注目，它的文化也正在竭力走出歐洲的陰影。

1836年9月他用化名出版小品《論自然》（Nature）。1837年愛默生以《美國學者》為題發表了一篇著名的演講辭，宣告美國文學已脫離英國文學而獨立，告誡美國學者不要讓學究習氣蔓延，不要盲目地追隨傳統，不要進行純粹的摹仿；另外，這篇演講辭還抨擊了美國社會的拜金主義，強調人的價值；被譽為美國思想文化領域的「獨立宣言」。一年之後，愛默生在《神學院獻辭》中批評了基督教唯一神教派死氣沉沉的局面，竭力推崇人的至高無上，提倡靠直覺認識真理。

他的名言佳句有：

說到底，愛情就是一個人的自我價值在別人身上的反映。

你若是愛千古，你就應該愛現在；昨日不能喚回來，明日還是不實在；你能確有把握的，只有今日的現在。

人的一生就是進行嘗試，嘗試的越多，生活就越美好。

一個偉大的靈魂，會強化思想和生命。

所有的偉人都是從艱苦中脫穎而出的。

如果你要獲得成功，就應當以恆心為良友，以經驗為顧問，以小心為兄弟，以希望為守護者。

人類一切賺錢的職業與生意中都有罪惡的蹤跡。

家庭是父親的王國，母親的世界，兒童的樂園。

習慣是一個人思想與行為的領導者。

使時間充實就是幸福。

真正持久的勝利是和平，而不是戰爭。

生命的呼聲屬於每個人。

你信任人，人才對你忠實。以偉人的風度待人，人才表現出偉人的風度。——譯者注

⑪詹姆士·拉塞爾·洛威爾（James Russell Lowell，1819-1891），美國作家、批評家、編輯家和外交官，爐邊詩人之一。他自言「我是第一位努力表達美國思想的詩人」。《比格羅詩稿》（Biglow Papers）（1848、1867）是他最為知名的作品，是美國式幽默的傑出範例。

他在美國文學史上的重要地位主要取決於他的編輯工作和文學批評。很多評論家認為洛威爾的《哈佛大學校慶紀念會上的頌詩》（Ode Recited at the Harvard Commemoration）（1865）第六章是他最優秀的詩歌作品。這一章讚頌亞伯拉罕·林肯的偉大。

洛威爾出生於馬薩諸塞州的劍橋，其父是基督教唯一神教派的牧師。1838年他畢業於哈佛大學，1840年獲得該校法學院學位，但終其一生並未從事過法律工作。

1854年，洛威爾被任命為哈佛大學現代語言學史密斯教授（Smith professor），他擔任此職20餘年一直到1886年（但是，從1876年之後，他就沒有再教書）。他總結其間的教學方法：「真正的學識在於不知道事物存在什麼，而是知道它們的含義；不是記憶，而是判斷。」

1857年他成為直到今天都有世界影響力的《大西洋月刊》的首位編輯。在洛威爾任職的四年裡，該雜誌在理論批評和商業運作上都獲得了成功，吸引了當時許多美國一流作家。1864到1872年間，洛威爾與查理·艾略特·諾頓合編《北美評論》。

洛威爾在這兩份期刊上發表的文章，再加上其他一些文章，構成了他的第二部系列作品《比格羅詩稿》，他的文學批評散文則匯編為《在我的這些書中》（Among My Books）（1870）和《我的研究入口》（My Study Windows）（1871）。

他死後被安葬於奧本山墓園，緊鄰生前的好友兼鄰居朗費羅（Longfellow）的墓地。1905年，洛威爾入選美國偉人名錄。——譯者注

⑫朗費羅（Henry Wadsworth Longfellow，1807-1882），詩人和教育家。19世紀美國最偉大的浪漫主義詩人之一，爐邊詩人之一，第一位翻譯但丁《神曲》的美國人。

1807年2月27日出生於緬因州波特蘭城一個律師家庭。

1822年進入博德因學院，與霍桑是同班同學。畢業後去過法國、西班牙、意大利和德國等地，研究這些國家的語言和文學。1836年開始在哈佛大學講授語言、文學長達十八年，他致力於介紹歐洲文化和浪漫主義作家的作品，成為新英格蘭文化中心劍橋文學界和社交界的重要人物。他一生創作的大量抒情詩、敘事詩、歌謠和詩劇，曾在美國和歐洲廣泛流傳，受到讚賞。他的名言有：

「不要老嘆息過去，它是不再回來的；要明智地改善現在。要以不憂不懼的堅決意志投入撲朔迷離的未來。先相信你自己，然後別人才會相信你。」——譯者注

⑬威廉·詹姆斯（William James，1842-1910），美國本土第一位哲學家和心理學家，第一位在美國開設心理學課程的教育家，實用主義的倡導者，美國機能主義心理學派創始人之一，美國最早的實驗心理學家之一，「美國心理學之父」。1875年，建立美國第一個心理學實驗室。1904年當選為美國心理學會主席，1906年當選為國家科學院院士。2006年，詹姆斯被美國的權威期刊《大西洋月刊》評為影響美國的100位人物之一（第62位）。——譯者注

　　⑭香港浸會大學（Hong Kong Baptist University，HKBU）是香港第二所歷史最悠久的高等教育學府，前身為香港浸會學院，於1956年成立，是一所具有基督教教育傳統的公立大學，以「全人教育」為其教育目標及理想，其校訓為「篤信力行」。浸大在香港排名雖屬「二流」大學，但其傳理學院（School of Communication）的新聞系（Department of Journalism），在全港乃至全亞洲居於一流，無論師資還是設備都屬頂配。傳理學院於1991年由傳理學系升格而成；新聞專業亦成為新聞系，課程創辦於1968年，致力打造亞洲最優質的專業及理論並重的新聞課程。

第二部分　教育的目的（英文原版）

The Aims of Education

Alfred North Whitehead

Preface

The general topic of this volume is education on its intellectual side. One main idea runs through the various chapters, and is illustrated in them from many points of view. It can be stated briefly thus: The students are alive, and the purpose of education is to stimulate and guide their self-development. It follows as a corollary from this premiss, that the teachers also should be alive with living thoughts. The whole book is a protest against dead knowledge, that is to say, against inert ideas. The separate chapters have, with the exception of Chapter IX, been delivered as addresses at various conferences of educational bodies and of scientific societies. They are the outcome of practical experience, reflections on the practice of education and some criticisms on the meaning of the topics constituting its content.

The references to the educational system concern England. The failures and successes of the system in that country are somewhat different from those in America. But such references are merely illustrative: the general principles apply equally to both countries.

The earliest of the addresses was delivered in the year 1912 to the Educational Section of the International Congress of Mathe-maticians, meeting at Cambridge, England, and the latest in the year 1928 at the Business School of Harvard University, Cambridge, Massachusetts. Chapters I, IV, VI, VIII, IX, and X have been published in my book, *The Organisation of Thoughts* (Williams and Norgate, London, 1917). Chapter II, *The Rhythm of Education*, has been published as a separate pamphlet (Christophers, London, 1922). In this republication there are omissions but no other alterations. In particular, the three final chapters of the present book, with some omissions, stand as published in 1917. They are not to be constructed as commentaries on my writings since that date. The converse relation is the true one.

My thanks are due to the Editor of *The Hibbert Journal* for permission to republish Chapter III, *The Rhythmic Claims of Freedom and Discipline*, and Chapter V, *The Place of Classics in Education*, also to the Editor of *The Atlantic Monthly* for permission to republish Chapter VII, *Universities and Their Function*.

A. N. W.

Harvard University,
January, 1929.

CHAPTER I

The Aims of Education

Culture is activity of thought, and receptiveness to beauty and humane feeling. Scraps of information have nothing to do with it. A merely well-informed man is the most useless bore on God's earth. What we should aim at producing is men who possess both culture and expert knowledge in some special direction. Their expert knowledge will give them the ground to start from, and their culture will lead them as deep as philosophy and as high as art. We have to remember that the valuable intellectual development is self-development, and that it mostly takes place between the ages of sixteen and thirty. As to training, the most important part is given by mothers before the age of twelve. A saying due to Archbishop Temple illustrates my meaning. Surprise was expressed at the success in after-life of a man, who as a boy at Rugby had been somewhat undistinguished. He answered, "It is not what they are at eighteen, it is what they become afterwards that matters."

In training a child to activity of thought, above all things we must beware of what I will call "inert ideas" — that is to say, ideas that are merely received into the mind without being utilised, or tested, or thrown into fresh combinations.

In the history of education, the most striking phenomenon is that schools of learning, which at one epoch are alive with a ferment of genius, in a succeeding generation exhibit merely pedantry and routine. The reason is, that they are overladen with inert ideas. Education with inert ideas is not only useless: it is, above all things, harmful — *Corruptio optimi*, *pessima*. Except at rare intervals of intellectual ferment, education in the past has been radically infected with inert ideas. That is the reason why uneducated clever women, who have seen much of the world, are in middle life so much the most cultured part of the community. They have been saved from this horrible burden of inert ideas. Every intellectual revolution which has ever stirred humanity into greatness has been a passionate protest against inert ideas. Then, alas, with pathetic ignorance of human psychology, it has proceeded by some educational scheme to bind humanity afresh with inert ideas of its own fashioning.

Let us now ask how in our system of education we are to guard against this mental dryrot. We enunciate two educational commandments, "Do not teach too many subjects," and again, "What you teach, teach thoroughly."

The result of teaching small parts of a large number of subjects is the passive reception of disconnected ideas, not illumined with any spark of vitality. Let the main ideas which are introduced into a child's education be few and important, and let them be thrown into every combination possible. The child should make them his own, and should understand their application here and now in the circumstances of his actual life. From the very beginning of his education, the child should experience the joy of discovery. The discovery which he has to make, is that general ideas give an understanding of that stream of events which pours through his life, which is his life. By understanding I mean more than a mere logical analysis, though that is included. I mean "understanding" in the sense in which it is used in the French proverb, "To understand all, is to forgive all." Pedants sneer at an education which is useful. But if education is not useful, what is it? Is it a talent, to be hidden away in a napkin? Of course, education should be useful, whatever your aim in life. It was useful to Saint Augustine and it was useful to Napoleon. It is useful, because understanding is useful.

I pass lightly over that understanding which should be given by the literary side of education. Nor do I wish to be supposed to pronounce on the relative merits of a classical or a modern curriculum. I would only remark that the understanding which we want is an understanding of an insistent present. The only use of a knowledge of the past is to equip us for the present. No more deadly harm can be done to young minds than by depreciation of the present. The present contains all that there is. It is holy ground; for it is the past, and it is the future. At the same time it must be observed that an age is no less past if it existed two hundred years ago than if it existed two thousand years ago. Do not be deceived by the pedantry of dates. The ages of Shakespeare and of Molière are no less past than are the ages of Sophocles and of Virgil. The communion of saints is a great and inspiring assemblage, but it has only one possible hall of meeting, and that is, the present; and the mere lapse of time through which any particular group of saints must travel to reach that meeting-place, makes very little difference.

Passing now to the scientific and logical side of education, we remember that here also ideas which are not utilised are positively harmful. By utilising an idea, I mean relating it to that stream, compounded of sense perceptions, feelings, hopes, desires, and of mental activities adjusting thought to thought, which forms our life. I can imagine a set of beings which might fortify their souls by passively reviewing disconnected ideas. Humanity is not built that way — except perhaps some editors of newspapers.

In scientific training, the first thing to do with an idea is to prove it. But allow me for one moment to extend the meaning of "prove"; I mean — to prove its worth. Now an idea is not worth much unless the propositions in which it is embodied are true. Accordingly an essential part of the proof of an idea is the proof, either by experiment or by logic, of the truth of the propositions. But it is not essential that this proof of the truth should constitute the first introduction to the idea. After all, its assertion by the authority of respectable teachers is sufficient evidence to begin with. In our first contact with a set of propositions, we commence by appreciating their importance. That is what we all do in after-life. We do not attempt, in the strict sense, to prove or to disprove anything, unless its importance makes it worthy of that honour. These two processes of proof, in the narrow sense, and of appreciation, do not require a rigid separation in time. Both can be proceeded with nearly concurrently. But in so far as either process must have the priority, it should be that of appreciation by use.

Furthermore, we should not endeavour to use propositions in isolation. Emphatically I do not mean, a neat little set of experiments to illustrate Proposition I and then the proof of Proposition I, a neat little set of experiments to illustrate Proposition II and then the proof of Proposition II, and so on to the end of the book. Nothing could be more boring. Interrelated truths are utilised *en bloc*, and the various propositions are employed in any order, and with any reiteration. Choose some important applications of your theoretical subject; and study them concurrently with the systematic theoretical exposition. Keep the theoretical exposition short and simple, but let it be strict and rigid so far as it goes. It should not be too long for it to be easily known with thoroughness and accuracy. The consequences of a plethora of half-digested theoretical knowledge are deplorable. Also the theory should not be muddled up with the practice. The child should have no doubt when it is proving and when it is utilising. My point is that what is proved should be utilised, and that what is utilised should — so far, as is practicable — be proved. I am far from asserting that proof and utilisation are the same thing.

At this point of my discourse, I can most directly carry forward my argument in the outward form of a digression. We are only just realising that the art and science of education require a genius and a study of their own; and that this genius and this science are more than a bare knowledge of some branch of science or of literature. This truth was partially perceived in the past generation; and headmasters, somewhat crudely, were apt to supersede learning in their colleagues by requiring left-hand bowling and a taste for football. But culture is more than cricket, and more than football, and more than extent of knowledge.

Education is the acquisition of the art of the utilisation of knowledge. This is an art very difficult to impart. Whenever a textbook is written of real educational worth, you may be quite certain that some reviewer will say that it will be difficult to teach from it. Of course it will be difficult to teach from it. If it were easy, the book ought to be burned; for it cannot be educational. In education, as elsewhere, the broad primrose path leads to a nasty place. This evil path is represented by a book or a set of lectures which will practically enable the student to learn by heart all the questions likely to be asked at the next external examination. And I may say in passing that no educational system is possible unless every question directly asked of a pupil at any examination is either framed or modified by the actual teacher of that pupil in that subject. The external assessor may report on the curriculum or on the performance of the pupils, but never should be allowed to ask the pupil a question which has not been strictly supervised by the actual teacher, or at least inspired by a long conference with him. There are a few exceptions to this rule, but they are exceptions, and could easily be allowed for under the general rule.

We now return to my previous point, that theoretical ideas should always find important applications within the pupil's curriculum. This is not an easy doctrine to apply, but a very hard one. It contains within itself the problem of keeping knowledge alive, of preventing it from becoming inert, which is the central problem of all education.

The best procedure will depend on several factors, none of which can be neglected, namely, the genius of the teacher, the intellectual type of the pupils, their prospects in life, the opportunities offered by the immediate surroundings of the school, and allied factors of this sort. It is for this reason that the uniform external examination is so deadly. We do not denounce it because we are cranks, and like denouncing established things. We are not so childish. Also, of course, such examinations have their use in testing slackness. Our reason of dislike is very definite and very practical. It kills the best part of culture. When you analyse in the light of experience the central task of education, you find that its successful accomplishment depends on a delicate adjustment of many variable factors. The reason is that we are dealing with human minds, and not with dead matter. The evocation of curiosity, of judgment, of the power of mastering a complicated tangle of circumstances, the use of theory in giving foresight in special cases — all these powers are not to be imparted by a set rule embodied in one schedule of examination subjects.

I appeal to you, as practical teachers. With good discipline, it is always possible to pump into the minds of a class a certain quantity of inert knowledge. You take a text-book and make them learn it. So far, so good. The child then knows how to solve a quadratic equation. But what is the point of teaching a child to solve a quadratic equation? There is a traditional answer to this question. It runs thus: The mind is an instrument, you first sharpen it, and then use it; the acquisition of the power of solving a quadratic equation is part of the process of sharpening the mind. Now there is just enough truth in this answer to have made it live through the ages. But for all its half-truth, it embodies a radical error which bids fair to stifle the genius of the modern world. I do not know who was first responsible for this analogy of the mind to a dead instrument. For aught I know, it may have been one of the seven wise men of Greece, or a committee of the whole lot of them. Whoever was the originator, there can be no doubt of the authority which it has acquired by the continuous approval bestowed upon it by eminent persons. But whatever its weight of authority, whatever the high approval which it can quote, I have no hesitation in denouncing it as one of the most fatal, erroneous, and dangerous conceptions ever introduced into the theory of education. The mind is never passive; it is a perpetual activity, delicate, receptive, responsive to stimulus. You cannot postpone its life until you have sharpened it. Whatever interest attaches to your subject-matter must be evoked here and now; whatever powers you are strengthening in the pupil, must be exercised here and now; whatever possibilities of mental life your teaching should impart, must be exhibited here and now. That is the golden rule of education, and a very difficult rule to follow.

The difficulty is just this: the apprehension of general ideas, intellectual habits of mind, and pleasurable interest in mental achievement can be evoked by no form of words, however accurately adjusted. All practical teachers know that education is a patient process of the mastery of details, minute by minute, hour by hour, day by day. There is no royal road to learning through an airy path of brilliant generalisations. There is a proverb about the difficulty of seeing the wood because of the trees. That difficulty is exactly the point which I am enforcing. The problem of education is to make the pupil see the wood by means of the trees.

The solution which I am urging, is to eradicate the fatal disconnection of subjects which kills the vitality of our modern curriculum. There is only one subject-matter for education, and that is Life in all its manifestations. Instead of this single unity, we offer children — Algebra, from which nothing follows; Geometry, from which nothing follows; Science, from which nothing follows; History, from which nothing follows; a Couple of Languages, never mastered; and lastly, most dreary of all, Literature, represented by plays of Shakespeare, with philological notes and short analyses of plot and character to be in substance committed to memory. Can such a list be said to represent Life, as it is known in the midst of the living of it? The best that can be said of it is, that it is a rapid table of contents which a deity might run over in his mind while he was thinking of creating a world, and has not yet determined how to put it together.

Let us now return to quadratic equations. We still have on hand the unanswered question. Why should children be taught their solution? Unless quadratic equations fit into a connected curriculum, of course there is no reason to teach anything about them. Furthermore, extensive as should be the place of mathematics in a complete culture, I am a little doubtful whether for many types of boys algebraic solutions of quadratic equations do not lie on the specialist side of mathematics. I may here remind you that as yet I have not said anything of the psychology or the content of the specialism, which is so necessary a part of an ideal education. But all that is an evasion of our real question, and I merely state it in order to avoid being misunderstood in my answer.

Quadratic equations are part of algebra, and algebra is the intellectual instrument which has been created for rendering clear the quantitative aspects of the world. There is no getting out of it. Through and through the world is infected with quantity. To talk sense, is to talk in quantities. It is no use saying that the nation is large, — How large? It is no use saying that radium is scarce, — How scarce? You cannot evade quantity. You may fly to poetry and to music, and quantity and number will face you in your rhythms and your octaves. Elegant intellects which despise the theory of quantity, are but half developed. They are more to be pitied than blamed. The scraps of gibberish, which in their school-days were taught to them in the name of algebra, deserve some contempt.

This question of the degeneration of algebra into gibberish, both in word and in fact, affords a pathetic instance of the uselessness of reforming educational schedules without a clear conception of the attributes which you wish to evoke in the living minds of the children. A few years ago there was an outcry that school algebra was in need of reform, but there was a general agreement that graphs would put everything right. So all sorts of things were extruded, and graphs were introduced. So far as I can see, with no sort of idea behind them, but just graphs. Now every examination paper has one or two questions on graphs. Personally I am an enthusiastic adherent of graphs. But I wonder whether as yet we have gained very much. You cannot put life into any schedule of general education unless you succeed in exhibiting its relation to some essential characteristic of all intelligent or emotional perception. It is a hard saying, but it is true; and I do not see how to make it any easier. In making these little formal alterations you are beaten by the very nature of things. You are pitted against too skilful an adversary, who will see to it that the pea is always under the other thimble.

Reformation must begin at the other end. First, you must make up your mind as to those quantitative aspects of the world which are simple enough to be introduced into general education; then a schedule of algebra should be framed which will about find its exemplification in these applications. We need not fear for our pet graphs, they will be there in plenty when we once begin to treat algebra as a serious means of studying the world. Some of the simplest applications will be found in the quantities which occur in the simplest study of society. The curves of history are more vivid and more informing than the dry catalogues of names and dates which comprise the greater part of that arid school study. What purpose is effected by a catalogue of undistinguished kings and queens? Tom, Dick, or Harry, they are all dead. General resurrections are failures, and are better postponed. The quantitative flux of the forces of modern society is capable of very simple exhibition. Meanwhile, the idea of the variable, of the function, of rate of change, of equations and their solution, of elimination, are being studied as an abstract science for their own sake. Not, of course, in the pompous phrases with which I am alluding to them here, but with that iteration of simple special cases proper to teaching.

If this course be followed, the route from Chaucer to the Black Death, from the Black Death to modern Labour troubles, will connect the tales of the mediæval pilgrims with the abstract science of algebra, both yielding diverse aspects of that single theme, Life. I know what most of you are thinking at this point. It is that the exact course which I have sketched out is not the particular one which you would have chosen, or even see how to work. I quite agree. I am not claiming that I could do it myself. But your objection is the precise reason why a common external examination system is fatal to education. The process of exhibiting the applications of knowledge must, for its success, essentially depend on the character of the pupils and the genius of the teacher. Of course I have left out the easiest applications with which most of us are more at home. I mean the quantitative sides of sciences, such as mechanics and physics.

Again, in the same connection we plot the statistics of social phenomena against the time. We then eliminate the time between suitable pairs. We can speculate how far we have exhibited a real causal connection, or how far a mere temporal coincidence. We notice that we might have plotted against the time one set of statistics for one country and another set for another country, and thus, with suitable choice of subjects, have obtained graphs which certainly exhibited mere coincidence. Also other graphs exhibit obvious causal connections. We wonder how to discriminate. And so are drawn on as far as we will.

But in considering this description, I must beg you to remember what I have been insisting on above. In the first place, one train of thought will not suit all groups of children. For example, I should expect that artisan children will want something more concrete and, in a sense, swifter than I have set down here. Perhaps I am wrong, but that is what I should guess. In the second place, I am not contemplating one beautiful lecture stimulating, once and for all, an admiring class. That is not the way in which education proceeds. No; all the time the pupils are hard at work solving examples, drawing graphs, and making experiments, until they have a thorough hold on the whole subject. I am describing the interspersed explanations, the directions which should be given to their thoughts. The pupils have got to be made to feel that they are studying something, and are not merely executing intellectual minuets.

Finally, if you are teaching pupils for some general examination, the problem of sound teaching is greatly complicated. Have you ever noticed the zig-zag moulding round a Norman arch? The ancient work is beautiful, the modern work is hideous. The reason is, that the modern work is done to exact measure, the ancient work is varied according to the idiosyncrasy of the workman. Here it is crowded, and there it is expanded. Now the essence of getting pupils through examinations is to give equal weight to all parts of the schedule. But mankind is naturally specialist. One man sees a whole subject, where another can find only a few detached examples. I know that it seems contradictory to allow for specialism in a curriculum especially designed for a broad culture. Without contradictions the world would be simpler, and perhaps duller. But I am certain that in education wherever you exclude specialism you destroy life.

We now come to the other great branch of a general

mathematical education, namely Geometry. The same principles apply. The theoretical part should be clear-cut, rigid, short, and important. Every proposition not absolutely necessary to exhibit the main connection of ideas should be cut out, but the great fundamental ideas should be all there. No omission of concepts, such as those of Similarity and Proportion. We must remember that, owing to the aid rendered by the visual presence of a figure, Geometry is a field of unequalled excellence for the exercise of the deductive faculties of reasoning. Then, of course, there follows Geometrical Drawing, with its training for the hand and eye.

But, like Algebra, Geometry and Geometrical Drawing must be extended beyond the mere circle of geometrical ideas. In an industrial neighbourhood, machinery and workshop practice form the appropriate extension. For example, in the London Polytechnics this has been achieved with conspicuous success. For many secondary schools I suggest that surveying and maps are the natural applications. In particular, plane-table surveying should lead pupils to a vivid apprehension of the immediate application of geometric truths. Simple drawing apparatus, a surveyor's chain, and a surveyor's compass, should enable the pupils to rise from the survey and mensuration of a field to the construction of the map of a small district. The best education is to be found in gaining the utmost information from the simplest apparatus. The provision of elaborate instruments is greatly to be deprecated. To have constructed the map of a small district, to have considered its roads, its contours, its geology, its climate, its relation to other districts, the effects on the status of its inhabitants, will teach more history and geography than any knowledge of Perkin Warbeck or of Behren's Straits. I mean not a nebulous lecture on the subject, but a serious investigation in which the real facts are definitely ascertained by the aid of accurate theoretical knowledge. A typical mathematical problem should be: Survey such and such a field, draw a plan of it to such and such a scale, and find the area. It would be quite a good procedure to impart the necessary geometrical propositions without their proofs. Then, concurrently in the same term, the proofs of the propositions would be learnt while the survey was being made.

Fortunately, the specialist side of education presents an easier problem than does the provision of a general culture. For this there are many reasons. One is that many of the principles of procedure to be observed are the same in both cases, and it is unnecessary to recapitulate. Another reason is that specialist training takes place — or should take place — at a more advanced stage of the pupil's course, and thus there is easier material to work upon. But undoubtedly the chief reason is that the specialist study is normally a study of peculiar interest to the student. He is studying it because, for some reason, he wants to know it. This makes all the difference. The general culture is designed to foster an activity of mind; the specialist course utilises this activity. But it does not do to lay too much stress on these neat antitheses. As we have already seen, in the general course foci of special interest will arise; and similarly in the special study, the external connections of the subject drag thought outwards.

Again, there is not one course of study which merely gives general culture, and another which gives special knowledge. The subjects pursued for the sake of a general education are special subjects specially studied; and, on the other hand, one of the ways of encouraging general mental activity is to foster a special devotion. You may not divide the seamless coat of learning. What education has to impart is an intimate sense for the power of ideas, for the beauty of ideas, and for the structure of ideas, together with a particular body of knowledge which has peculiar reference to the life of the being possessing it.

The appreciation of the structure of ideas is that side of a cultured mind which can only grow under the influence of a special study. I mean that eye for the whole chess-board, for the bearing of one set of ideas on another. Nothing but a special study can give any appreciation for the exact formulation of general ideas, for their relations when formulated, for their service in the comprehension of life. A mind so disciplined should be both more abstract and more concrete. It has been trained in the comprehension of abstract thought and in the analysis of facts.

Finally, there should grow the most austere of all mental qualities; I mean the sense for style. It is an æsthetic sense, based on admiration for the direct attainment of a foreseen end, simply and without waste. Style in art, style in literature, style in science, style in logic, style in practical execution have fundamentally the same aesthetic qualities, namely, attainment and restraint. The love of a subject in itself and for itself, where it is not the sleepy pleasure of pacing a mental quarter-deck, is the love of style as manifested in that study.

Here we are brought back to the position from which we started, the utility of education. Style, in its finest sense, is the last acquirement of the educated mind; it is also the most useful. It pervades the whole being. The administrator with a sense for style hates waste; the engineer with a sense for style economises his material; the artisan with a sense for style prefers good work. Style is the ultimate morality of mind.

But above style, and above knowledge, there is something, a vague shape like fate above the Greek gods. That something is Power. Style is the fashioning of power, the restraining of power. But, after all, the power of attainment of the desired end is fundamental. The first thing is to get there. Do not bother about your style, but solve your problem, justify the ways of God to man, administer your province, or do whatever else is set before you.

Where, then, does style help? In this, with style the end is attained without side issues, without raising undesirable inflammations. With style you attain your end and nothing but your end. With style the effect of your activity is calculable, and foresight is the last gift of gods to men. With style your power is increased, for your mind is not distracted with irrelevancies, and you are more likely to attain your object. Now style is the exclusive privilege of the expert. Whoever heard of the style of an amateur painter, of the style of an amateur poet? Style is always the product of specialist study, the peculiar contribution of specialism to culture.

English education in its present phase suffers from a lack of definite aim, and from an external machinery which kills its vitality. Hitherto in this address I have been considering the aims which should govern education. In this respect England halts between two opinions. It has not decided whether to produce amateurs or experts. The profound change in the world which the nineteenth century has produced is that the growth of knowledge has given foresight. The amateur is essentially a man with appreciation and with immense versatility in mastering a given routine. But he lacks the foresight which comes from special knowledge. The object of this address is to suggest how to produce the expert without loss of the essential virtues of the amateur. The machinery of our secondary education is rigid where it should be yielding, and lax where it should be rigid. Every school is bound on pain of extinction to train its boys for a small set of definite examinations. No headmaster has a free hand to develop his general education or his specialist studies in accordance with the opportunities of his school, which are created by its staff, its environment, its class of boys, and its endowments. I suggest that no system of external tests which aims primarily at examining individual scholars can result in anything but educational waste.

Primarily it is the schools and not the scholars which should be inspected. Each school should grant its own leaving certificates, based on its own curriculum. The standards of these schools should be sampled and corrected. But the first requisite for educational reform is the school as a unit, with its approved curriculum based on its own needs, and evolved by its own staff. If we fail to secure that, we simply fall from one formalism into another, from one dung-hill of inert ideas into another.

In stating that the school is the true educational unit in any national system for the safeguarding of efficiency, I have conceived the alternative system as being the external examination of the individual scholar. But every Scylla is faced by its Charybdis — or, in more homely language, there is a ditch on both sides of the road. It will be equally fatal to education if we fall into the hands of a supervising department which is under the impression that it can divide all schools into two or three rigid categories, each type being forced to adopt a rigid curriculum. When I say that the school is the educational unit, I mean exactly what I say, no larger unit, no smaller unit. Each school must have the claim to be considered in relation to its special circumstances. The classifying of schools for some purposes is necessary. But no absolutely rigid curriculum, not modified by its own staff, should be permissible. Exactly the same principles apply, with the proper modifications, to universities and to technical colleges.

When one considers in its length and in its breadth the importance of this question of the education of a nation's young, the broken lives, the defeated hopes, the national failures, which result from the frivolous inertia with which it is treated, it is difficult to restrain within oneself a savage rage. In the conditions of modern life the rule is absolute, the race which does not value trained intelligence is doomed. Not all your heroism, not all your social charm, not all your wit, not all your victories on land or at sea, can move back the finger of fate. To-day we maintain ourselves. To-morrow science will have moved forward yet one more step, and there will be no appeal from the judgment which will then be pronounced on the uneducated.

We can be content with no less than the old summary of educational ideal which has been current at any time from the dawn of our civilisation. The essence of education is that it be religious.

Pray, what is religious education?

A religious education is an education which inculcates duty and reverence. Duty arises from our potential control over the course of events. Where attainable knowledge could have changed the issue, ignorance has the guilt of vice. And the foundation of reverence is this perception, that the present holds within itself the complete sum of existence, backwards and forwards, that whole amplitude of time, which is eternity.

CHAPTER II

The Rhythm of Education

By the Rhythm of Education I denote a certain principle which in its practical application is well known to everyone with educational experience. Accordingly, when I remember that I am speaking to an audience of some of the leading educationalists in England, I have no expectation that I shall be saying anything that is new to you. I do think, however, that the principle has not been subjected to an adequate discussion taking account of all the factors which should guide its application.

I first seek for the baldest statement of what I mean by the Rhythm of Education, a statement so bald as to exhibit the point of this address in its utter obviousness. The principle is merely this — that different subjects and modes of study should be undertaken by pupils at fitting times when they have reached the proper stage of mental development. You will agree with me that this is a truism, never doubted and known to all. I am really anxious to emphasise the obvious character of the foundational idea of my address; for one reason, because this audience will certainly find it out for itself. But the other reason, the reason why I choose this subject for discourse, is that I do not think that this obvious truth has been handled in educational practice with due attention to the psychology of the pupils.

The Tasks of Infancy

I commence by challenging the adequacy of some principles by which the subjects for study are often classified in order.

By this I mean that these principles can only be accepted as correct if they are so explained as to be explained away. Consider first the criterion of difficulty. It is not true that the easier subjects should precede the harder. On the contrary, some of the hardest must come first because nature so dictates, and because they are essential to life. The first intellectual task which confronts an infant is the acquirement of spoken language. What an appalling task, the correlation of meanings with sounds! It requires an anlysis of ideas and an analysis of sounds. We all know that the infant does it, and that the miracle of his achievement is explicable. But so are all miracles, and yet to the wise they remain miracles. All I ask is that with this example staring us in the face we should cease talking nonsense about postponing the harder subjects.

What is the next subject in the education of the infant minds? The acquirement of written language; that is to say, the correlation of sounds with shapes. Great heavens! Have our educationists gone mad? They are setting babbling mites of six years old to tasks which might daunt a sage after lifelong toil. Again, the hardest task in mathematics is the study of the elements of algebra, and yet this stage must precede the comparative simplicity of the differential calculus.

I will not elaborate my point further; I merely restate it in the form, that the postponement of difficulty is no safe clue for the maze of educational practice.

The alternative principle of order among subjects is that of necessary antecedence. There we are obviously on firmer ground. It is impossible to read *Hamlet* until you can read; and the study of integers must precede the study of fractions. And yet even this firm principle dissolves under scrutiny. It is certainly true, but it is only true if you give an artificial limitation to the concept of a subject for study. The danger of the principle is that it is accepted in one sense, for which it is almost a necessary truth, and that it is applied in another sense for which it is false. You cannot read Homer before you can read; but many a child, and in ages past many a man, has sailed with Odysseus over the seas of Romance by the help of the spoken word of a mother, or of some wandering bard. The uncritical application of the principle of the necessary antecedence of some subjects to others has, in the hands of dull people with a turn for organisation, produced in education the dryness of the Sahara.

Stages of Mental Growth

The reason for the title which I have chosen for this address, the Rhythm of Education, is derived from yet another criticism of current ideas. The pupil's progress is often conceived as a uniform steady advance undifferentiated by change of type or alteration in pace; for example, a boy may be conceived as starting Latin at ten years of age and by a uniform progression steadily developing into a classical scholar at the age of eighteen or twenty. I hold that this conception of education is based upon a false psychology of the process of mental development which has gravely hindered the effectiveness of our methods. Life is essentially periodic. It comprises daily periods, with their alternations of work and play, of activity and of sleep, and seasonal periods, which dictate our terms and our holidays; and also it is composed of well-marked yearly periods. These are the gross obvious periods which no one can overlook. There are also subtler periods of mental growth, with their cyclic recurrences, yet always different as we pass from cycle to cycle, though the subordinate stages are reproduced in each cycle. That is why I have chosen the term "rhythmic," as meaning essentially the conveyance of difference within a framework of repetition. Lack of attention to the rhythm and character of mental growth is a main source of wooden futility in education. I think that Hegel was right when he analysed progress into three stages, which he called Thesis, Antithesis, and Synthesis; though for the purpose of the application of his idea to educational theory I do not think that the names he gave are very happily suggestive. In relation to intellectual progress I would term them, the stage of romance, the stage of precision, and the stage of generalisation.

The Stage of Romance

The stage of romance is the stage of first apprehension. The subject-matter has the vividness of novelty; it holds within itself unexplored connexions with possibilities half-disclosed by glimpses and half-concealed by the wealth of material. In this stage knowledge is not dominated by systematic procedure. Such system as there must be is created piecemeal *ad hoc*. We are in the presence of immediate cognisance of fact, only intermittently subjecting fact to systematic dissection. Romantic emotion is essentially the excitement consequent on the transition from the bare facts to the first realisations of the import of their unexplored relationships. For example, Crusoe was a mere man, the sand was mere sand, the footprint was a mere footprint, and the island a mere island, and Europe was the busy world of men. But the sudden perception of the half-disclosed and half-hidden possibilities relating Crusoe and the sand and the footprint and the lonely island secluded from Europe constitutes romance. I have had to take an extreme case for illustration in order to make my meaning perfectly plain. But construe it as an allegory representing the first stage in a cycle of progress. Education must essentially be a setting in order of a ferment already stirring in the mind: you cannot educate mind in *vacuo*. In our conception of education we tend to confine it to the second stage of the cycle; namely, to the stage of precision. But we cannot so limit our task without misconceiving the whole problem. We are concerned alike with the ferment, with the acquirement of precision, and with the subsequent fruition.

The Stage of Precision

The stage of precision also represents an addition to

knowledge. In this stage, width of relationship is subordinated to exactness of formulation. It is the stage of grammar, the grammar of language and the grammar of science. It proceeds by forcing on the students' acceptance a given way of analysing the facts, bit by bit. New facts are added, but they are the facts which fit into the analysis.

It is evident that a stage of precision is barren without a previous stage of romance: unless there are facts which have already been vaguely apprehended in their broad generality, the previous analysis in an analysis of nothing. It is simply a series of meaningless statements about bare facts, produced artificially and without and further relevance. I repeat that in this stage we do not merely remain within the circle of the facts elicited in the romantic epoch. The facts of romance have disclosed ideas with possibilities of wide significance, and in the stage of precise progress we acquire other facts in a systematic order, which thereby form both a disclosure and an analysis of the general subject-matter of the romance.

The Stage of Generalisation

The final stage of generalisation is Hegel's synthesis. It is a return to romanticism with added advantage of classified ideas and relevant technique. It is the fruition which has been the goal of the precise training. It is the final success. I am afraid that I have had to give a dry analysis of somewhat obvious ideas. It has been necessary to do so because my subsequent remarks presuppose that we have clearly in our minds the essential character of this threefold cycle.

The Cyclic Processes

Education should consist in a continual repetition of such cycles. Each lesson in its minor way should form an eddy cycle issuing in its own subordinate process. Longer periods should issue in definite attainments, which then form the starting-grounds for fresh cycles. We should banish the idea of a mythical, far-off end of education. The pupils must be continually enjoying some fruition and starting afresh — if the teacher is stimulating in exact proportion to his success in satisfying the rhythmic cravings of his pupils.

An infant's first romance is its awakening to the apprehension of objects and to the appreciation of their connexions. Its growth in mentality takes the exterior form of occupying itself in the co-ordination of its perceptions with its bodily activities. Its first stage of precision is mastering spoken language as an instrument for classifying its contemplation of objects and for strengthening its apprehension of emotional relations with other beings. Its first stage of generalisation is the use of language for a classified and enlarged enjoyment of objects.

This first cycle of intellectual progress from the achievement of perception to the acquirement of language, and from the acquirement of language to classified thought and keener perception, will bear more careful study. It is the only cycle of progress which we can observe in its purely natural state. The later cycles are necessarily tinged by the procedure of the current mode of education. There is a characteristic of it which is often sadly lacking in subsequent education; I mean, that it achieves complete success. At the end of it the child *can* speak, its ideas *are* classified, and its perceptions *are* sharpened. The cycle achieves its object. This is a great deal more than can be said for most systems of education as applied to most pupils. But why should this be so? Certainly, a new-born baby looks a most unpromising subject for intellectual progress when we remember the difficulty of the task before it. I suppose it is because nature, in the form of surrounding circumstances, sets it a task for which the normal development of its brain is exactly fitted. I do not think that there is any particular mystery about the fact of a child learning to speak and in consequence thinking all the better; but it does offer food for reflection.

In the subsequent education we have not sought for cyclic processes which in a finite time run their course and within their own limited sphere achieve a complete success. This completion is one outstanding character in the natural cycle for infants. Later on we start a child on some subject, say Latin, at the age of ten, and hope by a uniform system of formal training to achieve success at the age of twenty. The natural result is failure, both in interest and in acquirement. When I speak of failure, I am comparing our results with the brilliant success of the first natural cycle. I do not think that it is because our tasks are intrinsically too hard, when I remember that the infant's cycle is the hardest of all. It is because our tasks are set in an unnatural way, without rhythm and without the stimulus of intermediate successes and without concentration.

I have not yet spoken of this character of concentration which so conspicuously attaches to the infant's progress. The whole being of the infant is absorbed in the practice of its cycle. It has nothing else to divert its mental development. In this respect there is a striking difference between this natural cycle and the subsequent history of the student's development. It is perfectly obvious that life is very various and that the mind and brain naturally develop so as to adapt themselves to the many-hued world in which their lot is cast. Still, after making allowance for this consideration, we will be wise to preserve some measure of concentration for each of the subsequent cycles. In particular, we should avoid a competition of diverse subjects in the same stage of their cycles. The fault of the older education was unrhythmic concentration on a single undifferentiated subject. Our modern system, with its insistence on a preliminary general education, and with its easy toleration of the analysis of knowledge into distinct subjects, is an equally unrhythmic collection of distracting scraps. I am pleading that we shall endeavour to weave in the learner's mind a harmony of patterns, by co-ordinating the various elements of instruction into subordinate cycles each of intrinsic worth for the immediate appre-hension of the pupil. We must garner our crops each in its due season.

The Romance of Adolescence

We will now pass to some concrete applications of the ideas which have been developed in the former part of my address.

The first cycle of infancy is succeeded by the cycle of adolescence, which opens with by far the greatest stage of romance which we ever experience. It is in this stage that the lines of character are graven. How the child emerges from the romantic stage of adolescence is how the subsequent life will be moulded by ideals and coloured by imagination. It rapidly follows on the generalisation of capacity produced by the acquirement of spoken language and of reading. The stage of generalisation belonging to the infantile cycle is comparatively short because the romantic material of infancy is so scanty. The initial knowledge of the world in any developed sense of the word "knowledge" really commences after the achievement of the first cycle, and thus issues in the tremendous age of romance. Ideas, facts, relationships, stories, histories, possibilities, artistry in words, in sounds, in form and in colour, crowd into the child's life, stir his feelings, excite his appreciation, and incite his impulses to kindred activities. It is a saddening thought that on this golden age there falls so often the shadow of the crammer. I am thinking of a period of about four years of the child's life, roughly, in ordinary cases, falling between the ages of eight and twelve or thirteen. It is the first great period of the utilisation of the native language, and of developed powers of observation and of manipulation. The infant cannot manipulate, the child can; the infant cannot observe, the child can; the infant cannot retain thoughts by the recollection of words, the child can. The child thus enters upon a new world.

Of course, the stage of precision prolongs itself as recurring in minor cycles which form eddies in the great romance. The perfecting of writing, of spelling, of the elements of arithmetic, and of lists of simple facts, such as the Kings of England, are all elements of precision, very necessary both as training in concentration and as useful acquirements However, these are essentially fragmentary in character, whereas the great romance is the flood which bears on the child towards the life of the spirit.

The success of the Montessori system is due to its recognition of the dominance of romance at this period of growth. If this be the explanation, it also points to the limitations in the usefulness of that method. It is the system which in some measure is essential for every romantic stage. Its essence is browsing and the encouragement of vivid freshness. But it lacks the restraint which is necessary for the great stages of precision.

The Mastery of Language

As he nears the end of the great romance the cyclic course of growth is swinging the child over towards an aptitude for exact knowledge. Language is now the natural subject-matter for concentrated attack. It is the mode of expression with which he is thoroughly familiar. He is acquainted with stories, histories, and poems illustrating the lives of other people and of other civilisations. Accordingly, from the age of eleven onwards there is wanted a gradually increasing concentration towards precise knowledge of language. Finally, the three years from twelve to fifteen should be dominated by a mass attack upon language, so planned that a definite result, in itself worth having, is thereby achieved. I should guess that within these limits of time, and given adequate concentration, we might ask that at the end of that period the children should have command of English, should be able to read fluently fairly simple French, and should have completed the elementary stage of Latin; I mean, a precise knowledge of the more straight-forward parts of Latin grammar, the knowledge of the construction of Latin sentences, and the reading of some parts of appropriate Latin authors, perhaps simplified and largely supplemented by the aid of the best literary translations so that their reading of the original, plus translation, gives them a grip of the book as a literary whole. I conceive that such a measure of attainment in these three languages is well within the reach of the ordinary child, provided that he has not been distracted by the effort at precision in a multiplicity of other subjects. Also some more gifted children could go further. The Latin would come to them easily, so that it would be possible to start Greek before the end of the period, always provided that their bent is literary and that they mean later to pursue that study at least for some years. Other subjects will occupy a subordinate place in the time-table and will be undertaken in a different spirit. In the first place, it must be remembered that the semi-literary subjects, such as history, will largely have been provided in the study of the languages. It will be hardly possible to read some English, French, and Latin literature without imparting some knowledge of European history. I do not mean that all special history teaching should be abandoned. I do, however, suggest that the subject should be exhibited in what I have termed the romantic spirit, and that the pupils should not be subjected to the test of precise recollection of details on any large systematic scale.

At this period of growth science should be in its stage of romance. The pupils should see for themselves, and experiment for themselves, with only fragmentary precision of thought. The essence of the importance of science, both for interest in theory or for technological purposes, lies in its application to concrete detail, and every such application evokes a novel problem for research. Accordingly, all training in science should begin as well as end in research, and in getting hold of the subject-matter as it occurs in nature. The exact form of guidance suitable to this age and the exact limitations of experiment are matters depending on experience. But I plead that this period is the true age for the romance of science.

Concentration on Science

Towards the age of fifteen the age of precision in language and of romance in science draws to its close, to be succeeded by a period of generalisation in language and of precision in science. This should be a short period, but one of vital importance. I am thinking of about one year's work, and I suggest that it would be well decisively to alter the balance of the preceding curriculum. There should be a concentration on science and a decided diminution of the linguistic work. A year's work on science, coming on the top of the previous romantic study, should make everyone understand the main principles which govern the development of mechanics, physics, chemistry, algebra and geometry. Understand that they are not beginning these subjects, but they are putting together a previous discursive study by an exact formulation of their main ideas. For example, take algebra and geometry, which I single out as being subjects with which I have some slight familiarity. In the previous three years there has been work on the applications of the simplest algebraic formulæ and geometrical propositions to problems of surveying, or of some other scientific work involving calculations. In this way arithmetic has been carefully strengthened by the insistence on definite numerical results, and familiarity with the ideas of literal formulæ and of geometrical properties has been gained; also some minor methods of manipulation have been inculcated. There is thus no long time to be wasted in getting used to the ideas of the sciences. The pupils are ready for the small body of algebraic and geometrical truths which they ought to know thoroughly. Furthermore, in the previous period some boys will have shown an aptitude for mathematics and will have pushed on a little more, besides in the final year somewhat emphasising their mathematics at the expense of some of the other subjects. I am simply taking mathematics as an illustration.

Meanwhile, the cycle of language is in its stage of generalisation. In this stage the precise study of grammar and composition is discontinued, and the language study is confined to reading the literature with emphasised attention to its ideas and to the general history in which it is embedded; also the time allotted to history will pass into the precise study of a short definite period, chosen to illustrate exactly what does happen at an important epoch and also to show how to pass the simpler types of judgments on men and policies.

I have now sketched in outline the course of education from babyhood to about sixteen and a half, arranged with some attention to the rhythmic pulses of life. In some such way a general education is possible in which the pupil throughout has the advantage of concentration and of freshness. Thus precision will always illustrate subject-matter already apprehended and crying out for drastic treatment. Every pupil will have concentrated in turn on a variety of different subjects, and will know where his strong points lie. Finally — and this of all the objects to be attained is the most dear to my heart — the science students will have obtained both an invaluable literary education and also at the most impressionable age an early initiation into habits of thinking for themselves in the region of science.

After the age of sixteen new problems arise. For literary students science passes into the stage of generalisation, largely in the form of lectures on its main results and general ideas. New cycles of linguistic, literary, and historical study commence. But further detail is now unnecessary. For the scientists the preceding stage of precision maintains itself to the close of the school period with an increasing apprehension of wider general ideas.

However, at this period of education the problem is too individual, or at least breaks up into too many cases, to be susceptible of broad general treatment. I do suggest, nevertheless, that all scientists should now keep up their French, and initiate the study of German if they have not already acquired it.

University Education

I should now like, if you will bear with me, to make some remarks respecting the import of these ideas for a University education.

The whole period of growth from infancy to manhood forms one grand cycle. Its stage of romance stretches across the first dozen years of life, its stage of precision comprises the whole school period of secondary education, and its stage of generalisation is the period of entrance into manhood. For those whose formal education is prolonged beyond the school age, the University course or its equivalent is the great period of generalisation. The spirit of generalisation should dominate a University. The lectures should be addressed to those to whom details and procedure are familiar; that is to say, familiar at least in the sense of being so congruous to pre-existing training as to be easily acquirable. During the school period the student has been mentally bending over his desk; at the University he should stand up and look around. For this reason it is fatal if the first year at the University be frittered away in going over the old work in the old spirit. At school the boy painfully rises from the particular towards glimpses at general ideas; at the University he should start from general ideas and study their applications to concrete cases. A well-planned University course is a study of the wide sweep of generality. I do not mean that it should be abstract in the sense of divorce from concrete fact, but that concrete fact should be studied as illustrating the scope of general ideas.

Cultivation of Mental Power

This is the aspect of University training in which theoretical interest and practical utility coincide. Whatever be the detail with which you cram your student, the chance of his meeting in after-life exactly that detail is almost infinitesimal; and if he does meet it, he will probably have forgotten what you taught him about it. The really useful training yields a comprehension of a few general principles with a thorough grounding in the way they apply to a variety of concrete details. In subsequent practice the men will have forgotten your particular details; but they will remember by an unconscious common sense how to apply principles to immediate circumstances. Your learning is useless to you till you have lost your text-books, burnt your lecture notes, and forgotten the minutiæ which you learnt by heart for the examination. What, in the way of detail, you continually require will stick in your memory as obvious facts like the sun and moon; and what you casually require can be looked up in any work of reference. The function of a University is to enable you to shed details in favour of principles. When I speak of principles I am hardly even thinking of verbal formulations. A principle which has thoroughly soaked into you is rather a mental habit than a formal statement. It becomes the way the mind reacts to the appropriate stimulus in the form of illustrative circumstances. Nobody goes about with his knowledge clearly and consciously before him. Mental cultivation is nothing else than the satisfactory way in which the mind will function when it is poked up into activity. Learning is often spoken of as if we are watching the open pages of all the books which we have ever read, and then, when occasion arises, we select the right page to read aloud to the universe.

Luckily, the truth is far otherwise from this crude idea; and for this reason the antagonism between the claims of pure knowledge and professional acquirement should be much less acute than a faulty view of education would lead us to anticipate. I can put my point otherwise by saying that the ideal of a University is not so much knowledge, as power. Its business is to convert the knowledge of a boy into the power of a man.

The Rhythmic Character of Growth

I will conclude with two remarks which I wish to make by way of caution in the interpretation of my meaning. The point of this address is the rhythmic character of growth. The interior spiritual life of man is a web of many strands. They do not all grow together by uniform extension. I have tried to illustrate this truth by considering the normal unfolding of the capacities of a child in some what favourable circumstances but otherwise with fair average capacities. Perhaps I have misconstrued the usual phenomena. It is very likely that I have so failed, for the evidence is complex and difficult. But do not let any failure in this respect prejudice the main point which I am here to enforce. It is that the development of mentality exhibits itself as a rhythm involving an interweaving of cycles, the whole process being dominated by a greater cycle of the same general character as its minor eddies. Furthermore, this rhythm exhibits certain ascertainable general laws which are valid for most pupils, and the quality of our teaching should be so adapted as to suit the stage in the rhythm to which our pupils have advanced. The problem of a curriculum is not so much the succession of subjects; for all subjects should in essence be begun with the dawn of mentality. The truly important order is the order of quality which the educational procedure should assume.

My second caution is to ask you not to exaggerate into sharpness the distinction between the three stages of a cycle. I strongly suspect that many of you, when you heard me detail the three stages in each cycle, said to yourselves — How like a mathematician to make such formal divisions! I assure you that it is not mathematics but literary incompetence that may have led me into the error against which I am warning you. Of course, I mean throughout a distinction of emphasis, of pervasive quality — romance, precision, generalisation, are all present throughout. But there is an alternation of dominance, and it is this alternation which constitutes the cycles.

CHAPTER III

The Rhythmic Claims of Freedom and Discipline

The fading of ideals is sad evidence of the defeat of human endeavour. In the schools of antiquity philosophers aspired to impart wisdom, in modern colleges our humbler aim is to teach subjects. The drop from the divine wisdom, which was the goal of the ancients, to text-book knowledge of subjects, which is achieved by the moderns, marks an educational failure, sustained through the ages. I am not maintaining that in the practice of education the ancient were more successful that ourselves. You have only to read Lucian, and to note his satiric dramatizations of the pretentious claims of philosophers, to see that in this respect the ancients can boast over us no superiority. My point is that, at the dawn of our European civilisation, men started with the full ideals which should inspire education, and that gradually our ideals have sunk to square with our practice.

But when ideals have sunk to the level of practice, the result is stagnation. In particular, so long as we conceive intellectual education as merely consisting in the acquirement of mechanical mental aptitudes, and of formulated statements of useful truths, there can be no progress; though there will be much activity, amid aimless re-arrangement of syllabuses, in the fruitless endeavour to dodge the inevitable lack of time. We must take it as an unavoidable fact, that God has so made the world that there are more topics desirable for knowledge than any one person can possibly acquire. It is hopeless to approach the problem by the way of the enumeration of subjects which every one ought to have mastered. There are too many of them, all with excellent title-deeds. Perhaps, after all, this plethora of material is fortunate; for the world is made interesting by a delightful ignorance of important truths. What I am anxious to impress on you is that though knowledge is one chief aim of intellectual education, there is another ingredient, vaguer but greater, and more dominating in its importance. The ancients called it "wisdom". You cannot be wise without some basis of knowledge; but you may easily acquire knowledge and remain bare of wisdom.

Now wisdom is the way in which knowledge is held. It concerns the handling of knowledge, its selection for the determination of relevant issues, its employment to add value to our immediate experience. This mastery of knowledge, which is wisdom, is the most intimate freedom obtainable. The ancients saw clearly — more clearly than we do — the necessity for dominating knowledge by wisdom. But, in the pursuit of wisdom in the region of practical education, they erred sadly. To put the matter simply, their popular practice assumed that wisdom could be imparted to the young by procuring philosophers to spout at them. Hence the crop of shady philosophers in the schools of the ancient world. The only avenue towards wisdom is by freedom in the presence of knowledge. But the only avenue towards knowledge is by discipline in the acquirement of ordered fact. Freedom and discipline are the two essentials of education, and hence the title of my discourse to-day, "The Rhythmic Claims of Freedom and Discipline."

The antithesis in education between freedom and discipline is not so sharp as a logical analysis of the meanings of the terms might lead us to imagine. The pupil's mind is a growing organism. On the one hand, it is not a box to be ruthlessly packed with alien ideas; and, on the other hand, the ordered acquirement of knowledge is the natural food for a developing intelligence. Accordingly, it should be the aim of an ideally constructed education that the discipline should be the voluntary issue of free choice, and that the freedom should gain an enrichment of possibility as the issue of discipline. The two principles, freedom and discipline, are not antagonists, but should be so adjusted in the child's life that they correspond to a natural sway, to and fro, of the developing personality. It is this adaptation of freedom and discipline to the natural sway of development that I have elsewhere called The Rhythm of Education. I am convinced that much disappointing failure in the past has been due to neglect of attention to the importance of this rhythm. My main position is that the dominant note of education at its beginning and at its end is freedom, but that there is an intermediate stage of discipline with freedom in subordination; Furthermore, that there is not one unique threefold cycle of freedom, discipline, and freedom; but that all mental development is composed of such cycles, and of cycles of such cycles. Such a cycle is a unit cell, or brick; and the complete stage of growth is an organic structure of such cells. In analysing any one such cell, I call the first period of freedom the "stage of Romance," the intermediate period of discipline I call the "stage of Precision," and the final period of freedom is the "stage of Generalisation."

Let me now explain myself in more detail. There can be no mental development without interest. Interest is the *sine qua non* for attention and apprehension. You may endeavour to excite interest by means of birch rods, or you may coax it by the incitement of pleasurable activity. But without interest there will be no progress. Now the natural mode by which living organisms are excited towards suitable self-development is enjoyment. The infant is lured to adapt itself to its environment by its love of its mother and its nurse; we eat because we like a good dinner: we subdue the forces of nature because we have been lured to discovery by an insatiable curiosity: we enjoy exercise: and we enjoy the unchristian passion of hating our dangerous enemies. Undoubtedly pain is one subordinate means of arousing an organism to action. But it only supervenes on the failure of pleasure. Joy is the normal healthy spur for the *élan vital*. I am not maintaining that we can safely abandon ourselves to the allurement of the greater immediate joys. What I do mean is that we should seek to arrange the development of character along a path of natural activity, in itself pleasurable. The subordinate stiffening of discipline must be directed to secure some long-time good: although an adequate object must not be too far below the horizon, if the necessary interest is to be retained.

The second preliminary point which I wish to make, is the unimportance — indeed the evil — of barren knowledge. The importance of knowledge lies in its use, in our active mastery of it — that is to say, it lies in wisdom. It is a convention to speak of mere knowledge, apart from wisdom, as of itself imparting a peculiar dignity to its possessor. I do not share in this reverence for knowledge as such. It all depends on who has the knowledge and what he does with it. That knowledge which adds greatness to character is knowledge so handled as to transform every phase of immediate experience. It is in respect to the activity of knowledge that an over-vigorous discipline in education is so harmful. The habit of active thought, with freshness, can only be generated by adequate freedom. Undiscriminating discipline defeats its own object by dulling the mind. If you have much to do with the young as they emerge from school and from the university, you soon note the dulled minds of those whose education has consisted in the acquirement of inert knowledge. Also the deplorable tone of English society in respect to learning is a tribute to our educational failure. Furthermore, this overhaste to impart mere knowledge defeats itself. The human mind rejects knowledge imparted in this way. The craving for expansion, for activity, inherent in youth is disgusted by a dry imposition of disciplined knowledge. The discipline, when it comes, should satisfy a natural craving for the wisdom which adds value to bare experience.

But let us now examine more closely the rhythm of these natural cravings of the human intelligence. The first procedure of the mind in a new environment is a somewhat discursive activity amid a welter of ideas and experience. It is a process of discovery, a process of becoming used to curious thoughts, of shaping questions, of seeking for answers, of devising new experiences of noticing what happens as the result of new ventures. This general process is both natural and of absorbing interest. We must often have noticed children between the ages of eight and thirteen absorbed in its ferment. It is dominated by wonder, and cursed be the dullard who destroys wonder. Now undoubtedly this stage of development requires help, and even discipline. The environment within which the mind is working must be carefully selected. It must, of course, be chosen to suit the child's stage of growth, and must be adapted to individual needs. In a sense it is an imposition from without; but in a deeper sense it answers to the call of life within the child. In the teacher's consciousness the child has been sent to his telescope to look at the stars, in the child's consciousness he has been given free access to the glory of the heavens. Unless, working somewhere, however obscurely, even in the dullest child, there is this transfiguration of imposd routine, the child's nature will refuse to assimilate the alien material. It must never be forgotten that education is not a process of packing articles in a trunk. Such a simile is entirely inapplicable. It is, of course, a process completely of its own peculiar genus. Its nearest analogue is the assimilation of food by a living organism: and we all know how necessary to health is palatable food under suitable conditions. When you have put your boots in a trunk, they will stay there till you take them out again; but this is not at all the case if you feed a child with the wrong food.

This initial stage of romance requires guidance in another way. After all the child is the heir to long ages of civilisation, and it is absurd to let him wander in the intellectual maze of men in the Glacial Epoch. Accordingly, a certain pointing out of important facts, and of simplifying ideas, and of usual names, really strengthens the natural impetus of the pupil. In no part of education can you do without discipline or can you do without freedom; but in the stage of romance the emphasis must always be on freedom, to allow the child to see for itself and to act for itself. My point is that a block in the assimilation of ideas inevitably arises when a discipline of precision is imposed before a stage of romance has run its course in the growing mind. There is no comprehension apart from romance. It is my strong belief that the cause of so much failure in the past has been due to the lack of careful study of the due place of romance. Without the adventure of romance, at the best you get inert knowledge without initiative, and at the worst you get contempt of ideas — without knowledge.

But when this stage of romance has been properly guided another craving grows. The freshness of inexperience has worn off; there is general knowledge of the groundwork of fact and theory; and, above all, there has been plenty of independent browsing amid first-hand experiences, involving adventures of thought and of action. The enlightenment which comes from precise knowledge can now be understood. It corresponds to the obvious requirements of common sense, and deals with familiar material. Now is the time for pushing on, for knowing the subject exactly, and for retaining in the memory its salient features. This is the stage of precision. This stage is the sole stage of learning in the traditional scheme of education, either at school or university. You had to learn your subject, and there was nothing more to be said on the topic of education. The result of such an undue extension of a most necessary period of development was the production of a plentiful array of dunces, and of a few scholars whose natural interest had survived the car of Juggernaut. There is, indeed, always the temptation to teach pupils a little more of fact and of precise theory than at that stage they are fitted to assimilate. If only they could, it would be so useful. We — I am talking of schoolmasters and of university dons — are apt to forget that we are only subordinate elements in the education of a grown man; and that, in their own good time, in later life our pupils will learn for themselves. The phenomena of growth cannot be hurried beyond certain very narrow limits. But an unskilful practitioner can easily damage a sensitive organism. Yet, when all has been said in the way of caution, there is such a thing as pushing on, of getting to know the fundamental details and the main exact generalisations, and of acquiring an easy mastery of technique. There is no getting away from the fact that things have been found out, and that to be effective in the modern world you must have a store of definite acquirement of the best practice. To write poetry you must study metre, and to build bridges you must be learned in the strength of material. Even the Hebrew prophets had learned to write probably in those days requiring no mean effort. The untutored art of genius is — in the words of the Prayer Book — a vain thing, fondly invented.

During the stage of precision, romance is the background. The stage is dominated by the inescapable fact that there are right ways and wrong ways, and definite truths to be known. But romance is not dead, and it is the art of teaching to foster it amidst definite application to appointed task. It must be fostered for one reason, because romance is after all a necessary ingredient of that balanced wisdom which is the goal to be attained. But there is another reason: The organism will not absorb the fruits of the task unless its powers of apprehension are kept fresh by romance. The real point is to discover in practice that exact balance between freedom and discipline which will give the greatest rate of progress over the things to be known. I do not believe that there is any abstract formula which will give information applicable to all subjects, to all types of pupils, or to each individual pupil; except indeed the formula of rhythmic sway which I have been insisting on, namely, that in the earlier stage the progress requires that the emphasis be laid on freedom, and that in the later middle stage the emphasis be laid on the definite acquirement of allotted tasks. I freely admit that if the stage of romance has been properly managed, the discipline of the second stage is much less apparent, that the children know how to go about their work, want to make a good job of it, and can be safely trusted with the details. Furthermore, I hold that the only discipline, important for its own sake, is self-discipline, and that this can only be acquired by a wide use of freedom. But yet — so many are the delicate points to be considered in education — it is necessary in life to have acquired the habit of cheerfully undertaking imposed tasks. The conditions can be satisfied if the tasks correspond to the natural cravings of the pupil at his stage of progress, if they keep his powers at full stretch, and if they attain an obviously sensible result, and if reasonable freedom is allowed in the mode of execution.

The difficulty of speaking about the way a skilful teacher will keep romance alive in his pupils arises from the fact that what takes a long time to describe, takes a short time to do. The beauty of a passage of Virgil may be rendered by insisting on beauty of verbal enunciation, taking no longer than prosy utterance. The emphasis on the beauty of a mathematical argument, in its marshalling of general considerations to unravel complex fact, is the speediest mode of procedure. The responsibility of the teacher at this stage is immense. To speak the truth, except in the rare case of genius in the teacher, I do not think that it is possible to take a whole class very far along the road of precision without some dulling of the interest. It is the unfortunate dilemma that initiative and training are both necessary, and that training is apt to kill initiative.

But this admission is not to condone a brutal ignorance of methods of mitigating this untoward fact. It is not a theoretical necessity, but arises because perfect tact is unattainable in the treatment of each individual case. In the past the methods employed assassinated interest; we are discussing how to reduce the evil to its smallest dimensions. I merely utter the warning that education is a difficult problem, to be solved by no one simple formula.

In this connection there is, however, one practical consideration which is largely neglected. The territory of romantic interest is large, ill-defined, and not to be controlled by any explicit boundary. It depends on the chance flashes of insight. But the area of precise knowledge, as exacted in any general educational system, can be, and should be, definitely determined. If you make it too wide you will kill interest and defeat your own object; if you make it too narrow your pupils will lack effective grip. Surely, in every subject in each type of curriculum, the precise knowledge required should be determined after the most anxious inquiry. This does not now seem to be the case in any effective way. For example, in the classical studies of boys destined for a scientific career — a class of pupils in whom I am greatly interested — What is the Latin vocabulary which they ought definitely to know? Also what are the grammatical rules and constructions which they ought to have mastered? Why not determine these once and for all, and then bend every exercise to impress just these on the memory, and to understand their derivatives, both in Latin and also in French and English. Then, as to other constructions and words which occur in the reading of texts, supply full information in the easiest manner. A certain ruthless definiteness is essential in education. I am sure that one secret of a successful teacher is that he has formulated quite clearly in his mind what the pupil has got to know in precise fashion. He will then cease from half-hearted attempts to worry his pupils with memorising a lot of irrelevant stuff of inferior importance. The secret of success is pace, and the secret of pace is concentration. But, in respect to precise knowledge, the watchword is pace, pace, pace. Get your knowledge quickly, and then use it. If you can use it, you will retain it.

We have now come to the third stage of the rhythmic cycle, the stage of generalisation. There is here a reaction towards romance. Something definite is now known; aptitudes have been acquired; and general rules and laws are clearly apprehended both in their formulation and their detailed exemplification. The pupil now wants to use his new weapons. He is an effective individual, and it is effects that he wants to produce. He relapses into the discursive adventures of the romantic stage, with the advantage that his mind is now a disciplined regiment instead of a rabble. In this sense, education should begin in research and end in research. After all, the whole affair is merely a preparation for battling with the immediate experiences of life, a preparation by which to qualify each immediate moment with relevant ideas and appropriate actions. An education which does not begin by evoking initiative and end by encouraging it must be wrong. For its whole aim is the production of active wisdom.

In my own work at universities I have been much struck by the paralysis of thought induced in pupils by the aimless accumulation of precise knowledge, inert and unutilised. It should be the chief aim of a university professor to exhibit himself in his own true character — that is, as an ignorant man thinking, actively utilising his small share of knowledge. In a sense, knowledge shrinks as wisdom grows: for details are swallowed up in principles. The details of knowledge which are important will be picked up *ad hoc* in each avocation of life, but the habit of the active utilisation of well-understood principles is the final possession of wisdom. The stage of precision is the stage of growing into the apprehension of principles by the acquisition of a precise knowledge of details. The stage of generalisations is the stage of shedding details in favour of the active application of principles, the details retreating into subconscious habits. We don't go about explicitly retaining in our own minds that two and two make four, though once we had to learn it by heart. We trust to habit for our elementary arithmetic. But the essence of this stage is the emergence from the comparative passivity of being trained into the active freedom of application. Of course, during this stage, precise knowledge will grow, and more actively than ever before, because the mind has experienced the power of definiteness, and responds to the acquisition of general truth, and of richness of illustration. But the growth of knowledge becomes progressively unconscious, as being an incident derived from some active adventure of thought.

So much for the three stages of the rhythmic unit of development. In a general way the whole period of education is dominated by this threefold rhythm. Till the age of thirteen or fourteen there is the romantic stage, from fourteen to eighteen the stage of precision, and from eighteen to two and twenty the stage of generalisation. But these are only average characters, tinging the mode of development as a whole. I do not think that any pupil completes his stages simultaneously in all subjects. For example, I should plead that while language it initiating its stage of precision in the way of acquisition of vocabulary and of grammar, science should be in its full romantic stage. The romantic stage of language begins in infancy with the acquisition of speech, so that it passes early towards a stage of precision; while science is a late comer. Accordingly a precise inculcation of science at an early age wipes out initiative and interest, and destroys any chance of the topic having any richness of content in the child's apprehension. Thus, the romantic stage of science should persist for years after the precise study of language has commenced.

There are minor eddies, each in itself a threefold cycle, running its course in each day in each week, and in each term. There is the general apprehension of some topic in its vague possibilities, the mastery of the relevant details, and finally the putting of the whole subject together in the light of the relevant knowledge. Unless the pupils are continually sustained by the evocation of interest, the acquirement of technique, and the excitement of success, they can never make progress, and will certainly lose heart. Speaking generally, during the last thirty years the schools of England have been sending up to the universities a disheartened crowd of young folk, inoculated against any outbreak of intellectual zeal. The universities have seconded the efforts of the schools and emphasised the failure. Accordingly, the cheerful gaiety of the young turns to other topics, and thus educated England is not hospitable to ideas. When we can point to some great achievement of our nation — let us hope that it may be something other than a war — which has been won in the class-room of our schools, and not in their playing-fields, then we may feel content with our modes of education.

So far I have been discussing intellectual education, and my argument has been cramped on too narrow a basis. After all, our pupils are alive, and cannot be chopped into separate bits, like the pieces of a jig-saw puzzle. In the production of a mechanism the constructive energy lies outside it, and adds discrete parts to discrete parts. The case is far different for a living organism which grows by its own impulse towards self-development. This impulse can be stimulated and guided from outside the organism, and it can also be killed. But for all your stimulation and guidance the creative impulse towards growth comes from within, and is intensely characteristic of the individual. Education is the guidance of the individual towards a comprehension of the art of life; and by the art of life I mean the most complete achievement of varied activity expressing the potentialities of that living creature in the face of its actual environment. This completeness of achievement involves an artistic sense, subordinating the lower to the higher possibilities of the indivisible personality. Science, art, religion, morality, take their rise from this sense of values within the structure of being. Each individual embodies an adventure of existence. The art of life is the guidance of this adventure. The great religions of civilisation include among their original elements revolts against the inculcation of morals as a set of isolated prohibitions. Morality, in the petty negative sense of the term, is the deadly enemy of religion. Paul denounces the Law, and the Gospels are vehement against the Pharisees. Every outbreak of religion exhibits the same intensity of antagonism — an antagonism diminishing as religion fades. No part of education has more to gain from attention to the rhythmic law of growth than has moral and religious education. Whatever be the right way to formulate religious truths, it is death to religion to insist on a premature stage of precision. The vitality of religion is shown by the way in which the religious spirit has survived the ordeal of religious education.

The problem of religion in education is too large to be discussed at this stage of my address. I have referred to it to guard against the suspicion that the principles here advocated are to be conceived in a narrow sense. We are analysing the general law of rhythmic progress in the higher stages of life, embodying the initial awakening, the discipline, and the fruition on the higher plane. What I am now insisting is that the principle of progress is from within; the discovery is made by ourselves, the discipline is self-discipline, and the fruition is the outcome of our own initiative. The teacher has a double function. It is for him to elicit the enthusiasm by resonance from his own personality, and to create the environment of a larger knowledge and a firmer purpose. He is there to avoid the waste, which in the lower stages of existence is nature's way of evolution. The ultimate motive power, alike in science, in morality, and in religion, is the sense of value, the sense of importance. It takes the various forms of wonder, of curiosity, of reverence, or worship, of tumultuous desire for merging personality in something beyond itself. This sense of value imposes on life incredible labours, and apart from it life sinks back into the passivity of its lower types. The most penetrating exhibition of this force is the sense of beauty, the æsthetic sense of realised perfection. This thought leads me to ask, whether in our modern education we emphasise sufficiently the functions of art.

The typical education of our public schools was devised for boys from well-to-do cultivated homes. They travelled in Italy, in Greece, and in France, and often their own homes were set amid beauty. None of these circumstances hold for modern national education in primary or secondary schools, or even for the majority of boys and girls in our enlarged system of public schools. You cannot, without loss, ignore in the life of the spirit so great a factor as art. Our æsthetic emotions provide us with vivid apprehensions of value. If you maim these, you weaken the force of the whole system of spiritual apprehensions. The claim for freedom in education carries with it the corollary that the development of the whole personality must be attended to. You must not arbitrarily refuse its urgent demands. In these days of economy, we hear much of the futility of our educational efforts and of the possibility of curtailing them. The endeavour to develop a bare intellectuality is bound to issue in a large crop of failure. This is just what we have done in our national schools. We do just enough to excite and not enough to satisfy. History shows us that an efflorescence of art is the first activity of nations on the road to civilisation. Yet, in the face of this plain fact we practically shut out art from the masses of the population. Can we wonder that such an education, evoking and defeating cravings, leads to failure and discontent? The stupidity of the whole procedure is, that art in simple popular forms is just what we can give to the nation without undue strain on our resources. You may, perhaps, by some great reforms, obviate the worse kind of sweated labour and the insecurity of employment. But you can never greatly increase average incomes. On that side all hope of Utopia is closed to you. It would, however, require no very great effort to use our schools to produce a population with some love of music, some enjoyment of drama, and some joy in beauty of form and colour. We could also provide means for the satisfaction of these emotions in the general life of the population. If you think of the simplest ways, you will see that the strain on material resources would be negligible; and when you have done that, and when your population widely appreciates what art can give — its joys and its terrors — do you not think that your prophets and your clergy and your statesmen will be in a stronger position when they speak to the population of the love of God, of the inexorableness of duty, and of the call of patriotism?

Shakespeare wrote his plays for English people reared in the beauty of the country, amid the pageant of life as the Middle Age merged into the Renaissance, and with a new world across the ocean to make vivid the call of romance. To-day we deal with herded town populations, reared in a scientific age. I have no doubt that unless we can meet the new age with new methods, to sustain for our populations the life of the spirit, sooner or later, amid some savage outbreak of defeated longings, the fate of Russia will be the fate of England. Historians will write as her epitaph that her fall issued from the spiritual blindness of her governing classes, from their dull materialism, and from their Pharisaic attachment to petty formulæ of statesmanship.

CHAPTER IV

Technical Education and Its Relation to Science and Literature

The subject of this address is Technical Education. I wish to examine its essential nature and also its relation to a liberal education. Such an inquiry may help us to realise the conditions for the successful working of a national system of technical training. It is also a very burning question among mathematical teachers; for mathematics is included in most technological courses.

Now it is unpractical to plunge into such a discussion without framing in our own minds the best ideal towards which we desire to work, however modestly we may frame our hopes as to the result which in the near future is likely to be achieved.

People are shy of ideals; and accordingly we find a formulation of the ideal state of mankind placed by a modern dramatist[①] in the mouth of a mad priest. "In my dreams it is a country where the State is the Church and the Church the people: three in one and one in three. It is a commonwealth in which work is play and play is life: three in one and one in three. It is a temple in which the priest is the worshipper and the worshipper the worshipped: three in one and one in three. It is a godhead in which all life is human and all humanity divine: three in one and one in three. It is, in short, the

---

① Cf. BERNARD SHAW: *John Bull's Other Island*.

dream of a madman."

Now the part of this speech to which I would direct attention is embodied in the phrase, "It is a commonwealth in which work is play and play is life." This is the ideal of technical education. It sounds very mystical when we confront it with the actual facts, the toiling millions, tired, discontented, mentally indifferent, and then the employers — I am not undertaking a social analysis, but I shall carry you with me when I admit that the present facts of society are a long way off this ideal. Furthermore, we are agreed that an employer who conducted his workshop on the principle that "work should be play" would be ruined in a week.

The curse that has been laid on humanity, in fable and in fact, is, that by the sweat of its brow shall it live. But reason and moral intuition have seen in this curse the foundation for advance. The early Benedictine monks rejoiced in their labours because they conceived themselves as thereby made fellow-workers with Christ.

Stripped of its theological trappings, the essential idea remains, that work should be transfused with intellectual and moral vision and thereby turned into a joy, triumphing over is weariness and its pain. Each of us will re-state this abstract formulation in a more concrete shape in accordance with his private outlook. State it how you like, so long as you do not lose the main point in your details. However you phrase it, it remains the sole real hope of toiling humanity; and it is in the hands of technical teachers, and of those who control their spheres of activity, so to mould the nation that daily it may pass to its labours in the spirit of the monks of old.

The immediate need of the nation is a large supply of skilled workmen, of men with inventive genius, and of employers alert in the development of new ideas.

There is one — and only one — way to obtain these admirable results. It is by producing workmen, men of science, and employers who enjoy their work. View the matter practically in the light of our knowledge of average human nature. Is it likely that a tired, bored workman, however skilful his hands, will produce a large output of first-class work? He will limit his production, will scamp his work, and be an adept at evading inspection, he will be slow in adapting himself to new methods; he will be a focus of discontent, full of unpractical revolutionary ideas, controlled by no sympathetic apprehension of the real working of trade conditions. If, in the troubled times which may be before us, you wish appreciably to increase the chance of some savage upheaval, introduce widespread technical education and ignore the Benedictine ideal. Society will then get what it deserves.

Again, inventive genius requires pleasurable mental activity as a condition for its vigorous exercise. "Necessity is the mother of invention" is a silly proverb. "Necessity is the mother of futile dodges" is much nearer to the truth. The basis of the growth of modern invention is science, and science is almost wholly the outgrowth of pleasurable intellectual curiosity.

The third class are the employers, who are to be enterprising. Now it is to be observed that it is the successful employers who are the important people to get at, the men with business connections all over the world, men who are already rich. No doubt there will always be a continuous process of rise and fall of businesses. But it is futile to expect flourishing trade, if in the mass the successful houses of business are suffering from atrophy. Now if these men conceive their businesses as merely indifferent means for acquiring other disconnected opportunities of life, they have no spur to alertness. They are already doing very well, the mere momentum of their present business engagements will carry them on for their time. They are not at all likely to bother themselves with the doubtful chances of new methods. Their real soul is in the other side of their life. Desire for money will produce hard-fistedness and not enterprise. There is much more hope for humanity from manufacturers who enjoy their work than from those who continue in irksome business with the object of founding hospitals.

Finally, there can be no prospect of industrial peace so long as masters and men in the mass conceive themselves as engaged in a soulless operation of extracting money from the public. Enlarged views of the work performed, and of the communal service thereby rendered, can be the only basis on which of found sympathetic co-operation.

The conclusion to be drawn from this discussion is, that alike for masters and for men a technical or technological education, which_ is to have any chance of satisfying the practical needs of the nation, must be conceived in a liberal spirit as a real intellectual enlightenment in regard to principles applied and services rendered. In such an education geometry and poetry are as essential as turning laths.

The mythical figure of Plato may stand for modern liberal education as does that of St. Benedict for technical education. We need not entangle ourselves in the qualifications necessary for a balanced representation of the actual thoughts of the actual men. They are used here as symbolic figures typical of antithetical notions. We consider Plato in the light of the type of culture he now inspires.

In its essence a liberal education is an education for thought and for æsthetic appreciation. It proceeds by imparting a knowledge of the masterpieces of thought, of imaginative literature, and of art. The action which it contemplates is command. It is an aristocratic education implying leisure. This Platonic ideal has rendered imperishable services to European civilisation. It has encouraged art, it has fostered that spirit of disinterested curiosity which is the origin of science, it has maintained the dignity of mind in the face of material force, a dignity which claims freedom of thought. Plato did not, like St. Benedict, bother himself to be a fellow-worker with his slaves; but he must rank among the emancipators of mankind.

His type of culture is the peculiar inspiration of the liberal aristocrat, the class from which Europe derives what ordered liberty it now possesses. For centuries, from Pope Nicholas V to the school of the Jesuits, and from the Jesuits to the modern headmasters of English public schools, this educational ideal has had the strenuous support of the clergy.

For certain people it is a very good education. It suits their type of mind and the circumstances amid which their life is passed. But more has been claimed for it than this. All education has been judged adequate or defective according to its approximation to this sole type.

The essence of the type is a large discursive knowledge of the best literature. The ideal product of the type is the man who is acquainted with the best that has been written. He will have acquired the chief languages, he will have considered the histories of the rise and fall of nations, the poetic expression of human feeling, and have read the great dramas and novels. He will also be well grounded in the chief philosophies, and have attentively read those philosophic authors who are distinguished for lucidity of style.

It is obvious that, except at the close of a long life, he will not have much time for anything else if any approximation is to be made to the fulfilment of this programme. One is reminded of the calculation in a dialogue of Lucian that, before a man could be justified in practising any one of the current ethical systems, he should have spent a hundred and fifty years in examining their credentials.

Such ideals are not for human beings. What is meant by a liberal culture is nothing so ambitious as a full acquaintance with the varied literary expression of civilised mankind from Asia to Europe, and from Europe to America. A small selection only is required; but then, as we are told, it is a selection of the very best. I have my doubts of a selection which includes Xenophon and omits Confucius, but then I have read through neither in the original. The ambitious programme of a liberal education really shrinks to a study of some fragments of literature included in a couple of important languages.

But the expression of the human spirit is not confined to literature. There are the other arts, and there are the sciences. Also education must pass beyond the passive reception of the ideas of others. Powers of initiative must be strengthened. Unfortunately initiative does not mean just one acquirement — there is initiative in thought, initiative in action, and the imaginative initiative of art; and these three categories require many subdivisions.

The field of acquirement is large, and the individual so fleeting and so fragmentary: classical scholars, scientists, headmasters are alike ignoramuses.

There is a curious illusion that a more complete culture was possible when there was less to know. Surely the only gain was, that it was more possible to remain unconscious of ignorance. It cannot have been a gain to Plato to have read neither Shakespeare, nor Newton, nor Darwin. The achievements of a liberal education have in recent times not been worsened. The change is that its pretensions have been found out.

My point is, that no course of study can claim any position of ideal completeness. Nor are the omitted factors of subordinate importance. The insistence in the Platonic culture on disinterested intellectual appreciation is a psychological error. Action and our implication in the transition of events amid the inevitable bond of cause to effect are fundamental. An education which strives to divorce intellectual or æsthetic life from these fundamental facts carries with it the decadence of civilisation. Essentially culture should be for action, and its effect should be to divest labour from the associations of aimless toil. Art exists that we may know the deliverances of our senses as good. It heightens the sense-world.

Disinterested scientific curiosity is a passion for an ordered intellectual vision of the connection of events. But the goal of such curiosity is the marriage of action to thought. This essential intervention of action even in abstract science is often overlooked. No man of science wants merely to know. He acquires knowledge to appease his passion for discovery. He does not discover in order to know, he knows in order to discover. The pleasure which art and science can give to toil is the enjoyment which arises from successfully directed intention. Also it is the same pleasure which is yielded to the scientist and to the artist.

The antithesis between a technical and a liberal education is fallacious. There can be no adequate technical education which is not liberal, and no liberal education which is not technical; that is, no education which does not impart both technique and intellectual vision. In simpler language, education should turn out the pupil with something he knows well and something he can do well. This intimate union of practice and theory aids both. The intellect does not work best in a vacuum. The stimulation of creative impulse requires, especially in the case of a child, the quick transition to practice. Geometry and mechanics, followed by workshop practice, gain that reality without which mathematics is verbiage.

There are three main methods which are required in a national system of education, namely, the literary curriculum, the scientific curriculum, the technical curriculum. But each of these curricula should include the other two. What I mean is, that every form of education should give the pupil a technique, a science, an assortment of general ideas, and æsthetic appreciation and that each of these sides of his training should be illuminated by the others. Lack of time, even for the most favoured pupil, makes it impossible to develop fully each curriculum. Always there must be a dominant emphasis. The most direct æsthetic training naturally falls in the technical curriculum in those cases when the training is that requisite for some art or artistic craft. But it is of high importance in both a literary and a scientific education.

The educational method of the literary curriculum is the study of language, that is, the study of our most habitual method of conveying to others our states of mind. The technique which should be acquired is the technique of verbal expression, the science is the study of the structure of language and the analysis of the relations of language to the states of mind conveyed. Furthermore, the subtle relations of language to feeling, and the high development of the sense organs to which written and spoken words appeal, lead to keen æsthetic appreciations being aroused by the successful employment of language. Finally, the wisdom of the world is preserved in the masterpieces of linguistic composition.

This curriculum has the merit of homogeneity. All its various parts are co-ordinated and play into each other's hands. We can hardly be surprised that such a curriculum, when once broadly established, should have claimed the position of the sole perfect type of education. Its defect is unduly to emphasise the importance of language. Indeed the varied importance of verbal expression is so overwhelming that its sober estimation is difficult. Recent generations have been witnessing the retreat of literature, and of literary forms of expression, from their position of unique importance in intellectual life. In order truly to become a servant and a minister of nature something more is required than literary aptitudes.

A scientific education is primarily a training in the art of observing natural phenomena, and in the knowledge and deduction of laws concerning the sequence of such phenomena. But here, as in the case of a liberal education, we are met by the limitations imposed by shortness of time. There are many types of natural phenomena, and to each type there corresponds a science with its peculiar modes of observation, and its peculiar types of thought employed in the deduction of laws. A study of science in general is impossible in education, all that can be achieved is the study of two or three allied sciences. Hence the charge of narrow specialism urged against any education which is primarily scientific. It is obvious that the charge is apt to be well-founded; and it is worth considering how, within the limits of a scientific education and to the advantage of such an education, the danger can be avoided.

Such a discussion requires the consideration of technical education. A technical education is in the main a training in the art of utilising knowledge for the manufacture of material products. Such a training emphasises manual skill, and the co-ordinated action of hand and eye, and judgment in the control of the process of construction. But judgment necessitates knowledge of those natural processes of which the manufacture is the utilisation. Thus somewhere in technical training an education in scientific knowledge is required. If you minimise the scientific side, you will confine it to the scientific experts; if you maximise it, you will impart it in some measure to the men, and — what is of no less importance — to the directors and managers of the businesses.

Technical education is not necessarily allied exclusively to science on its mental side. It may be an education for an artist or for apprentices to an artistic craft. In that case æsthetic appreciation will have to be cultivated in connection with it.

An evil side of the Platonic culture has been its total neglect of technical education as an ingredient in the complete development of ideal human beings. This neglect has arisen from two disastrous antitheses, namely, that between mind and body, and that between thought and action. I will here interject, solely to avoid criticism, that I am well aware that the Greeks highly valued physical beauty and physical activity. They had however, that perverted sense of values which is the nemesis of slave-owning.

I lay it down as an educational axiom that in teaching you will come to grief as soon as you forget that your pupils have bodies. This is exactly the mistake of the post-renaissance Platonic curriculum. But nature can be kept at bay by no pitchfork; so in English education, being expelled from the class-room, she returned with a cap and bells in the form of all-conquering athleticism.

The connections between intellectual activity and the body, though diffused in every bodily feeling, are focussed in the eyes, the ears, the voice, and the hands. There is a co-ordination of senses and thought, and also a reciprocal influence between brain activity and material creative activity. In this reaction the hands are peculiarly important. It is a moot point whether the human hand created the human brain, or the brain created the hand. Certainly the connection is intimate and reciprocal. Such deep-seated relations are not widely atrophied by a few hundred years of disuse in exceptional families.

The disuse of hand-craft is a contributory cause to the brain-lethargy of aristocracies, which is only mitigated by sport where the concurrent brain-activity is reduced to a minimum and the handcraft lacks subtlety. The necessity for constant writing and vocal exposition is some slight stimulus to the thought-power of the professional classes. Great readers, who exclude other activities, are not distinguished by subtlety of brain. They tend to be timid conventional thinkers. No doubt this is partly due to their excessive knowledge outrunning their powers of thought; but it is partly due to the lack of brain-stimulus from the productive activities of hand or voice.

In estimating the importance of technical education we must rise above the exclusive association of learning with book-learning. First-hand knowledge is the ultimate basis of intellectual life. To a large extent book-learning conveys second-hand information, and as such can never rise to the importance of immediate practice. Our goal is to see the immediate events of our lives as instances of our general ideas. What the learned world tends to offer is one second-hand scrap of information illustrating ideas derived from another second-hand scrap of information. The second-handedness of the learned world is the secret of its mediocrity. It is tame because it has never been scared by facts. The main importance of Francis Bacon's influence does not lie in any peculiar theory of inductive reasoning which he happened to express, but in the revolt against second-hand information of which he was a leader.

The peculiar merit of a scientific education should be, that it bases thought upon first-hand observation; and the corresponding merit of a technical education is, that it follows our deep natural instinct to translate thought into manual skill, and manual activity into thought.

The thought which science evokes is logical thought. Now logic is of two kinds: the logic of discovery and the logic of the discovered.

The logic of discovery consists in the weighing of probabilities, in discarding details deemed to be irrelevant, in divining the general rules according to which events occur, and in testing hypotheses by devising suitable experiments. This is inductive logic.

The logic of the discovered is the deduction of the special events which, under certain circumstances, would happen in obedience to the assumed laws of nature. Thus when the laws are discovered or assumed, their utilisation entirely depends on deductive logic. Without deductive logic science would be entirely useless. It is merely a barren game to ascend from the particular to the general, unless afterwards we can reverse the process and descend from the general to the particular, ascending and descending like the angels on Jacob's ladder. When Newton had divined the law of gravitation he at once proceeded to calculate the earth's attractions on an apple at its surface and on the moon. We may note in passing that inductive logic would be impossible without deductive logic. Thus Newton's calculations were an essential step in his inductive verification of the great law.

Now mathematics is nothing else than the more complicated parts of the art of deductive reasoning, especially where it concerns number, quantity, and space.

In the teaching of science, the art of thought should be taught: namely, the art of forming clear conceptions applying to first-hand experience, the art of divining the general truths which apply, the art of testing divinations, and the art of utilising general truths by reasoning to more particular cases of some peculiar importance. Furthermore, a power of scientific exposition is necessary, so that the relevant issues from a confused mass of ideas can be stated clearly, with due emphasis on important points.

By the time a science, or a small group of sciences, has been taught thus amply, with due regard to the general art of thought, we have gone a long way towards correcting the specialism of science. The worst of a scientific education based, as necessarily must be the case, on one or two particular branches of science, is that the teachers under the influence of the examination system are apt merely to stuff their pupils with the narrow results of these special sciences. It is essential that the generality of the method be continually brought to light and contrasted with the speciality of the particular application. A man who only knows his own science, as a routine peculiar to that science, does not even know that. He has no fertility of thought, no power of quickly seizing the bearing of alien ideas. He will discover nothing, and be stupid in practical applications.

This exhibition of the general in the particular is extremely difficult to effect, especially in the case of younger pupils. The art of education is never easy. To surmount its difficulties, especially those of elementary education, is a task worthy of the highest genius. It is the training of human souls.

Mathematics, well taught, should be the most powerful instrument in gradually implanting this generality of idea. The essence of mathematics is perpetually to be discarding more special ideas in favour of more general ideas, and special methods in favour of general methods. We express the conditions of a special problem in the form of an equation, but that equation will serve for a hundred other problems, scattered through diverse sciences. The general reasoning is always the powerful reasoning, because deductive cogency is the property of abstract form.

Here, again, we must be careful. We shall ruin mathematical education if we use it merely to impress general truths. The general ideas are the means of connecting particular results. After all, it is the concrete special cases which are important. Thus in the handing of mathematics in your results you cannot be too concrete, and in your methods you cannot be too general. The essential course of reasoning is to generalise what is particular, and then to particularise what is general. Without generality there is no reasoning, without concreteness there is no importance.

Concreteness is the strength of technical education. I would remind you that truths which lack the highest generality are not necessarily concrete facts. For example, $x + y = y + x$ is an algebraic truth more general than $2 + 2 = 4$. But "two and two make four" is itself a highly general proposition lacking any element of concreteness. To obtain a concrete proposition immediate intuition of a truth concerning particular objects is requisite; for example, "these two apples and those apples together make four apples" is a concrete proposition, if you have direct perception or immediate memory of the apples.

In order to obtain the full realisation of truths as applying, and not as empty formulæ, there is no alternative to technical education. Mere passive observation is not sufficient. In creation only is there vivid insight into the properties of the object thereby produced. If you want to understand anything, make it yourself, is a sound rule. Your faculties will be alive, your thoughts gain vividness by an immediate translation into acts. Your ideas gain that reality which comes from seeing the limits of their application.

In elementary education this doctrine has long been put into practice. Young children are taught to familiarise themselves with shapes and colours by simple manual operations of cutting out and of sorting. But good though this is, it is not quite what I mean. That is practical experience before you think, experience antecedent to thought in order to create ideas, a very excellent discipline. But technical education should be much more than that: it is creative experience while you think, experience which realises your thought, experience which teaches you to co-ordinate act and thought, experience leading you to associate thought with foresight and foresight with achievement. Technical education gives theory, and a shrewd insight as to where theory fails.

A technical education is not to be conceived as a maimed alternative to the perfect Platonic culture: namely as a defective training unfortunately made necessary by cramped conditions of life. No human being can attain to anything but fragmentary knowledge and a fragmentary training of his capacities. There are, however, three main roads along which we can proceed with good hope of advancing towards the best balance of intellect and character: these are the way of literary culture, the way of scientific culture, the way of technical culture. No one of these methods can be exclusively followed without grave loss of intellectual activity and of character. But a mere mechanical mixture of the three curricula will produce bad results in the shape of scraps of information never interconnected or utilised. We have already noted as one of the strong points of the traditional literary culture that all its parts are co-ordinated. The problem of education is to retain the dominant emphasis, whether literary, scientific or technical, and without loss of co-ordination to infuse into each way of education something of the other two.

To make definite the problem of technical education fix attention on two ages: one thirteen, when elementary education ends; and the other seventeen, when technical education ends so far as it is compressed within a school curriculum. I am aware that for artisans in junior technical schools a three-years' course would be more usual. On the other hand, for naval officers, and for directing classes generally, a longer time can be afforded. We want to consider the principles to govern a curriculum which shall land these children at the age of seventeen in the position of having technical skill useful to the community.

Their technical manual training should start at thirteen, bearing a modest proportion to the rest of their work, and should increase in each year finally to attain to a substantial proportion. Above all things it should not be too specialised. Workshop finish and workshop dodges, adapted to one particular job, should be taught in the commercial workshop, and should form no essential part of the school course. A properly trained worker would pick them up in no time. In all education the main cause of failure is staleness. Technical education is doomed if we conceive it as a system for catching children young and for giving them one highly specialised manual aptitude. The nation has need of a fluidity of labour, not merely from place to place, but also within reasonable limits of allied aptitudes, from one special type of work to another special type. I know that here I am on delicate ground, and I am not claiming that men while they are specialising on one sort of work should spasmodically be set to other kinds. That is a question of trade organisation with which educationalists have no concern. I am only asserting the principles that training should be broader than the ultimate specialisation, and that the resulting power of adaptation to varying demands is advantageous to the workers, to the employers, and to the nation.

In considering the intellectual side of the curriculum we must be guided by the principle of the co-ordination of studies. In general, the intellectual studies most immediately related to manual training will be some branches of science. More than one branch will, in fact, be concerned; and even if that be not the case, it is impossible to narrow down scientific study to a single thin line of thought. It is possible, however, provided that we do not press the classification too far, roughly to classify technical pursuits according to the dominant science involved. We thus find a sixfold division, namely, (1) Geometrical techniques, (2) Mechanical techniques, (3) Physical techniques, (4) Chemical techniques, (5) Biological techniques, (6) Techniques of commerce and of social service.

By this division, it is meant that apart from auxiliary sciences some particular science requires emphasis in the training for most occupations. We can, for example, reckon carpentry, ironmongery, and many artistic crafts among geometrical techniques. Similarly agriculture is a biological technique. Probably cookery, if it includes food catering, would fall midway between biological, physical, and chemical sciences, though of this I am not sure.

The sciences associated with commerce and social service would be partly algebra, including arithmetic and statistics, and partly geography and history. But this section is somewhat heterogeneous in its scientific affinities. Any how the exact way in which technical pursuits are classified in relation to science is a detail. The essential point is, that with some thought it is possible to find scientific courses which illuminate most occupations. Furthermore, the problem is well understood, and has been brilliantly solved in many of the schools of technology and junior technical schools throughout the country.

In passing from science to literature, in our review of the intellectual elements of technical education, we note that many studies hover between the two: for example, history and geography. They are both of them very essential in education, provided that they are the right history and the right geography. Also books giving descriptive accounts of general results, and trains of thought in various sciences fall in the same category. Such books should be partly historical and partly expository of the main ideas which have finally arisen. Their value in education depends on their quality as mental stimulants. They must not be inflated with gas on the wonders of science, and must be informed with a broad outlook.

It is unfortunate that the literary element in education has rarely been considered apart from grammatical study. The historical reason is, that when the modern Platonic curriculum was being formed Latin and Greek were the sole keys which rendered great literature accessible. But there is no necessary connection between literautre and grammar. The great age of Greek literature was already past before the arrival of the grammarians of Alexandria. Of all types of men to-day existing, classical scholars are the most remote from the Greeks of the Periclean times.

Mere literary knowledge is of slight importance. The only thing that matters is, how it is known. The facts related are nothing. Literature only exists to express and develop that imaginative world which is our life, the kingdom which is within us. It follows that the literary side of a technical education should consist in an effort to make the pupils enjoy literature. It does not matter what they know, but the enjoyment is vita. The great English Universities, under whose direct authority school-children are examined in plays of Shakespeare to the certain destruction of their enjoyment, should be prosecuted for soul murder.

Now there are two kinds of intellectual enjoyment: the enjoyment of creation, and the enjoyment of relaxation. They are not necessarily separated. A change of occupation may give the full tide of happiness which comes from the concurrence of both forms of pleasure. The appreciation of literature is really creation. The written word, its music, and its associations, are only the stimuli. The vision which they evoke is our own doing. No one, no genius other than our own, can make our own life live. But except for those engaged in literary occupations, literature is also a relaxation. It gives exercise to that other side which any occupation must suppress during the working hours. Art also has the same function in life as has literature.

To obtain the pleasure of relaxation requires no help. The pleasure is merely to cease doing. Some such pure relaxation is a necessary condition of health. Its dangers are notorious, and to the greater part of the necessary relaxation nature has affixed, not enjoyment, but the oblivion of sleep. Creative enjoyment is the outcome of successful effort and requires help for its initiation. Such enjoyment is necessary for high-speed work and for original achievement.

To speed up production with unrefreshed workmen is a disastrous economic policy. Temporary success will be at the expense of the nation, which, for long years of their lives, will have to support worn-out artisans-unemployables. Equally disastrous is the alternation of spasms of effort with periods of pure relaxation. Such periods are the seed-times of degeneration, unless rigorously curtailed. The normal recreation should be change of activity, satisfying the cravings of instincts. Games afford such activity. Their disconnection emphasises the relaxation, but their excess leaves us empty.

It is here that literature and art should play an essential part in a healthily organised nation. Their services to economic production would be only second to those of sleep or of food. I am not now talking of the training of an artist, but of the use of art as a condition of healthy life. It is analogous to sunshine in the physical world.

When we have once rid our minds of the idea that knowledge is to be exacted, there is no especial difficulty or expense involved in helping the growth of artistic enjoyment. All school-children could be sent at regular intervals to neighbouring theatres where suitable plays could be subsidised. Similarly for concerts and cinema films. Pictures are more doubtful in their popular attraction; but interesting representations of scenes or ideas which the children have read about would probably appeal. The pupils themselves should be encouraged in artistic efforts. Above all the art of reading aloud should be cultivated. The Roger de Coverley essays of Addison are perfect examples of readable prose.

Art and literature have not merely an indirect effect on the main energies of life. Directly, they give vision. The world spreads wide beyond the deliverances of material sense, with subtleties of reaction and with pulses of emotion. Vision is the necessary antecedent to control and to direction. In the contest of races which in its final issues will be decided in the workshops and not on the battlefield, the victory will belong to those who are masters of stores of trained nervous energy, working under conditions favourable to growth. One such essential condition is Art.

If there had been time, there are other things which I should like to have said: for example, to advocate the inclusion of one foreign language in all education. From direct observation I know this to be possible for artisan children. But enough has been put before you to make plain the principles with which we should undertake national education.

In conclusion, I recur to the thought of the Benedictines, who saved for mankind the vanishing civilisation of the ancient world by linking together knowledge, labour, and moral energy. Our danger is to conceive practical affairs as the kingdom of evil, in which success is only possible by the extrusion of ideal aims. I believe that such a conception is a fallacy directly negatived by practical experience. In education this error takes the form of a mean view of technical training. Our forefathers in the dark ages saved themselves by embodying high ideals in great organisations. It is our task，without servile imitation，boldly to exercise our creative energies.

CHAPTER V

The Place of Classics in Education

The future of classics in this country is not going mainly to be decided by the joy of classics to a finished scholar, and by the utility of scholarly training for scholarly avocations. The pleasure and the discipline of character to be derived from an education based mainly on classical literature and classical philosophy has been demonstrated by centuries of experience. The danger to classical learning does not arise because classical scholars now love classics less than their predecessors. It arises in this way. In the past classics reigned throughout the whole sphere of higher education. There were no rivals; and accordingly all students were steeped in classics throughout their school life, and its domination at the universities was only challenged by the narrow discipline of mathematics. There were many consequences to this state of things. There was a large demand for classical scholars for the mere purposes of tution, there was a classical tone in all learned walks of life, so that aptitude for classics was a synonym for ability; and finally every boy who gave the slightest promise in that direction cultivated his natural or acquired interest in classical learning. All this is gone, and gone for ever. Humpty Dumpty was a good egg so long as he was on the top of the wall, but you can never set him up again. There are now other disciplines each involving topics of wide-spread interest, with complex relationships, and exhibiting in their development the noblest feats of genius in its stretch of imagination and its philosophic intuition. Almost every walk of life is now a learned profession, and demands one or more of these disciplines as the substratum for its technical skill. Life is short, and the plastic period when the brain is apt for acquirement is still shorter. Accordingly, even if all children were fitted for it, it is absolutely impossible to maintain a system of education in which a complete training as a classical scholar is the necessary preliminary to the acquirement of other intellectual disciplines. As a member of the Prime Minister's Committee on the Place of Classics in Education it was my misfortune to listen to much ineffectual wailing from witnesses on the mercenary tendencies of modern parents. I do not believe that the modern parent of any class is more mercenary than his predecessors. When classics was the road to advancement, classics was the popular subject for study. Opportunity has now shifted its location, and classics is in danger. Was is not Aristotle who said that a good income was a desirable adjunct to an intellectual life? I wonder how Aristotle, as a parent, would have struck a headmaster of one of our great public schools. From my slight knowledge of Aristotle, I suspect that there would have been an argument, and that Aristotle would have got the best of it. I have been endeavouring to appreciate at its full value the danger which besets classics in the educational curriculum. The conclusion that I draw is that the future classics will be decided during the next few years in the secondary schools of this country. Within a generation the great public schools will have to follow suit, whether they like it or not.

The situation is dominated by the fact that in the future ninety per cent. of the pupils who leave school at the age of eighteen will never again read a classical book in the original. In the case of pupils leaving at an earlier age, the estimate of ninety per cent. may be changed to one of ninety-nine per cent. I have heard and read many a beautiful exposition or the value of classics to the scholar who reads Plato and Virgil in his armchair. But these people will never read classics either in their armchairs or in any other situation. We have got to produce a defence of classics which applies to this ninety per cent. of the pupils. If classics is swept out of the curriculum for this section, the remaining ten per cent. will soon vanish. No school will have the staff to teach them. The problem is urgent.

It would, however, be a great mistake to conclude that classics is faced with a hostile opinion either in the learned professions or from leaders of industry who have devoted attention to the relation between education and efficiency. The last discussion, public or private, on this subject, at which I have been present was a short and vigorous one at one of the leading committees of a great modern university. The three representatives of the Faculty of Science energetically urged the importance of classics on the ground of its value as a preliminary discipline for scientists. I mention this incident because in my experience it is typical.

We must remember that the whole problem of intellectual education is controlled by lack of time. If Methuselah was not a well-educated man, it was his own fault or that of his teachers. But our task is to deal with five years of secondary school-life. Classics can only be defended on the ground that within that period, and sharing that period with other subjects, it can produce a necessary enrichment of intellectual character more quickly than any alternative discipline directed to the same object.

In classics we endeavour by a thorough study of language to develop the mind in the regions of logic, philosophy, history and of æsthetic apprehension of literary beauty. The learning of the languages — Latin or Greek — is a subsidiary means for the furtherance of this ulterior object. When the object has been obtained, the languages can be dropped unless opportunity and choice lead to their further pursuit. There are certain minds, and among them some of the best, for which the analysis of language is not the avenue of approach to the goal of culture. For these a butterfly or a steam-engine has a wider range of significance than a Latin sentence. This is especially the case where there is a touch of genius arising from vivid apprehensions stimulating originality of thought. The assigned verbal sentence almost always says the wrong thing for such people, and confuses them by its trivial irrelevance.

But on the whole the normal avenue is the analysis of language. It represents the greatest common measure for the pupils, and by far the most manageable job for the teachers.

At this point I must cross-question myself. My other self asks me, Why do you not teach the children logic, if you want them to learn that subject? Wouldn't that be the obvious procedure? I answer in the words of a great man who to our infinite loss has recently died, Sanderson, the late headmaster of Oundle. His phrase was, They learn by contact. The meaning to be attached to this saying goes to the root of the true practice of education. It must start from the particular fact, concrete and definite for individual apprehension, and must gradually evolve towards the general idea. The devil to be avoided is the cramming of general statements which have no reference to individual personal experiences.

Now apply this principle to the determination of the best method to help a child towards a philosophical analysis of thought. I will put it in more homely style, What is the best way to make a child clear-headed in its thoughts and its statements? The general statements of a logic book have no reference to anything the child has ever heard of. They belong to the grown-up stage of education at — or not far from — the university. You must begin with the analysis of familiar English sentences. But this grammatical procedure, if prolonged beyond its elementary stages, is horribly dry. Furthermore, it has the disadvantage that it only analyses so far as the English language analyses. It does nothing to throw light upon the complex significance of English phrases, and words, and habits of mental procedure. Your next step is to teach the child a foreign language. Here you gain an enormous advantage. You get away from the nauseating formal drill for the drill's sake. The analysis is now automatic, while the pupil's attention is directed to expressing his wants in the language, or to understanding someone who is speaking to him, or to making out what an author has written. Every language embodies a definite type of mentality, and two languages necessarily display to the pupil some contrast between their two types. Common sense dictates that you start with French as early as possible in the child's life. If you are wealthy, you will provide a French nursery-governess. Less fortunate children will start French in a secondary school about the age of twelve. The direct method is probably used, by which the child is immersed in French throughout the lesson and is taught to think in French without the intervention of English between the French words and their significations. Even an average child will get on well, and soon acquires the power of handling and understanding simple French sentences. As I have said before, the gain is enormous; and, in addition, a useful instrument for after life is acquired. The sense for language grows, a sense which is the subconscious appreciation of language as an instrument of definite structure.

It is exactly now that the initiation of Latin is the best stimulus for mental expansion. The elements of Latin exhibit a peculiarly plain concrete case of language as a structure. Provided that your mind has grown to the level of that idea, the fact stares you in the face. You can miss it over English and French. Good English of a simple kind will go straight into slipshod French, and conversely good French will go into slipshod English. The difference between the slipshod French of the literal translation and the good French, which ought to have been written, is often rather subtle for that stage of mental growth, and is not always easy to explain. Both languages have the same common modernity of expression. But in the case of English and Latin the contrast of structure is obvious, and yet not so wide as to forman insuperable difficulty.

According to the testimony of schoolmasters, Latin is rather a popular subject; I know that as a schoolboy I enjoyed it myself. I believe that this popularity is due to the sense of enlightenment that accompanies its study. You know that you are finding out something. The words somehow stick in the sentences in a different way to what they do either in English or French, with odd queer differences of connotation. Of course in a way Latin is a more barbaric language than English. It is one step nearer to the sentence as the unanalysed unit.

This brings me to my next point. In my catalogue of the gifts of Latin I placed philosophy between logic and history. In this connection, that is its true place. The philosophic instinct which Latin evokes, hovers between the two and enriches both. The analysis of thought involved in translation, English to Latin or Latin to English, imposes that type of experience which is the necessary introduction to philosophic logic. If in after life your job is to think, render thanks to Providence which ordained that, for five years of your youth, you did a Latin prose once a week and daily construed some Latin author. The introduction to any subject is the process of learning by contact. To that majority of people for whom language is the readiest stimulus to thought-activity, the road towards enlightenment of understanding runs from simple English grammar to French, from French to Latin, and also traverses the elements of Geometry and of Algebra. I need not remind my readers that I can claim Plato's authority for the general principle which I am upholding.

From the philosophy of thought we now pass to the philosophy of history. I again recur to Sanderson's great saying, They learn by contact. How on earth is a child to learn history by contact? The original documents, charters and laws and diplomatic correspondence, are double Dutch to it. A game of football is perhaps a faint reflection of the Battle of Marathon. But that is only to say that human life in all ages and circumstances has common qualities. Furthermore, all this diplomatic and political stuff with which we cram children is a very thin view of history. What is really necessary is that we should have an instinctive grasp of the flux of outlook, and of thought, and of æsthetic and racial impulses, which have controlled the troubled history of mankind. Now the Roman Empire is the bottleneck through which the vintage of the past has passed into modern life. So far as European civilisation is concerned the key to history is a comprehension of the mentality of Rome and the work of its Empire.

In the language of Rome, embodying in literary form the outlook of Rome, we possess the simplest material, by contact with which we can gain appreciation of the tides of change in human affairs. The mere obvious relations of the languages, French and English, to Latin are in themselves a philosophy of history. Consider the contrast which English presents to French: the entire break of English with the civilised past of Britain and the slow creeping back of words and phrases of Mediterranean origin with their cargoes of civilised meaning: in French we have continuity or development, amid obvious traces of rude shock. I am not asking for pretentious abstract lectures on such points. The thing illustrates itself. An elementary knowledge of French and Latin with a mother-tongue of English imparts the requisite atmosphere of reality to the story of the racial wanderings which created our Europe. Language is the incarnation of the mentality of the race which fashioned it. Every phrase and word embodies some habitual idea of men and women as they ploughed their fields, tended their homes, and built their cities. For this reason there are no true synonyms as between words and phrases in different languages. The whole of what I have been saying is merely an embroidery upon this single theme, and our endeavour to emphasise its critical importance. In English, French, and Latin we possess a triangle, such that one pair of vertices, English and French, exhibits a pair of diverse expressions of two chief types of modern mentality, and the relations of these vertices to the third exhibit alternative processes of derivation from the Mediterranean civilisation of the past. This is the essential triangle of literary culture, containing within itself freshness of contrast, embracing both the present and the past. It ranges through space and time. These are the grounds by which we justify the assertion, that in the acquirement of French and Latin is to be found the easiest mode of learning by contact the philosophy of logic and the philosophy of history. Apart from some such intimate experience, your analyses of thought and your histories of actions are mere sounding brasses. I am not claiming, and I do not for a moment believe, that this route of education is more than the simplest, easiest route for the majority of pupils. I am certain that there is a large minority for which the emphasis should be different. But I do believe that it is the route which can give the greatest success for the largest majority. It has also the advantage of having survived the test of experience. I believe that large modifications require to be introduced into existing practice to adapt it for present needs. But on the whole this foundation of literary education involves the best understood tradition and the largest corps of experienced scholarly teachers who can realise it in practice.

The reader has perhaps observed that I have as yet said nothing of the glories of Roman literature. Of course the teaching of Latin must proceed by the means of reading Latin literature with the pupils. This literature possesses vigorous authors who have succeeded in putting across the footlights the Roman mentality on a variety of topics, including its appreciation of Greek thought. One of the merits of Roman literature is its comparative lack of outstanding genius. There is very little aloofness about its authors, they express their race and very little which is beyond all differences of race. With the exception of Lucretius, you always feel the limitations under which they are working. Tacitus expressed the views of the Die-hards of the Roman Senate, and, blind to the achievements of Roman provincial administration, could only see that Greek freedmen were replacing Roman aristocrats. The Roman Empire and the mentality which created it absorbed the genius of Romans. Very little of Roman literature will find its way into the kingdom of heaven, when the events of this world will have lost their importance. The languages of heaven will be Chinese, Greek, French, German, Italian, and English, and the blessed Saints will dwell with delight on these golden expressions of eternal life. They will be wearied with the moral fervour of Hebrew literature in its battle with a vanished evil, and with Roman authors who have mistaken the Forum for the footstool of the living God.

We do not teach Latin in the hope that Roman authors, read in the original, may be for our pupils companions through life. English literature is so much greater: it is richer, deeper, and more subtle. If your tastes are philosophic, would you abandon Bacon and Hobbes, Locke, Berkeley, Hume, and Mill for the sake of Cicero? Not unless your taste among the moderns would lead you to Martin Tupper. Perhaps you crave for reflection on the infinite variety of human existence and the reaction of character to circumstance. Would you exchange Shakespeare and the English novelists for Terence, Plautus, and the banquet of Trimalchio? Then there are our humorists, Sheridan, Dickens, and others. Did anyone ever laugh like that as he read a Latin author? Cicero was a great orator, staged amid the pomp of Empire. England also can show statesmen inspired to expound policies with imagination. I will not weary you with an extended catalogue embracing poetry and history. I simply wish to justify my scepticism as to the claim for Latin literature that it expresses with outstanding perfection the universal element in human life. It cannot laugh and it can hardly cry.

You must not tear it from its context. It is not a literature in the sense that Greece and England have produced literatures, expressions of universal human feeling. Latin has one theme and that is Rome — Rome, the mother of Europe, and the great Babylon, the harlot whose doom is described by the writer of the Apocalypse: "Standing afar off for the fear of her torment, saying, Alas, alas, that great city Babylon, that mighty city! for in one hour is thy judgment come. And the merchants of the earth shall weep and mourn over her; for no man buyeth their merchandise any more:

"The merchandise of gold, and silver, and precious stones, and of pearls, and fine linen, and purple, and silk, and scarlet, and all thyine wood, and all manner vessels of ivory, and all manner vessels of most precious wood, and of brass, and iron, and marble;

" And cinnamon, and odours, and ointments, and frankincense, and wine, and oil, and fine flour, and wheat, and beasts, and sheep, and horses, and chariots, and slaves, and souls of men. "

This is the way Roman civilisation appeared to an early Christian. But then Christianity itself is part of the outcrop of the ancient world which Rome passed on to Europe. We inherit the dual aspect of the civilisations of the eastern Mediterranean.

The function of Latin literature is its expression of Rome. When to England and France your imagination can add Rome in the background, you have laid firm the foundations of culture. The understanding of Rome leads back to that Mediterranean civilisation of which Rome was the last phase, and it automatically exhibits the geography of Europe, and the functions of seas and rivers and mountains and plains. The merit of this study in the education of youth is its concreteness, its inspiration to action, and the uniform greatness of persons, in their characters and their staging. Their aims were great, their virtues were great, and their vices were great. They had the saving merit of sinning with cart-ropes. Moral education is impossible apart from the habitual vision of greatness. If we are not great, it does not matter what we do or what is the issue. Now the sense of greatness is an immediate intuition and not the conclusion of an argument. It is permissible for youth in the agonies of religious conversion to entertain the feeling of being a worm and no man, so long as there remains the conviction of greatness sufficient to justify the eternal wrath of God. The sense of greatness is the groundwork of morals. We are at the threshold of a democratic age, and it remains to be determined whether the equality of man is to be realised on a high level or a low level. There was never a time in which it was more essential to hold before the young the vision of Rome: in itself a great drama, and with issues greater than itself. We are now already immersed in the topic of æsthetic appreciation of literary quality. It is here that the tradition of classical teaching requires most vigorous reformation for adaptation to new conditions. It is obsessed with the formation of finished classical scholars. The old tradition was remorselessly to devote the initial stages to the acquirement of the languages and then to trust to the current literary atmosphere to secure enjoyment of the literature. During the latter part of the nineteenth century other subjects encroached on the available time. Too often the result has been merely time wasted in the failure to learn the language. I often think that the ruck of pupils from great. English schools show a deplorable lack of intellectual zest, arising from this sense of failure. The school course of classics must be planned so that a definite result is clearly achieved. There has been too great a product of failures on the road to an ambitious ideal of scholarship.

In approaching every work of art we have to comport

ourselves suitably in regard to two factors, scale and pace. It is not fair to the architect if you examine St. Peter's at Rome with a microscope, and the Odyssey becomes insipid if you read it at the rate of five lines a day. Now the problem before us is exactly this. We are dealing with pupils who will never know Latin well enough to read it quickly, and the vision to be illumed is of vast scale, set in the history of all time. A careful study of scale and pace, and of the correlative functions of various parts of our work, should appear to be essential. I have not succeeded in hitting upon any literature which deals with this question with reference to the psychology of the pupils. Is it a masonic secret?

I have often noticed that, if in an assembly of great scholars the topic of translations be introduced, they function as to their emotions and sentiments in exactly the same way as do decent people in the presence of a nasty sex-problem. A mathematician has no scholastic respectability to lose, so I will face the question.

It follows from the whole line of thought which I have been developing, that an exact appreciation of the meanings of Latin words, of the ways in which ideas are connected in grammatical constructions, and of the whole hang of a Latin sentence with its distribution of emphasis, forms the very backbone of the merits which I ascribe to the study of Latin. Accordingly and woolly vagueness of teaching, slurring over the niceties of language defeats the whole ideal which I have set before you. The use of a translation to enable the pupils to get away from the Latin as quickly as possible, or to avoid the stretch of mind in grappling with construction, is erroneous. Exactness, definiteness, and independent power of analysis are among the main prizes of the whole study.

But we are still confronted with the inexorable problem of pace, and with the short four or five years of the whole course. Every poem is meant to be read within certain limits of time. The contrasts, and the images, and the transition of moods must correspond with the sway of rhythms in the human spirit. These have their periods, which refuse to be stretched beyond certain limits. You may take the noblest poetry in the world, and, if you stumble through it at snail's pace, it collapses from a work of art into a rubbish heap. Think of the child's mind as he pores over his work: he reads "as when," then follows a pause with a reference to the dictionary, then he goes on — "an eagle," then another reference to the dictionary, followed by a period of wonderment over the construction, and so on, and so on. Is that going to help him to the vision of Rome? Surely, surely, common sense dictates that you procure the best literary translation you can, the one which best preserves the charm and vigour of the original, and that you read it aloud at the right pace, and append such comments as will elucidate the comprehension. The attack on the Latin will then be fortified by the sense that it enshrines a living work of art.

But someone objects that a translation is woefully inferior to the original. Of course it is, that is why the boy has to master the Latin original. When the original has been mastered, it can be given its proper pace. I plead for an initial sense of the unity of the whole, to be given by a translation at the right pace, and for a final appreciation of the full value of the whole to be given by the original at the right place. Wordsworth talks of men of science who "murder to dissect." In the past, classical scholars have been veritable assassins compared to them. The sense to beauty is eager and vehement, and should be treated with the reverence which is its due. But I go further. The total bulk of Latin literature necessary to convey the vision of Rome is much greater than the students can possibly accomplish in the original. They should read more Virgil than they can read in Latin, more Lucretius than they can read in Latin, more history than they can read in Latin, more Cicero than they can read in Latin. In the study of an author the selected portions in Latin should illumine a fuller disclosure of his whole mind, although without the force of his own words in his own language. It is, however, a grave evil if no part of an author be read in his own original words.

The difficulty of scale is largely concerned in the presentation of classical history. Everything set before the young must be rooted in the particular and the individual. Yet we want to illustrate the general characters of whole periods. We must make students learn by contact. We can exhibit the modes of life by visual representations. There are photographs of buildings, casts of statues, and pictures from vases or frescoes illustrating religious myths or domestic scenes. In this way we can compare Rome with the preceding civilisation of the eastern Mediterranean, and with the succeeding period of the Middle Ages. It is essential to get into the children's minds how men altered, in their appearance, their dwellings, their technology, their art, and their religious beliefs. We must imitate the procedure of the zoologists who have the whole of animal creation on their hands. They teach by demonstrating typical examples. We must do likewise, to exhibit the position of Rome in history.

The life of man is founded on Technology, Science, Art and Religion. All four are inter-connected and issue from his total mentality. But there are particular intimacies between Science and Technology, and between Art and Religion. No social organisation can be understood without reference to these four underlying factors. A modern steam-engine does the work of a thousand slaves in the ancient world. Slave-raiding was the key to much of the ancient imperialism. A modern printing-press is an essential adjunct to a modern democracy. The key to modern mentality is the continued advance of science with the consequential shift of ideas and progress of technology. In the ancient world Mesopotamia and Egypt were made possible by irrigation. But the Roman Empire existed by virtue of the grandest application of technology that the world had hitherto seen: its roads, its bridges, its aqueducts, its tunnels, its sewers, its vast buildings, its organised merchant navies, its military science, its metallurgy, and its agriculture. This was the secret of the extension and the unity of Roman civilisation. I have often wondered why Roman engineers did not invent the steam-engine. They might have done it at any time, and then how different would have been the history of the world. I ascribe it to the fact that they lived in a warm climate and had not introduced tea and coffee. In the eighteenth century thousands of men sat by fires and watched their kettles boil. We all know of course that Hiero of Alexandria invented some slight anticipation. All that was wanted was that the Roman engineers should have been impressed with the motive force of steam by the humble process of watching their kettles.

The history of mankind has yet to be set in its proper relation to the gathering momentum of technological advance. Within the last hundred years, a developed science has wedded itself to a developed technology and a new epoch has opened.

Similarly about a thousand years before Christ the first great literary epoch commenced when the art of writing was finally popularised. In its earlier dim origins the art had been used for traditional hieratic formulæ and for the formal purposes of governmental record and chronicle. It is a great mistake to think that in the past the full sweep of a new invention has even been anticipated at its first introduction. It is not even so at the present day, when we are all trained to meditate on the possibilities of new ideas. But in the past, with its different direction of thought, novelty slowly ate its way into the social system. Accordingly writing, as a stimulus to the preservation of individual novelty of thought, was but slowly grasped on the borders of the eastern Mediterranean. When the realisation of its possibilities was complete, in the hands of the Greeks and the Hebrews, civilisation took a new turn; though the general influence of Hebrew mentality was delayed for a thousand years till the advent of Christianity. But it was now that their prophets were recording their inward thoughts, when Greek civilisation was beginning to take shape.

What I want to illustrate is that in the large scale treatment of history necessary for the background and the foreground of the vision of Rome, the consecutive chronicle of political events on the scale traditional to our histories absolutely vanishes. Even verbal explanations partly go into the background. We must utilise models, and pictures, and diagrams, and charts to exhibit typical examples of the growth of technology and its impact on the current modes of life. In the same way art, in its curious fusion with utility and with religion, both expresses the actual inward life of imagination and changes it by its very expression. The children can see the art of previous epochs in models and pictures, and sometimes the very objects in museums. The treatment of the history of the past must not start with generalised statements but with concrete examples exhibiting the slow succession of period to period, and of mode of life to mode of life, and of race to race.

The same concreteness of treatment must apply when we come to the literary civilisations of the eastern Mediterranean. When you come to think of it, the whole claim for the importance of classics rests on the basis that there is no substitute for first-hand knowledge. In so far as Greece and Rome are the founders of European civilisation, a knowledge of history means above all things a first-hand knowledge of the thoughts of Greeks and Romans. Accordingly, to put the vision of Rome into its proper setting, I urge that the pupils should read at first hand some few examples of Greek literature. Of course it must be in translation. But I prefer a translation of what a Greek actually said, to any talk about the Greeks written by an Englishman, however well he has done it. Books about Greece should come after some direct knowledge of Greece.

The sort of reading I mean is a verse translation of the Odyssey, some Herodotus, some choruses of plays translated by Gilbert Murray, some lives of Plutarch, especially the part about Archimedes in the life of Marcellus, and the definitions and axioms and one or two propositions from Euclid's Elements in the exact scholarly translation of Heath. In all this, just enough explanation is wanted to give the mental environment of the authors. The marvellous position of Rome in relation to Europe comes from the fact that it has transmitted to us a double inheritance. It received the Hebrew religious thought, and has passed on to Europe its fusion with Greek civilisation. Rome itself stands for the impress of organization and unity upon diverse fermenting elements. Roman Law embodies the secret of Roman greatness in its Stoic respect for intimate rights of human nature within an iron framework of empire. Europe is always flying apart because of the diverse explosive character of its inheritance, and coming together because it can never shake off that impress of unity it has received from Rome. The history of Europe is the history of Rome curbing the Hebrew and the Greek, with their various impulses of religion, and of science, and of art, and of quest for material comfort, and of lust of domination, which are all at daggers drawn with each other. The vision of Rome is the vision of the unity of civilisation.

CHAPTER VI

The Mathematical Curriculum

The situation in regard to education at the present time cannot find its parallel without going back for some centuries to the breakup of the mediæval traditions of learning. Then, as now, the traditional intellectual outlook, despite the authority which it had justly acquired from its notable triumphs, had grown to be too narrow for the interests of mankind. The result of this shifting of human interest was a demand for a parallel shifting of the basis of education, so as to fit the pupils for the ideas which later in life would in fact occupy their minds. Any serious fundamental change in the intellectual outlook of human society must necessarily be followed by an educational revolution. It may be delayed for a generation by vested interests or by the passionate attachment of some leaders of thought to the cycle of ideas within which they received their own mental stimulus at an impressionable age. But the law is inexorable that education to be living and effective must be directed to informing pupils with those ideas, and to creating for them those capacities which will enable them to appreciate the current thought of their epoch.

There is no such thing as a successful system of education in a vacuum, that is to say, a system which is divorced from immediate contact with the existing intellectual atmosphere. Education which is not modern shares the fate of all organic things which are kept too long.

But the blessed word "modern" does not really solve our

difficulties. What we mean is, relevant to modern thought, either in the ideas imparted or in the aptitudes produced. Something found out only yesterday may not really be modern in this sense. It may belong to some bygone system of thought prevalent in a previous age, or, what is very much more likely, it may be too recondite. When we demand that education should be relevant to modern thought, we are referring to thoughts broadly spread throughout cultivated society. It is this question of the unfitness of recondite subjects for use in general education which I wish to make the keynote of my address this afternoon.

It is in fact rather a delicate subject for mathematicians. Outsiders are apt to accuse our subject of being recondite. Let us grasp the nettle at once and frankly admit that in general opinion it is the very typical example of reconditeness. By this word I do not mean difficulty, but that the ideas involved are of highly special application, and rarely influence thought.

This liability to reconditeness is the characteristic evil which is apt to destroy the utility of mathematics in liberal education. So far as it clings to the educational use of the subject, so far we must acquiesce in a miserably low level of mathematical attainment among cultivated people in general. I yield to no one in my anxiety to increase the educational scope of mathematics. The way to achieve this end is not by a mere blind demand for more mathematics. We must face the real difficulty which obstructs its extended use.

Is the subject recondite? Now, viewed as a whole, I think it is. *Securus judicat orbis terrarum* — the general judgment of mankind is sure.

The subject as it exists in the minds and in the books of students of mathematics *is* recondite. It proceeds by deducing innumerable special results from general ideas, each result more recondite than the preceding. It is not my task this afternoon to defend mathematics as a subject for profound study. It can very well take care of itself. What I want to emphasise is, that the very reasons which make this science a delight to its students are reasons which obstruct its use as an educational instrument — namely, the boundless wealth of deductions from the interplay of general theorems, their complication, their apparent remoteness from the ideas from which the argument started, the variety of methods, and their purely abstract character which brings, as its gift, eternal truth.

Of course, all these characteristics are of priceless value to students; for ages they have fascinated some of the keenest intellects. My only remark is that, except for a highly selected class, they are fatal in education. The pupils are bewildered by a multiplicity of detail, without apparent relevance either to great ideas or to ordinary thoughts. The extension of this sort of training in the direction of acquiring more detail is the last measure to be desired in the interests of education.

The conclusion at which we arrive is, that mathematics, if it is to be used in general education, must be subjected to a rigorous process of selection and adaptation. I do not mean, what is of course obvious, that however much time we devote to the subject the average pupil will not get very far. But that, however limited the progress, certain characteristics of the subject, natural at any stage, must be rigorously excluded. The science as presented to young pupils must lose its aspect of reconditeness. It must, on the fact of it, deal directly and simply with a few general ideas of farreaching importance.

Now, in this matter of the reform of mathematical instruction, the present generation of teachers may take a very legitimate pride in its achievements. It has shown immense energy in reform, and has accomplished more than would have been thought possible in so short a time. It is not always recognised how difficult is the task of changing a well-established curriculum entrenched behind public examinations.

But for all that, great progress has been made, and, to put the matter at its lowest, the old dead tradition has been broken up. I want to indicate this afternoon the guiding idea which should direct our efforts at reconstruction. I have already summed it up in a phrase, namely, we must aim at the elimination of reconditeness from the educational use of the subject.

Our courses of instruction should be planned to illustrate simply a succession of ideas of obvious importance. All pretty divagations should be rigorously excluded. The goal to be aimed at is that the pupil should acquire familiarity with abstract thought, should realise how it applies to particular concrete circumstances, and should know how to apply general methods to its logical investigation. With this educational ideal nothing can be worse than the aimless accretion of theorems in our text-books, which acquire their position merely because the children can be made to learn them and examiners can set neat questions on them. The bookwork to be learnt should all be very important as illustrating ideas. The examples set — and let there be as many examples as teachers find necessary — should be direct illustrations of the theorems, either by way of abstract particular cases or by way of application to concrete phenomena. Here it is worth remarking that it is quite useless to simplify the bookwork, if the examples set in examinations in fact require an extended knowledge of recondite details. There is a mistaken idea that problems test ability and genius, and that bookwork tests cram. This is not my experience. Only boys who have been specially crammed for scholarships can ever do a problem paper successfully. Bookwork properly set, not in mere snippets according to the usual bad plan, is a far better test of ability, provided that it is supplemented by direct examples. But this is a digression on the bad influence of examinations on teaching.

The main ideas which lie at the base of mathematics are not at all recondite. They are abstract. But one of the main objects of the inclusion of mathematics in a liberal education is to train the pupils to handle abstract ideas. The science constitutes the first large group of abstract ideas which naturally occur to the mind in any precise form. For the purposes of education, mathematics consists of the relations of number, the relations of quantity, and the relations of space. This is not a general definition of mathematics, which, in my opinion, is a much more general science. But we are now discussing the use of mathematics in education. These three groups of relations, concerning number, quantity, and space, are interconnected.

Now, in education we proceed from the particular to the general. Accordingly, children should be taught the use of these ideas by practice among simple examples. My point is this: The goal should be, not an aimless accumulation of special mathematical theorems, but the final recognition that the preceding years of work have illustrated those relations of number, and of quantity, and of space, which are of fundamental importance. Such a training should lie at the base of all philosophical thought. In fact elementary mathematics rightly conceived would give just that philosophical discipline of which the ordinary mind is capable. But what at all costs we ought to avoid, is the pointless accumulation of details. As many examples as you like; let the children work at them for terms, or for years. But these examples should be direct illustrations of the main ideas. In this way, and this only, can the fatal reconditeness be avoided.

I am not now speaking in particular of those who are to be professional mathematicians, o or of those who for professional reasons require a knowledge of certain mathematical details. We are considering the liberal education of all students, including these two classes. This general use of mathematics should be the simple study of a few general truths, well illustrated by practical examples. This study should be conceived by itself, and completely separated in idea from the professional study mentioned above, for which it would make a most excellent preparation. Its final stage should be the recognition of the general truths which the work done has illustrated. As far as I can make out, at present the final stage is the proof of some property of circles connected with triangles. Such properties are immensely interesting to mathematicians. But are they not rather recondite, and what is the precise relation of such theorems to the ideal of a liberal education? The end of all the grammatical studies of the student in classics is to read Virgil and Horace — the greatest thoughts of the greatest men. Are we content, when pleading for the adequate representation in education of our own science, to say that the end of a mathematical training is that the student should know the properties of the nine-point circle? I ask you frankly, is it not rather a "come down"?

This generation of mathematical teachers has done so much strenuous work in the way of reorganising mathematical instruction that there is no need to despair of its being able to elaborate a curriculum which shall leave in the minds of the pupils something even nobler than "the ambiguous case."

Let us think how this final review, closing the elementary course, might be conducted for the more intelligent pupils. Partly no doubt it requires a general oversight of the whole work done, considered without undue detail so as to emphasise the general ideas used, and their possibilities of importance when subjected to further study. Also the analytical and geometrical ideas find immediate application in the physical laboratory where a course of simple experimental mechanics should have been worked through. Here the point of view is twofold, the physical ideas and the mathematical ideas illustrate each other.

The mathematical ideas are essential to the precise formulation of the mechanical laws. The idea of a precise law of nature, the extent to which such laws are in fact verified in our experience, and the role of abstract thought in their formulation, then become practically apparent to the pupil. The whole topic of course requires detailed development with full particular illustration, and is not suggested as requiring merely a few bare abstract statements.

It would, however, be a grave error to put too much emphasis on the mere process of direct explanation of the previous work by way of final review. My point is, that the latter end of the course should be so selected that in fact the general ideas underlying all the previous mathematical work should be brought into prominence. This may well be done by apparently entering on a new subject. For example, the ideas of quantity and the ideas of number are fundamental to all precise thought. In the previous stages they will not have been sharply separated; and children are, rightly enough, pushed on to algebra without too much bother and quantity. But the more intelligent among them at the end of their curriculum would gain immensely by a careful consideration of those fundamental properties of quantity in general which lead to the introduction of numerical measurement. This is a topic which also has the advantage that the necessary books are actually to hand. Euclid's fifth book is regarded by those qualified to judge as one of the triumphs of Greek mathematics. It deals with this very point. Nothing can be more characteristic of the hopelessly illiberal character of the traditional mathematical education than the fact that this book has always been omitted. It deals with ideas, and therefore was ostracised. Of course a careful selection of the more important propositions and a careful revision of the argument are required. The whole book would not be wanted, but just the few propositions which embody the fundamental ideas. The subject is not fit for backward pupils; but certainly it could be made interesting to the more advanced class. There would be great scope for interesting discussion as to the nature of quantity, and the tests which we should apply to ascertain when we are dealing with quantities. The work would not be at all in the air, but would be illustrated at every stage by reference to actual examples of cases where the quantitative character is absent, or obscure, or doubtful, or evident. Temperature, heat, electricity, pleasure and pain, mass and distance could all be considered.

Another idea which requires illustration is that of functionality. A function in analysis is the counterpart of a law in the physical universe, and of a curve in geometry. Children have studied the relations of functions to curves from the first beginning of their study of algebra, namely in drawing graphs. Of recent years there has been a great reform in respect to graphs. But at its present stage it has either gone too far or not far enough. It is not enough merely to draw a graph. The idea behind the graph — like the man behind the gun — is essential in order to make it effective. At present there is some tendency merely to set the children to draw curves, and there to leave the whole question.

In the study of simple algebraic functions and of trigonometrical functions we are initiating the study of the precise expression of physical laws. Curves are another way of representing these laws. The simple fundamental laws — such as the inverse square and the direct distance — should be passed under review, and the applications of the simple functions to express important concrete cases of physical laws considered. I cannot help thinking that the final review of this topic might well take the form of a study of some of the main ideas of the differential calculus applied to simple curves. There is nothing particularly difficult about the conception of a rate of change; and the differentiation of a few powers of x, such as x^2, x^3, etc., could easily be effected; perhaps by the aid of geometry even $\sin x$ and $\cos x$ could be differentiated. If we once abandon our fatal habit of cramming the children with theorems which they do not understand, and will never use, there will be plenty of time to concentrate their attention on really important topics. We can give them familiarity with conceptions which really influence thought.

Before leaving this topic of physical laws and mathematical

VI *The Mathematical Curriculum*

functions, there are other points to be noticed. The fact that the precise law is never really verified by observation in its full precision is capable of easy illustration and of affording excellent examples. Again, statistical laws, namely laws which are only satisfied on the average by large numbers, can easily be studied and illustrated. In fact a slight study of statistical methods and their application to social phenomena affords one of the simplest examples of the application of algebraic ideas.

Another way in which the students' ideas can be generalised is by the use of the History of Mathematics, conceived not as a mere assemblage of the dates and names of men, but as an exposition of the general current of thought which occasioned the subjects to be objects of interest at the time of their first elaboration. I merely draw attention to it now, to point out that perhaps it is the very subject which may best obtain the results for which I am pleading.

We have indicated two main topics, namely general ideas of quantity and of laws of nature, which should be an object of study in the mathematical curriculum of a liberal education. But there is another side to mathematics which must not be overlooked. It is the chief instrument for discipline in logical method.

Now, what is logical method, and how can any one be trained in it?

Logical method is more than the mere knowledge of valid types of reasoning and practice in the concentration of mind necessary to follow them. If it were only this, it would still be very important; for the human mind was not evolved in the bygone ages for the sake of reasoning, but merely to enable manking with more art to hunt between meals for fresh food supplies. Accordingly few people can follow close reasoning without considerable practice.

More than this is wanted to make a good reasoner, or even to enlighten ordinary people with knowledge of what constitutes the essence of the art. The art of reasoning consists in getting hold of the subject at the right end, of seizing on the few general ideas which illuminate the whole, and of persistently marshalling all subsidiary facts round them. Nobody can be a good reasoner unless by constant practice he has realised the importance of getting hold of the big ideas and of hanging on to them like grim death. For this sort of training geometry is, I think, better than algebra. The field of thought of algebra is rather obscure, whereas space is an obvious insistent thing evident to all. Then the process of simplification, or abstraction, by which all irrelevant properties of matter, such as colour, taste, and weight, are put aside is an education in itself. Again, the definitions, and the propositions assumed without proof, illustrate the necessity of forming clear notions of the fundamental facts of the subject-matter and of the relations between them. All this belongs to the mere prolegomena of the subject. When we come to its development, its excellence increases. The learner is not initially confronted with any symbolism which bothers the memory by its rules, however simple they may be. Also, from the very beginning the reasoning, if properly conducted, is dominated by well-marked ideas which guide each stage of development. Accordingly the essence of logical method receives immediate exemplification.

Let us now put aside for the moment the limitations introduced by the dullness of average pupils and the pressure on time due to other subjects, and consider what geometry has to offer in the way of a liberal education. I will indicate some stages in the subject, without meaning that necessarily they are to be studied in this exclusive order. The first stage is the study of *congruence*. Our perception of congruence is in practice dependent on our judgments of the invariability of the intrinsic properties of bodies when their external circumstances are varying. But however it arises, congruence is in essence the correlation of two regions of space, point by point, so that all homologous distances and all homologous angles are equal. It is to be noticed that the definition of the equality of lengths and angles is their congruence, and all tests of equality, such as the use of the yard measure, are merely devices for making immediate judgments of congruence easy. I make these remarks to suggest that apart from the reasoning connected with it, congruence, both as an example of a larger and very far-reaching idea and also for its own sake, is well worthy of attentive consideration. The propositions concerning it elucidate the elementary properties of the triangle, the parallelogram, and the circle, and of the relations of two planes to each other. It is very desirable to restrict the proved propositions of this part within the narrowest bounds, partly by assuming redundant axiomatic propositions, and partly by introducing only those propositions of absolutely fundamental importance.

The second stage is the study of similarity. This can be reduced to three or four fundamental propositions. Similarity is an enlargement of the idea of congruence, and, like that idea, is another example of a one-to-one correlation of points of spaces. Any extension of study of this subject might well be in the direction of the investigation of one or two simple properties of similar and similarly situated rectilinear figures. The whole subject receives its immediate applications in plans and maps. It is important, however, to remember that trigonometry is really the method by which the main theorems are made available for use.

The third stage is the study of the elements of trigonometry. This is the study of the periodicity introduced by rotation and of properties preserved in a correlation of similar figures. Here for the first time we introduce a slight use of the algebraic analysis founded on the study of number and quantity. The importance of the periodic character of the functions requires full illustration. The simplest properties of the functions are the only ones required for the solution of triangles, and the consequent applications to surveying. The wealth of formulæ, often important in themselves, but entirely useless for this type of study, which crowd our books should be rigorously excluded, except so far as they are capable of being proved by the pupils as direct examples of the bookwork.

This question of the exclusion of formulæ is best illustrated by considering this example of Trigonometry, though of course I may well have hit on an unfortunate case in which my judgment is at fault. A great part of the educational advantage of the subject can be obtained by confining study to Trigonometry of one angle and by exclusion of the addition formulæ for the sine and cosine and the sum of two angles. The functions can be graphed, and the solution of triangles effected. Thus the aspects of the science as (1) embodying analytically the immediate results of some of the theorems deduced from congruence and similarity, (2) as a solution of the main problem of surveying, (3) as a study of the fundamental functions required to express periodicity and wave motion, will all be impressed on the pupils' minds both by bookwork and example.

If it be desired to extend this course, the addition formulæ should be added. But great care should be taken to exclude specialising the pupils in the wealth of formulæ which comes in their train. By "exclude" is meant that the pupils should not have spent time or energy in acquiring any facility in their deduction. The teacher may find it interesting to work a few such examples before a class. But such results are not among those which learners need retain. Also, I would exclude the whole subject of circumscribed and inscribed circles both from Trigonometry and from the previous geometrical courses. It is all very pretty, but I do not understand what its function is in an elementary non-professional curriculum.

Accordingly, the actual bookwork of the subject is reduced to very manageable proportions. I was told the other day of an American college where the students are expected to know by heart ninety formulæ or results in Trigonometry alone. We are not quite so bad as that. In fact, in Trigonometry we have nearly approached the ideal here sketched out as far as our elementary courses are concerned.

The fourth stage introduces Analytical Geometry. The study of graphs in algebra has already employed the fundamental notions, and all that is now required is a rigorously pruned course on the straight line, the circle, and the three types of conic sections, defined by the forms of their equations. At this point there are two remarks to be made. It is often desirable to give our pupils mathematical information which we do not prove. For example, in co-ordinate geometry, the reduction of the general equation of the second degree is probably beyond the capacities of most of the type of students whom we are considering. But that need not prevent us from explaining the fundamental position of conics, as exhausting the possible types of such curves.

The second remark is to advocate the entire sweeping away of 'geometrical conics' as a separate subject. Naturally, on suitable occasions the analysis of analytical geometry will be lightened by the use of direct deduction from some simple figure. But geometrical conics, as developed from the definition of a conic section by the focus and directrix property, suffers from glaring defects. It is hopelessly recondite. The fundamental definition of a conic, $SP = e \cdot PM$, usual in this subject at this stage, is thoroughly bad. It is very recondite, and has no obvious importance. Why should such curves be studied at all, any more than those defined by an indefinite number of other formulæ? But when we have commenced the study of the Cartesian methods, the equations of the first and second degrees are naturally the first things to think about.

In this ideal course of Geometry, the fifth stage is occupied with the elements of Projective Geometry. The general ideas of cross ratio and of projection are here fundamental.

Projection is yet a more general instance of that one-to-one correlation which we have already considered under congruence and similarity. Here again we must avoid the danger of being led into a bewildering wealth of detail.

The intellectual idea which projective geometry is to illustrate is the importance in reasoning of the correlation of all cases which can be proved to possess in common certain identical properties. The preservation of the projective properties in projection is the one important educational idea of the subject. Cross ratio only enters as the fundamental metrical property which is preserved. The few propositions considered are selected to illustrate the two allied processes which are made possible by this procedure. One is proof by simplification. Here the simplification is psychological and not logical — for the general case is logically the simplest. What is meant is: Proof by considering the case which is in fact the most familiar to us, or the easiest to think about. The other procedure is the deduction of particular cases from known general truths, as soon as we have a means of discovering such cases or a criterion for testing them.

The projective definition of conic sections and the identity of the results obtained with the curves derived from the general equation of the second degree are capable of simple exposition, but lie on the border-line of the subject. It is the sort of topic on which information can be given, and the proofs suppressed.

The course of geometry as here conceived in its complete ideal — and ideals can never be realised — is not a long one. The actual amount of mathematical deduction at each stage in the form of bookwork is very slight. But much more explanation would be given, the importance of each proposition being illustrated by examples, either worked out or for students to work, so selected as to indicate the fields of thought to which it applies. By such a course the student would gain an analysis of the leading properties of space, and of the chief methods by which they are investigated.

The study of the elements of mathematics, conceived in this spirit, would constitute a training in logical method together with an acquisition of the precise ideas which lie at the base of the scientific and philosophical investigations of the universe. Would it be easy to continue the excellent reforms in mathematical instruction which this generation has already achieved, so as to include in the curriculum this wider and more philosophic spirit? Frankly, I think that this result would be very hard to achieve as the result of single individual efforts. For reasons which I have already briefly indicated, all reforms in education are very difficult to effect. But the continued pressure of combined effort, provided that the ideal is really present in the minds of the mass of teachers, can do much, and effects in the end surprising modification. Gradually the requisite books get written, still more gradually the examinations are reformed so as to give weight to the less technical aspects of the subject, and then all recent experience has shown that the majority of teachers are only too ready to welcome any practicable means of rescuing the subject from the reproach of being a mechanical discipline.

CHAPTER VII

Universities and Their Function

I

The expansion of universities is one marked feature of the social life in the present age. All countries have shared in this movement, but more especially America, which thereby occupies a position of honour. It is, however, possible to be overwhelmed even by the gifts of good fortune; and this growth of universities, in number of institutions, in size, and in internal complexity of organization, discloses some danger of destroying the very sources of their usefulness, in the absence of a widespread understanding of the primary functions which universities should perform in the service of a nation. These remarks, as to the necessity for reconsideration of the function of universities, apply to all the more developed countries. They are only more especially applicable to America, because this country has taken the lead in a development which, under wise guidance, may prove to be one of the most fortunate forward steps which civilisation has yet taken.

This article will only deal with the most general principles, though the special problems of the various departments in any university are, of course, innumerable. But generalities require illustration, and for this purpose I choose the business school of a university. This choice is dictated by the fact that business schools represent one of the newer developments of university activity. They are also more particularly relevant to the dominant social activities of modern nations, and for that reason are good examples of the way in which the national life should be affected by the activities of its universities. Also at Harvard, where I have the honour to hold office, the new foundation of a business school on a scale amounting to magnificence has just reached its completion.

There is a certain novelty in the provision of such a school of training, on this scale of magnitude, in one of the few leading universities of the world. It marks the culmination of a movement which for many years past has introduced analogous departments throughout American universities. This is a new fact in the university world; and it alone would justify some general reflections upon the purpose of a university education, and upon the proved importance of that purpose for the welfare of the social organism.

The novelty of business schools must not be exaggerated. At no time have universities been restricted to pure abstract learning. The University of Salerno in Italy, the earliest of European universities, was devoted to medicine. In England, at Cambridge, in the year 1316, a college was founded for the special purpose of providing 'clerks for the King's service.' Universities have trained clergy, medical men, lawyers, engineers. Business is now a highly intellectualized vocation, so it well fits into the series. There is, however, this novelty: the curriculum suitable for a business school, and the various modes of activity of such a school, are still in the experimental stage. Hence the peculiar importance of recurrence to general principles in connection with the moulding of these schools. It would, however, be an act of presumption on my part if I were to enter upon any consideration of details, or even upon types of policy affecting the balance of the whole training. Upon such questions I have no special knowledge, and therefore have no word of advice.

II

The universities are schools of education, and schools of research. But the primary reason for their existence is not to be found either in the mere knowledge conveyed to the students or in the mere opportunities for research afforded to the members of the faculty.

Both these functions could be performed at a cheaper rate, apart from these very expensive institutions. Books are cheap, and the system of apprenticeship is well understood. So far as the mere imparting of information is concerned, no university has had any justification for existence since the popularisation of printing in the fifteenth century. Yet the chief impetus to the foundation of universities came after that date, and in more recent times has even increased.

The justification for a university is that it preserves the connection between knowledge and the zest of life, by uniting the young and the old in the imaginative consideration of learning. The university imparts information, but it imparts it imaginatively. At least, this is the function which it should perform for society. A university which fails in this respect has no reason for existence. This atmosphere of excitement, arising from imaginative consideration, transforms knowledge. A fact is no longer a bare fact: it is invested with all its possibilities. It is no longer a burden on the memory: it is energising as the poet of our dreams, and as the architect of our purposes.

Imagination is not to be divorced from the facts: it is a way of illuminating the facts. It works by eliciting the general principles which apply to the facts, as they exist, and then by an intellectual survey of alternative possibilities which are consistent with those principles. It enables men to construct an intellectual vision of a new world, and it preserves the zest of life by the suggestion of satisfying purposes.

Youth is imaginative, and if the imagination be

strengthened by discipline this energy of imagination can in great measure be preserved through life. The tragedy of the world is that those who are imaginative have but slight experience, and those who are experienced have feeble imaginations. Fools act on imagination without knowledge; pedants act on knowledge without imagination. The task of a university is to weld together imagination and experience.

The initial discipline of imagination in its period of youthful vigour requires that there be no responsibility for immediate action. The habit of unbiased thought, whereby the ideal variety of exemplification is discerned in its derivation from general principles, cannot be acquired when there is the daily task of preserving a concrete organisation. You must be free to think rightly and wrongly, and free to appreciate the variousness of the universe undisturbed by its perils.

There reflections upon the general functions of a university can be at once translated in terms of the particular functions of a business school. We need not flinch from the assertion that the main function of such a school is to produce men with a greater zest for business. It is a libel upon human nature of conceive that zest for life is the product of pedestrian purposes directed toward the narrow routine of material comforts. Mankind by its pioneering instinct, and in a hundred other ways, proclaims the falsehood of that lie.

In the modern complex social organism, the adventure of life cannot be disjoined from intellectual adventure. Amid simpler circumstances, the pioneer can follow the urge of his instinct, directed toward the scene of his vision from the mountain top. But in the complex organisations of modern business the intellectual adventure of analysis, and of imaginative reconstruction, must precede any successful reorganisation. In a simpler world, business relations were simpler, being based on the immediate contact of man with man and on immediate confrontation with all relevant material circumstances. To-day business organisation requires an imaginative grasp of the psychologies of populations engaged in differing modes of occupation; of populations scattered through cities, through mountains, through plains; of populations on the ocean, and of populations in mines, and of populations in forests. It requires an imaginative grasp of conditions in the tropics, and of conditions in temperate zones. It requires an imaginative grasp of the interlocking interests or great organisations, and of the reactions of the whole complex to any change in one of its elements. It requires an imaginative understanding of laws of political economy, not merely in the abstract, but also with the power to construe them in terms of the particular circumstances of a concrete business. It requires some knowledge of the habits of government, and of the variations of those habits under diverse conditions. It requires an imaginative vision of the binding forces of any human organisation, a sympathetic vision of the limits of human nature and of the conditions which evoke loyalty of service. It requires some knowledge of the laws of health, and of the laws of fatigue, and of the conditions for sustained reliability. It requires an imaginative understanding of the social effects of the conditions of factories. It requires a sufficient conception of the rôle of applied science in modern society. It requires that discipline of character which can say 'yes' and 'no' to other men, not by reason of blind obstinacy, but with firmness derived from a conscious evaluation of relevant alternatives.

The universities have trained the intellectual pioneers of our civilisation — the priests, the lawyers, the statesmen, the doctors, the men of science, and the men of letters. They have been the home of those ideals which lead men to confront the confusion of their present times. The Pilgrim Fathers left England to found a state of society according to the ideals of their religious faith; and one of their earlier acts was the foundation of Harvard University in Cambridge, named after that ancient mother of ideals in England, to which so many of them owed their training. The conduct of business now requires intellectual imagination of the same type as that which in former times has mainly passed into those other occupations; and the universities are the organisations which have supplied this type of mentality for the service of the progress of the European races.

In early mediæval history the origin of universities was obscure and almost unnoticed. They were a gradual and natural growth. But their existence is the reason for the sustained, rapid progressiveness of European life in so many fields of activity. By their agency the adventure of action met the adventure of thought. It would not have been possible antecedently to have divined that such organisations would have been successful. Even now, amid the imperfections of all things human, it is sometimes difficult to understand how they succeed in their work. Of course there is much failure in the work of universities. But, if we take a broad view of history, their success has been remarkable and almost uniform. The cultural histories of Italy, of France, of Germany, of Holland, of Scotland, of England, of the United States, bear witness to the influence of universities. By 'cultural history' I am not chiefly thinking of the lives of scholars; I mean the energising of the lives of those men who gave to France, to Germany, and to other countries that impress of types of human achievement which, by their addition to the zest of life, form the foundation of our patriotism. We love to be members of a society which can do those things.

There is one great difficulty which hampers all the higher types of human endeavour. In modern times this difficulty has even increased in its possibilities for evil. In any large organisation the younger men, who are novices, must be set to jobs which consist in carrying out fixed duties in obedience to orders. No president of a large corporation meets his youngest employee at his office door with the offer of the most responsible job which the work of that corporation includes. The young men are set to work at a fixed routine, and only occasionally even see the president as he passes in and out of the building. Such work is a great discipline. It imparts knowledge, and it produces reliability of character; also it is the only work for which the young men, in that novice stage, are fit, and it is the work for which they are hired. There can be no criticism of the custom, but there may be an unfortunate effect — prolonged routine work dulls the imagination.

The result is that qualities essential at a later stage of a career are apt to be stamped out in an earlier stage. This is only an instance of the more general fact, that necessary technical excellence can only be acquired by a training which is apt to damage those energies of mind which should direct the technical skill. This is the key fact in education, and the reason for most of its difficulties.

The way in which a university should function in the preparation for an intellectual career, such as modern business or one of the older professions, is by promoting the imaginative consideration of the various general principles underlying that career. Its students thus pass into their period of technical apprenticeship with their imaginations already practised in connecting details with general principles. The routine then receives its meaning, and also illuminates the principles which give it that meaning. Hence, instead of a drudgery issuing in a blind rule of thumb, the properly trained man has some hope of obtaining an imagination disciplined by detailed facts and by necessary habits.

Thus the proper function of a university is the imaginative acquisition of knowledge. Apart from this importance of the imagination, there is no reason why business men, and other professional men, should not pick up their facts bit by bit as they want them for particular occasions. A university is imaginative or it is nothing — at least nothing useful.

III

Imagination is a contagious disease. It cannot be measured by the yard, or weighed by the pound, and then delivered to the students by members of the faculty. It can only be communicated by a faculty whose members themselves wear their learning with imagination. In saying this, I am only repeating one of the oldest of observations. More than two thousand years ago the ancients symbolised learning by a torch passing from hand to hand down the generations. That lighted torch is the imagination of which I speak. The whole art in the organisation of a university is the provision of a faculty whose learning is lighted up with imagination. This is the problem of problems in university education; and unless we are careful the recent vast extension of universities in number of students and in variety of activities — of which we are so justly proud — will fail in producing its proper results, by the mishandling of this problem.

The combination of imagination and learning normally requires some leisure, freedom from restraint, freedom from harassing worry, some variety of experiences, and the stimulation of other minds diverse in opinion and diverse in equipment. Also there is required the excitement of curiosity, and the self-confidence derived from pride in the achievements of the surrounding society in procuring the advance of knowledge. Imagination cannot be acquired once and for all, and then kept indefinitely in an ice box to be produced periodically in stated quantities. The learned and imaginative life is a way of living, and is not an article of commerce.

It is in respect to the provision and utilisation of these conditions for an efficient faculty that the two functions of education and research meet together in a university. Do you want your teachers to be imaginative? Then encourage them to research. Do you want your researchers to be imaginative? Then bring them into intellectual sympathy with the young at the most eager, imaginative period of life, when intellects are just entering upon their mature discipline. Make your researchers explain themselves to active minds, plastic and with the world before them; make your young students crown their period of intellectual acquisition by some contact with minds gifted with experience of intellectual adventure. Education is discipline for the adventure of life; research is intellectual adventure; and the universities should be homes of adventure shared in common by young and old. For successful education there must always be a certain freshness in the knowledge dealt with. It must either be new in itself or it must be invested with some novelty of application to the new world of new times. Knowledge does not keep any better that fish. You may be dealing with knowledge of the old species, with some old truth; but somehow or other it must come to the students, as it were, just drawn out of the sea and with the freshness of its immediate importance.

It is the function of the scholar to evoke into life wisdom and beauty which, apart from his magic, would remain lost in the past. A progressive society depends upon its inclusion of three groups — scholars, discoverers, inventors. Its progress also depends upon the fact that its educated masses are composed of members each with a tinge of scholarship, a tinge of discovery, and a tinge of invention. I am here using the term 'discovery' to mean the progress of knowledge in respect to truths of some high generality, and the term 'invention' to mean the progress of knowledge in respect to the application of general truths in particular ways subservient to present needs. It is evident that these three groups merge into each other, and also that men engaged in practical affairs are properly to be called inventors so far as they contribute to the progress of society. But any one individual has his own limitation of function, and his own peculiar needs. What is important for a nation is that there shall be a very close relation between all types of its progressive elements, so that the study may influence the market place, and the market place the study. Universities are the chief agencies for this fusion of progressive activities into an effective instrument of progress. Of course they are not the only agencies, but it is a fact that to-day the progressive nations are those in which universities flourish.

It must not be supposed that the output of a university in the form of original ideas is solely to be measured by printed papers and books labeled with the names of their authors. Mankind is as individual in its mode of output as in the substance of its thoughts. For some of the most fertile minds composition in writing, or in a form reducible to writing, seems to be an impossibility. In every faculty you will find that some of the more brilliant teachers are not among those who publish. Their originality requires for its expression direct intercourse with their pupils in the form of lectures, or of personal discussion. Such men exercise an immense influence; and yet, after the generation of their pupils has passed away, they sleep among the innumerable unthanked benefactors of humanity. Fortunately, one of them is immortal — Socrates.

Thus it would be the greatest mistake to estimate the value of each member of a faculty by the printed work signed with his name. There is at the present day some tendency to fall into this error; and an emphatic protest is necessary against an attitude on the part of authorities which is damaging to efficiency and unjust to unselfish zeal.

But, when all such allowances have been made, one good test for the general efficiency of a faculty is that as a whole it shall be producing in published form its quota of contributions of thought. Such a quota is to be estimated in weight of thought, and not in number of words.

This survey shows that the management of a university faculty has no analogy to that of a business organisation. The public opinion of the faculty, and a common zeal for the purposes of the university, form the only effective safeguards for the high level of university work. The faculty should be a band of scholars, stimulating each other, and freely determining their various activities. You can secure certain formal requirements, that lectures are given at stated times and that instructors and students are in attendance. But the heart of the matter lies beyond all regulation.

The question of justice to the teachers has very little to do with the case. It is perfectly just to hire a man to perform any legal services under any legal conditions as to times and salary. No one need accept the post unless he so desires.

The sole question is, What sort of conditions will produce the type of faculty which will run a successful university? The danger is that it is quite easy to produce a faculty entirely unfit — a faculty of very efficient pedants and dullards. The general public will only detect the difference after the university has stunted the promise of youth for scores of years.

The modern university system in the great democratic countries will only be successful if the ultimate authorities exercise singular restraint, so as to remember that universities cannot be dealt with according to the rules and policies which apply to the familiar business corporations. Business schools are no exception to this law of university life. There is really nothing to add to what the presidents of many American universities have recently said in public on this topic. But whether the effective portion of the general public, in America or other countries, will follow their advice appears to be doubtful. The whole point of a university, on its educational side, is to bring the young under the intellectual influence of a band of imaginative scholars. There can be no escape from proper attention to the conditions which — as experience has shown — will produce such a band.

IV

The two premier universities of Europe, in age and in dignity, are the University of Paris and the University of

Oxford. I will speak of my own country because I know it best. The University of Oxford may have sinned in many ways. But, for all her deficiencies, she has throughout the ages preserved one supreme merit, beside which all failures in detail are as dust in the balance: for century after century, throughout the long course of her existence, she has produced bands of scholars who treated learning imaginatively. For that service alone. no one who loves culture can think of her without emotion.

But it is quite unnecessary for me to cross the ocean for my examples. The author of the Declaration of Independence, Mr. Jefferson, has some claim to be the greatest American. The perfection of his various achievements certainly places him among the few great men of all ages. He founded a university, and devoted one side of his complex genius to placing that university amid every circumstance which could stimulate the imagination — beauty of buildings, of situation, and every other stimulation of equipment and organisation.

There are many other universities in America which can point my moral, but my final example shall be Harvard — the representative university of the Puritan movement. The New England Puritans of the seventeenth and eighteenth centuries were the most intensely imaginative people, restrained in their outward expression, and fearful of symbolism by physical beauty, but, as it were, racked with the intensity of spiritual truths intellectually imagined. The Puritan faculties of those centuries must have been imaginative indeed, and they produced great men whose names have gone round the world. In later times Puritanism softened, and, in the golden age of literary New England, Emerson, Lowell, and Long-fellow set their mark upon Harvard. The modern scientific age then gradually supervenes, and again in William James we find the typical imaginative scholar.

To-day business comes to Harvard; and the gift which the University has to offer is the old one of imagination, the lighted torch which passes from hand to hand. It is a dangerous gift, which has started many a conflagration. If we are timid as to that danger, the proper course is to shut down our universities. Imagination is a gift which has often been associated with great commercial peoples — with Greece, with Florence, with Venice, with the learning of Holland, and with the poetry of England. Commerce and imagination thrive together. It is a gift which all must pray for their country who desire for it that abiding greatness achieved by Athens: —

> Her citizens, imperial spirits,
> Rule the present from the past.

For American education no smaller ideal can suffice.

後　記

　　教育無論對國家民族，還是對家庭父母，或是對人本身而言，都是重中之重；可是教育，對於當代中國人來說，至為焦慮，不能承受之輕，甚至是可怕的夢魘——恐懼——學得好累——活得好累！

　　數十年來，我一直在體驗、觀察和思考中國教育！

　　近幾年來，我一直在想着，從教育的角度，來做點什麼？！

　　孩子慢慢長大，茁壯成長，我們怎樣面對應對他們未來的路？

　　響應號召，隨波逐流；圈定設限，划地為牢；無所適從，放任自流；無師自通，歪打正着；目的明晰，激發引導？

　　「無巧不成書」！

　　由於我策劃出版另一本書而結識的一位朋友——原中文戰略家網站站長——老參謀先生。他，不遠千里，專程從當時所在的甘肅省蘭州市到上海來看我這個策劃人，並贈送了我一本楚漁先生所著《中國人的思維批判》。我一口氣讀完，發現書中提及懷特海教育思想和《教育的目的》，並引用片斷若干。

　　我大呼：「得之矣！得之矣！」

　　我一定要好好地研究這本書！

　　我要弄明白這本書到底怎麼樣！

　　中文版找不到，很意外——這麼好的書沒人引進推廣？！

　　找英文版，登陸上海圖書館網站，沒有查到；登陸在北京的國家圖書館網站，沒有查到！

幸得傳曉的熱心幫助，從香港中央圖書館查到，她親往復印，並寄到內地給我。

我花了兩個星期，愛不釋手地翻閱，偶爾停下來咀嚼回味一番。過癮，過癮！

譯者莊蓮平，大學英語專業畢業，英文功底深厚；曾做過多年英語老師，有教書育人經驗。她邊工作邊擠出有限的時間，歷時半年多翻譯成稿。其間，我則充分學習和發揚著名翻譯家林琴南之風格，校對，編輯，注釋。二人同心，這本書中文版得以順利出版。

感謝《中國人的思維批判》著作者楚漁先生的啓發。

感謝傳曉小姐一直以來的熱心幫助與支持。她是一位港漂湖北人，香港浸會大學106新聞專業畢業生，香港中文大學跨文化專業碩士研究生畢業，嚮往自由、熱愛文化，在港從事媒體和跨文化傳播工作。

著名經濟學家茅于軾先生為本書中文版欣然做序，在此致以最真切的謝意！

本書初版譯本出版八年以來，各位方家的譯本紛至沓來，令譯者時有「拋磚引玉」的小小成就感。

張志華先生，我與他因本書而結緣，成為知音。他在大學任教期間，便不遺餘力地推廣本書；在本次修訂過程中，他提出了諸多寶貴的修改意見。

張祝全先生，資深編輯，內容專家，媒體出版策劃人，思想與文化傳播者，也是與我相知三十餘載、志同道合的同窗好友。本次修訂，特別邀請他對全書稿作加工潤色及編校把關，令本書內容更臻精確暢達。

期待您的進一步反饋和意見。

下一版——更好——最好！

懷特海的《教育的目的》是經典！

我們會努力做到，讓——

這本中文譯本，成為經典！

王立中

2020年6月，戰略家書苑

書　名：教育的目的

作　者：*Alfred North Whitehead* （懷特海）

譯　者：莊蓮平　王立中

總 策 劃：王立中

責任編輯：張祝全

特邀編輯：蒙　憲

排版設計：Rita Young

出　版：香港大華文化出版社

電　郵：info@dawaculture.com

版　次：2020年7月初版（香港）

國際書號：978-988-78473-8-0

印　刷：培基印刷鐳射分色公司